The Trace of
Political Representation

SUNY Series in Radical Social and Political Theory

Roger S. Gottlieb, editor

The Trace of
Political Representation

Brian Seitz

State University of New York Press

Published by
State University of New York Press, Albany

Printed in the United States of America

For information, address State University of New York Press,
State University Plaza, Albany, N.Y. 12246

Production by Christine Lynch
Marketing by Theresa Abad Swierzowski

Library of Congress Cataloging-in-Publication Data

Seitz, Brian, 1954-
    The trace of political representation / by Brian Seitz.
        p.   cm. — (SUNY series in radical social and political
    theory)
    Includes bibliographical references (p.   ) and index.
    ISBN 0-7914-2365-4 (acid-free paper). — ISBN 0-7914-2366-2 (pbk.
    acid-free paper)
    1. Representative government and representation.
    2. Representative government and representation—United States.
    I. Title. II. Series.
    JF1051.S427 1995
    328.3'347—dc20   94-10611
                                                                              CIP

10 9 8 7 6 5 4 3 2 1

*For Barbara Friedman and
Sabina Friedman-Seitz*

There is no possibility of understanding the problematic of representation if we seek the origin of representation outside of representation itself.

—Cornelius Castoriadis

Contents

PART TWO
Putting Some Pieces Together
(and Taking Them Apart Again)

Acknowledgments

While others have contributed in specific ways to my thoughts on the topic of political representation, I would particularly like to acknowledge the various ways this project has been informed by conversations with and comments from David B. Allison, Edward S. Casey, Dick Howard, Nickolas Pappas, Mary C. Rawlinson, and Thomas Thorp.

Preface

This investigation of political representation clearly dovetails into or is part of a much broader philosophical investigation of representation that has been going on in a variety of guises for some time on both sides of the Atlantic and in every imaginable philosophical style and context, including philosophy of language, aesthetics, social and political philosophy, cultural studies, and even the philosophy of science. If this particular investigation is an exercise in continental philosophy, the approach may be inspired by continental European thought, but the continent most in question is North America, specifically the United States.

Partly because of the eclectic range of sources and influences at work here and more specifically because of the conspicuously continental style, the approach I take may seem idiosyncratic to many American readers; the text is openly selective, ambiguously positioned (rather than neutral or unbiased), often polemical, sometimes playful, occasionally hyperbolic, cast as strategic, etc. Nevertheless, it seems to me that this book could serve for the uninitiated as an introduction to the general problematics of political representation. More to the point, I hope that my strategic engagement with it here encourages more philosophers working in the borderlines between continental philosophy and political thought to turn their attention to the kinds of issues associated with postmodern political representation. In every way, that encouragement is far more important than whether the perspective offered here is right or wrong. From the standpoint of the relation between communication and political reality, we are living in strange times, and it seems that there is more value in addressing these times on their own terms than in continuing to patch up and preserve the hollow architectonics of modern metaphysics. Our efforts could go into a defense of the integral political subject, the one associated with a rights-endowed, autonomous will, or they could go into a dissolution and abandonment of that subject. I do not think we can afford the luxury of either endeavor. Our precious time may be better spent trying to figure out what the political subject has become and how to respond to these developments. One of the most important lessons we must remember from phenomenology (a method not employed in this book) is that description is what renders the object to the philosophical gaze. I hope this book contributes something worthwhile to the descriptions of that peculiar object, the postmodern political subject.

Introduction

The Position of Representation

As a way of suggesting an orientation to the problem of
political representation and the perspective from which it will
be explored here, it may be useful to emphasize, as Jacques
Derrida has done,[1] and as work such as Hanna Pitkin's has
demonstrated,[2] that a philosophical or critical engagement
with representation—and with, perhaps, political representation in particular—cannot be formulated in terms of an affirmation or a denial, at least not initially. That is, a philosophical engagement with representation is not first of all a
question of trying to make a case or achieve a vote for or
against representation—is it good or bad?—or of aiming to
state definitively whether representation exists or not. For one
thing, it would be a mistake to assume in advance that representation is a singular, unitary, or general phenomenon. For
another, there is no clear way to avoid the inevitability that
the declaration of either affirmation or denial will already be
tied up with the discourses and practices of representation,
with its histories and the commitments embedded in them.
Casting a vote either way would be to decide about that which
has not yet been decided, that which has a more or less specific but nevertheless indecisive history, that which itself will
remain undecided.

On the yea side, to affirm that representation is what it
purports to be or that it is (or should be) identical with the
accounts that have traditionally been associated with and provided for it, would be simply to reinscribe representation or to
attempt to represent representation from the point of view of
representation without a difference.[3] More specifically and

graphically, political representation would probably remain predominantly represented by the instrumentalist image of a practical exchange or transfer, some sort of delegative microcosm, a kind of a mirror, an image of substitution or translation perhaps still loosely governed by the late eighteenth-century ideal of "in miniature an exact portrait of the people at large."[4]

On the nay side, the currently powerful denial of representation in some currents of postmodern thought is also a representational gesture, the offer of a representation, and an offering of representation. Further, the rejection of representation might also entail or be part of an ultimately reactionary and self-convinced nihilism, one that is perhaps 'passive' in a Nietzschean sense but certainly not reticent even if it succumbs to the oscillating images and accelerated velocities of postmodernism. This position announces that representation is dead, which seems to suggest that it was once alive or real, a persistently metaphysical claim, which may be translated "words used to mean something" and then "we have surpassed or gone beyond representation." This perspective is particularly problematic insofar as it seems to take for granted that representation is (or ever was) something self-evident and self-identical. That is, it presumes the very thing it denies.

On the other hand, in a very different vein, the rejection of representation might involve an attempt at the "rehabilitation of immediacy, of original simplicity, or presence without repetition or delegation."[5] This latter possibility, which may be detected in the discourse of "direct" democracy (e.g., characterized by the electronic town hall), revives an archaic, ontotheological image of unmediated presence or co-presence. This is an image of the political subject or political identity without difference or deviance, perhaps an unalienated, actualized, whole, autonomous, directly expressive, and pure self-identity. In a hi-tech context, this subject might call for political communication without distance, delay, substitution, or interference, for communication without static. However, practical suggestions, such as, for instance, "everyone will vote directly through personal computer workstations," clearly introduce technology and thus mediation into the political process, and with this (unavoidable) mediation they also introduce all kinds of deviance and difference into the political subject (in this case, one difference would have to do with access to both technology and information). Unavoidable procedural and organizational matters, such as the formation of the voting district (whether the nation, the political community as a whole, or a more traditional determination of the electoral district [next step, representation; at large? single member?]), ensure that even a "direct" democracy would render differences from some self-evident, self-identical, organic political subject, would introduce, that is, representation. The opposition between, on the one hand, a direct presence of the political subject, and, on the other, a mediated—represented or substituted—presence of the political subject, begins to unravel immediately because the political subject is itself a representation, and is inseparable from the specific configurations of representation in which it appears.

Both forms of the denial of representation—postmodernist nihilism and the advocacy of immediacy—remain thoroughly metaphysical, the former a nostalgic metaphysics of disappointment, the latter a nostalgic metaphysics of Enlightenment faith, which is not necessarily the same as optimism.[6] Neither alternative is conceptually adequate nor compatible with democracy, and part of this project is to suggest why not. We cannot simply choose to pass beyond representation.

Before or perhaps in the process of confronting why any sort of straightforward or decisive denial of representation would be problematic, it is necessary first to explore the problems with its simple affirmation. This process necessitates a philosophical assessment of some of the possibilities of political representation, which is to say of some of the things that representation is or has come to be. This assessment is one of the central tasks of this project, both in Part One, "Archaeological Fragments of Representation," which is overtly historical in focus, and in Part Two, "Putting Some Pieces Together (and Taking Them Apart Again)," which is oriented both to more directly philosophical dimensions of political representation and to contemporary political terrain. However, a philosophical exploration of what political representation is need not follow an ontological or eidetic path, by which I mean that it does not have to seek essences, structures, or other metaphysical self-identities. Instead, and informed by a diversity of sources,[7] such an exploration can investigate practices, organizations, ideas about, and effects of representation in political discourse and in specific institutions, including institutions of democracy. It can address the configurations of what Foucault calls "power/knowledge" that produce, incorporate, exercise, or are coextensive with representation. It can try to cultivate what has been made of representation and what it has been made into. Most generally speaking, then, it is a question of looking at some of the varied identities and possibilities of political representation, possibilities which, like all others and like all other processes of creation,[8] remain contingent and open-ended, never more than provisionally essential.

The most important field of identities and possibilities here is that of the political subject as it is constituted within the apparatuses of both past and present formations of representation. Against the backdrop of the historical material developed in Part One, I argue that the political subject—most simply, who or what a given political discourse is about—does not have an existence independent of a particular formation of political representation. Exploring the identity of the subject of political representation involves asking the following: What sort of an object is this subject and what are its characteristics and the conditions of its existence, of, that is, the constitution or exercise of its identity in the discourse and practice of political representation? The traditional modern image has been that what gets represented in the apparatuses and processes of representation is a political subject or identity (e.g., will, opinion, and agency) that exists fundamentally independent of and prior to the representative process, which at the same time is a process that has been predominantly viewed as an instrument—an often abused instrument—in the service of this political subject. In approaching representation, theorists have tended to concentrate on analyzing the relationship between the representative and the represented, with special attention usually given to the identity of the representative and, in particular, to its relations and practical obligations to its constituency (i.e., its obligations to what is represented, the subject). Meanwhile, what seems largely to have been taken for granted, even while viewed as problematic, is the identity of the subject represented. Consequently, the problem of representation tends to be addressed as one of translation (e.g., "good" or "bad" translation), which on the most general level means that it is a question of how to translate the originary political subject into a consolidating, effective, *true* representative, or, more simply, how to get government "to stand in the place of" the people in order to accurately reflect or express society.

While representation is necessarily an exchange, what I want to suggest is that the values or terms of this exchange do not exist independently of the productive exchange itself (more specifically, translation is never a simple or straightforward but always an intrinsically transformative and therefore productive affair). The political subject is not an autonomous creature, not an originary consciousness that simply uses representation as an instrument—uses it well or poorly—in order to achieve certain fundamentally rational ends. In contrast, this study probes the possibility that the discursive and practical mechanisms of political representation produce this political subject at the same time that they produce a representative for it. The study addresses some of the ramifications of such a possibility.

What I am most interested in exploring, then, is what is represented in a system of representation. Several important things will emerge here. First, historically, the subject represented in political discourse and practice has clearly not always been the same figure. There persists no self-identical political subject that gets embodied at different times and in different ways in the various forms of representative government, neither one that is essentially already constituted (and just needs a voice) nor one that is unfolding or coming into being as the body of a progressive, teleologically determined history of Reason or Freedom; the political subject is one that always appears in and is articulated by a particular political formation. There is no universal political subject and never was (outside of a discourse), neither actually nor potentially. Second, then, a given formation of representation produces and is coextensive with all of its elements and identities, and not with just that of the representative. As I will argue in the latter half of the book, this last point implies neither that discourse "invents" or makes up a political subject nor that the subject is a legislative phenomenon with an inaccessible noumenal content.[9] The identity of the political subject produced by representation is both real and positive, that is, really and effectively there (it is a power formation), even if it remains tenuous, inseparable from its organization, not independent, and not as given over to it via simple substitution or translation in the traditional sense of the term but as constituted by representation. Rather than approaching political representation as either a guiding (instrumental) concept or a given, ideal standard—the perfect translation of people into government or of society into state—rather, that is, than measuring reality against the rule of ideas, it makes more sense to view it from a perspective that is more historical in nature and to view representation as it has existed in different formations of political or power practices.

Before discussing the outline of the book, it is necessary to make a few general, prefatory remarks here, which pertain particularly to the historical section (i.e., Chapters II and III). Above all, it is important to emphasize that this is not intended to be a history of political representation. J. G. A. Pocock's contrast between "a history" and "a historical presentation" seems apt,[10] and what I am doing here is the latter. I am a philosopher, not a historian, and I openly acknowledge that this analysis is in no way exhaustive but openly partial.

For instance, while the three moments I have chosen to address—thirteenth-century England, eighteenth-century England, and eighteenth-century America—are important, prominent, and even canonized formations of representation, it would be a mistake to see them as, for instance, the rough outline of some sort of fundamental, progressive, logical development of representation (the logic embodied by representation is no more necessary than that associated with any retro-speculatively viewed complex of contingencies). As is the case with any choice, the selection of these particular three historical formations cannot avoid endowing them with a certain priority since choosing is prioritizing and evaluating is valuing. However, the motivation for these choices is not itself essentialist, insofar as they are not advanced as three archetypes or three fundamental moments, not in any decisive sort of sense. As part of the overall strategy of this book, the aim is to present them as examples or better as samplings rather than as fundamental essences. Clearly, they are not just any old examples—representation is finite and the analysis is finite—but, as samplings, they function as examples just the same. They are examples not of a universal but of themselves, which, articulated together, sketch out truly different formations of representation, clarified through comparison with other past formations and with the present. Partially determined by the contingent fact that I am American, my selection of them is itself contingent (not the same as arbitrary), by which I mean that other formations of political representation could have been alternatively selected. At the same time, these examples clearly constitute some nodal points in a history of representation, which again, like all histories, is finite even if it is open and never entirely definite, determinate, or determinable.

The main purpose here is not a celebration of difference for the sake of difference but to provide evidence that the political subject—the subject of representation—has been very different things in different discursive and practical contexts in history. This method seems like an effective way to substantiate the philosophical claim that there is no essential, perduring political subject. The point, then, is to tell a story (which is partly a history), one with only a provisional and not a fixed punch line. The general punch line of the story made up of the different formations of representation elaborated in Part One is that there is no subject independent of the different discourses to which it belongs. Here, then, "archaeology"—digging into a discursive formation—acquires an extra force when it is supplemented by the comparative materials provided by a genealogy.

Finally, Foucault's precautions about doing an "archaeology" of the present should be taken seriously since it is not possible to escape or take up a position outside of the very discourse that one would like to interrogate.[11] The genealogical dimension of Chapters II and III may help defuse at least some of the problems associated with an archaeology of the present, fragments of which appear in Part Two.

※

Chapter I is comprised of two sections. The initial section articulates some of the general features of my method and approach, which is determined by an orientation to history and to social or cultural formations that is influenced most of all by Foucault (and thus by Nietzsche). The identities under consideration are viewed as positive objects constituted in relation to and to be compared with or related to others as parts of a power formation. That is, these materials are treated as a complex of artifacts rather than as bearers of some fundamental essence, definiteness, or originary meaning ripe for reconstruction. I try to approach the narrative structure of history not as developmental in the traditional sense—that is, not as centered around the progressive epic of Reason—but as site specifically constitutive or productive in all of its terms, with an eye on the multiple dynamics of power.

The second section of Chapter I opens up political representation by cultivating certain philosophical dimensions of representation more generally. Through the sketch of a perspective on the traditional problem of the One and the many,

which involves discussion of Nietzsche's reading of Thales—
the end of philosophy encounters the beginning—I introduce
some of the important differences between the terms of representation, which are differences generated by the logic of
translation or substitution that representation embodies and
inscribes. As I have already suggested, the question is not so
much one of good or bad (or faithful or unfaithful) translation—that is the metaphysical way it has tended to be
viewed[12]—as it is of a sort of productive deviance associated
with the discourse and practice of substitution or, more specifically, of representation.

As a backdrop, the first historical formation engaged in
Chapter II is political representation as it emerges in thirteenth-century England. The English King's summons of
knights of the shire constitutes the representation of the
estates and then of the community of the realm and prefigures
the formal institution of Parliament. Throughout feudal times,
land coded in terms of bloodlines and in the blood of war had
been the ground in all senses. It can be argued that land, articulated in terms of territory, which is not reducible to property, was what was represented in medieval English representative assemblies. Power was the power of feudal territory and
of the land. Looking at certain developments of these medieval
English political practices will provide a picture of the identity
of the political subject in this particular representative apparatus, which is a subject quite unlike any form of popular
sovereignty, particularly one associated with a willful consciousness.

The rest of Chapter II examines the eighteenth-century
English discourse of virtual representation, whose most
famous proponent is Edmund Burke. This particular formation of representation is not the product of the logical, continuing development of what had emerged 400 years before
but is instead connected to the erosion of feudalism and the
new and massive forms of wealth—corporate forms—provided
by the growth of capitalism and overseas economic imperial-
ism. What is virtually represented in government as a whole
and in Parliament more specifically is common national inter-

ests, which are ultimately few in number, objective, and, given quality representation, objectively determinable. What is explicitly not represented is a popular sovereign or "the people." From the standpoint of its advocates, virtual representation was the only way to achieve "actual" representation, because representation of the interests of actual British subjects depended on representation of the true interests of the nation.

Of course, in strong and direct competition with this discourse of "virtual" representation was the emerging discourse of the natural rights of Man and the new possibilities of "actual" representation this new discourse implied. Thus, Chapter III shifts to America and to alternative political formations developing there, where the "crucial problem was defined as the question of *representation*."[13] While there was not consensus about the meaning of political representation in America either before or after the Revolution, many Americans were beginning to insist that only "actual" or "direct" representation was representation at all and so scoffed at England's invocation of virtual representation in response to the American protest of "no taxation without representation." That is, counterposed to the metaphysics of virtual representation, these Americans began developing their own metaphysic; the metaphysics of actual or direct representation articulated a configuration of the political subject very different from the common, objective national interest to which virtual representation devoted itself. The fundamental subject of actual representation is 'the people.' What this means is not as self-evident as it might seem, though, particularly set against the other, expressed subject of representation, which was property. In America, representation became an overtly doubled formation since what the government was designed to represent was both property and the people, which were articulated as neither synonymous nor necessarily in harmonious relation with each other. The political subject that emerged in America was something different from anything in Europe, something certainly strongly informed by European writers such as Locke and Rousseau but something also newly constituted. If it is not actually "actual," representation in America is not virtual either since the active political subject is radically rearticulated, a difference embodied in the periodic expansion of the all-important electorate. The people come into their own here, as they enter the heart of the political subject. The question remains, what is "the people"? This question becomes one of the keys to political representation in America.

Part Two pursues political representation on a different plane, one that is both more directly philosophical and more contemporary. Chapter IV begins with a discussion of representation as translation or as a logic of substitution. At issue is not whether representation is a translation of, e.g., the people into a government but whether such a translation is a straightforward substitution, in which one term simply takes the place of the other, or—a somewhat different point—in which one term can be used to take the place of the other. This issue leads into an address of certain dimensions of what the discourse and practice of political representation does, which is to rationalize itself, that is, to grant itself legitimation, to fabricate itself, and to cover this self-fabricating movement. However, these observations do not imply that representation is used by some specific, concealed power-identity in order to hide "reality," which is why the notion of ideology or false consciousness should not be relied upon, since, again, these figures must necessarily and inextricably be counterposed against and derived from an image of the Truth.

These last points lead into the last part of this chapter, which is a critique of the technological notion that representation is either an instrument used by conspiratorial or improper forces to fool the people or that it is an instrument used by some autonomous, definite (Proper) political subject in order to achieve its ends and account for itself. Representation does get used in many ways, but it is too productive in all of its dimensions to be viewed as, fundamentally or ideally, by itself a neutral tool. Does this mean that it is not a conduit of "communication"? Never neutral, the mediums and networks of "communication" inform the subject, which means more than just that the networks provide an autonomous subject with resources. The networks of communication contribute significantly to the determination of who she—the political subject—"is."

Chapter V explores some key profiles of the contemporary political subject. I criticize the notion that will is what represents itself via the mechanisms of representation and explore an alternative possibility, which begins with the observation that society (e.g. the people) is not fundamentally separate from either the state (e.g. the government) or the processes that constitute it. Carrying this point further and into a practical domain, I argue that the discourse and practice of selecting representatives renders "freedom of choice" as much as it presupposes it, and thus shapes consensual possibilities in a particular way (i.e., produces the consent of individual political subjects rather than provides a neutral conduit for its expression). However, to view this as a fundamentally inhibitive, distortive, alienating or otherwise essentially negative influence is to operate within a traditional paradigm of power as sovereign rather than as dispersed, relational, and productive and to miss the constitutive activity here in hopeful favor of instrumentality and Reason. Again, the political subject of representative democracy—popular sovereignty— is constituted by the very discourse and practice that constitutes the representative.

This particular discourse and practice is a practice of counting in at least two senses. First, there is a question of what, quite literally, is counted as part of the active, engaged and willful political agent by a given formation of representation. Second, there are the technical procedures of counting, which involve the determination of representative bodies (apportionment), voting practices, the involvement of opinion polls in politics, etc. The general discussion here revolves around the possibility of getting the numbers to line up, of tallying up a majority—the larger number—since these are what support representation. The point here is not that the numbers of representation express or communicate some willful thing that exists independently of the expression or of numbers but that numbers are the determinative political subject now.

If America were just a republic and not a democratic republic, there would be only one number, the number One (unity, unanimity, consensus, and peace). However, as always, the numbers are multiple and divided, which means that representative democracy in the Republic of the United States of America is conflictual in nature rather than, ultimately, consensually constituted. (Contrary to modern convictions, the social contract is a strategy of war rather than one opposed to it.) More specifically—and this is the theme of the final chapter, Chapter VI—because the political subject represented in its workings is multiple and divided, democracy is a form of warfare, and if its conflicts ever cease, democracy will be dead. This is a war that must continue, and, for better or worse, it cannot and will not continue without representation.

In the end, a position on modern and contemporary political representation will necessarily get traced out in the process of this investigation. There is no such thing as a discourse without a perspective, a discourse that represents or takes (up) no position. My discourse here marks a position on representation, which, for the time being, may turn out to mean generally democratic representation, embedded in or coextensive with a technologized culture and a global capitalist economy. Thus, while cautioning against pushing for a premature vote on representation, the prefatory remarks toward the beginning of this introduction are not meant to imply that we should refrain from taking a position on it. The open-endedness of the conflicted possibilities of representation neither implies, desires, nor leads to the kind of "openness" associated with neutrality, which in one of its liberal forms is a mode of openness effectively equivalent to impotence or vulnerability. In any event, it is above all not the dream of disinterested objectivity—of neutral desire—that inspires this particular analysis. For one thing, as Derrida has remarked,[14] one will always have to vote in the end, to make or take or mark a decision (included or excluded we get tallied whether we "decide" or not). We do not "choose" representation; it is, rather, something we are born into, a crucial part of the thrown world of political practices. Nevertheless, we must necessarily take up positions on it. Thus, at the moment of truth—the vote—an acknowledgment of the subject as number and as numbered, must establish an alliance with a cautious affirmation of the possibilities of representative democracy in America. These possibilities are uncontainable and irreducible because of *the one possibility that consists of every sort*,[15] which is not just the reductive, metaphysical, univocal and republican order of the One. This is an order that tends to work against even as it depends upon the democratic possibilities of open-ended multiplicity, which may transgress, clash with, and even threaten the polite, reasonable limitations of "pluralism."

I am not trying to offer a definitive argument or theory about representation here or to make some final sense of or conclusion about it. To do so would be to yield to the soothing answers offered by the One. Instead, the simpler, more direct intent is to contribute to the ongoing exploration of the questions generated by political representation. Philosophy has traditionally aimed for conclusions, but it becomes more untimely all the time. As it turns out, philosophy seems increasingly stuck with a conflicted imperative: to keep the talk going rather than reach a conclusion, to keep the talk going rather than come to an end.

Part One

Archaeological Fragments of
Political Representation

Chapter I

Introducing the
Metaphysics of Substitution

> Metaphor is less in the philosophical text (and the
> rhetorical text coordinated with it) than the philo-
> sophical text is within metaphor.
>
> —Jacques Derrida[1]

EXAMPLES AND SPECIFICS

This opening chapter aims to set up an approach to representation by exploring it initially as a general topic within
Western philosophical discourse. As always, such an approach
immediately confronts the problem of selection and exem-
plarity. What or whom, specifically, will I choose to talk
about? Are these choices "merely examples," neutral instruments in the service of an idea? That is, are they merely specific instances substituting for a general issue? Are they
merely representative or really representative? Is there something special about them? Do they serve a strategic purpose?
Or do they contribute more substantively to the development
of a philosophical position? Then there is the other critical
issue: Is representation really a general topic anyway, one
within which political representation functions as merely an
instance or version?

Examples are always special, and their selection necessarily involves some granting of privilege, some weighting of
an account. More specifically, examples do help constitute

rather than simply illustrate or represent an idea. It is important to acknowledge, for instance, that my decision to address Nietzsche later in this initial chapter serves the strategic purpose of introducing a particular approach to political representation. My decision not to engage "the great thinkers" here as a way of setting up the theme of representation has a similar purpose. The problems and issues do not originate from any particular philosopher or master set of philosophers, and an engagement with the masters at this stage might wind up diverting our focus onto a particular philosopher or society of philosophers and away from an issue that is not only metaphysical but part of a network of historical, social, political, and discursive contexts that are broader than philosophy itself. Philosophy often tends to inflate the originality, power, and value of ideas and to treat them as if they determine or illuminate and are ahead and even independent of specific discursive formations or of broader historical, social, economic, or libidinal (etc.) forces. Moreover, philosophy treats these concepts as if they were independent of specific networks of power and were causes rather than effects, functions, components, or signs (signs read as something like symptoms). It is important, then, to relate political representation to other species of representation, but it is simultaneously important to avoid reducing it to a mere instance of some general metaphysical configuration.

The aim at this point in the project is to display some of the complexes, currents, and general tendencies associated with representation as a theme in Western philosophy. In order to make sense of any particular representational system or network, it is necessary to begin to define the theme of representation as a philosophical problem. That is the task of this section of the investigation. This discussion is not an exhaustive history nor even a general account or overview. Rather, it is simply a suggestion and articulation of some select philosophical complexes related to representation. The turn to Nietzsche's Thales is not a return to an established origins but is a tour (or detour) of some beginnings or starts. These often provide remarkable contrasts as well as relations of continuity with what representation has become today in the age of "information" and "communication."

THE ONE AND THE MANY PROBLEMS

Recalling the General Particular

It might be a reductive imposition to equate representation in one context with its relatives from very different historical or narrative contexts, with, that is, distant cousins bearing family resemblances to what representation means today. Advocating such an equation might be one more instance of pushing a representational essence, a transcendental, ahistorical core of logic or meaning at the heart of representation, which one would like to be able to specify precisely. The ideal would be if it were possible to converse with, say, not only Hobbes about his notion of an 'artificial person,' but also Locke and Rousseau, as well as Wollstonecraft, Burke, Jefferson, Madison, and Paine, or even with members of the Athenian boule,[2] or Socrates, Plato, and Aristotle, or, to get to the root of things, with Heraclitus and Parmenides. It may be true that these figures are all particulars who do not together add up to a universal, but maybe a chat with each would help. After all, do we not share a common discipline, a certain language with them, the language of Western philosophy?

In an always ambiguous sense and at least retrospectively of course we philosophers participate in (even if we do not share) a language that is Parmenidean, Platonic, Aristotelian, indefinitely Socratic, and seldom Heraclitean enough. Thus, while it would be futile and absurd to attempt to posit a universal definition of representation—to present representation as ultimately independent of its historical variants—it should nevertheless be possible and helpful to explicate the philosophical domain or traditional concerns to which the phenomenon of political representation is related.

Here, while it is vital to affirm Foucault's insistence on attending to the specificity of discursive and power formations, we may also take a strategic tip from the Derridean reading of the history of Western metaphysics. This reading is also always specific in its cultivation of distinctions and differences, but it is a reading that simultaneously encounters something like a unity in Western philosophy in the form of a peculiar historical coherence in the economy of truth, which may be characterized as a hierarchically ordered exchange of values and correlative devaluations, a repeated trade or sacrifice in the name of _____ .[3] This "unity" is not derived from substance or being. That is, it is not derived from some ultimately singular object of thought or condition of thought or anything in between. The "unity" here is synonymous with a general economy of truth, which consists of the repetition of certain philosophical gestures that have no foundation outside of themselves or outside of the circuits constituted by their relations to each other (Derrida calls this "*différance*").[4] Tapping into Nietzsche, who is so critical of Western philosophy, Foucault indicates something like this "unity" even as he is questioning Unity when he refers to "this will to truth which has survived throughout so many centuries of our history. . . ."[5]

Foucault has become known as the philosopher of discontinuity, which, for various reasons, is not an entirely appropriate appellation.[6] Nevertheless, it is true that Foucault's approach to history is not an eidetic one. That is, Foucault does not seek to discover meanings or a meaning concealed in the depths of human history. As he describes it in *The Archaeology of Knowledge*, his is a method that "transforms documents into monuments,"[7] rather than treating

> discourse as *document*, as a sign of something else, as an element that ought to be transparent, but whose unfortunate opacity must often be pierced if one is to reach at last the depth of the essential in the place in which it is held in reserve; it is concerned with discourse in its own volume, as a *monument*. It is not an interpretative discipline: it does not seek another, better-hidden discourse.[8]

For Foucault, then, documents do not signify or represent something other than what they are on their surfaces, which must be articulated by the critical investigator. This may sound strange, perhaps even willfully naive, but what it means is that historical specificities, such as documents, are to be treated positivistically as objects or artifacts. They are not interpreted in order to recover autonomous meanings but analyzed in order to determine their positions in a given configuration of power/knowledge (of what might more concretely be called discourse-practice). Again, for Foucault, as for others, history is not woven from the strands of meaning immanent in historical specificities, which in proper sequence constitute progress, the ever-onward sense in which Mankind is going somewhere and the present is defined by the future, that is, by that which is not present. As Foucault suggests in "Truth and Power,"[9] our model for history should be war, not signs.

If there is a counterpart to the notion of progress in Foucault, it might be simply the sedimentary accumulation of marks and monuments (objects and "facts"); the archive does not get better, just bigger and more dense. Foucault's philosophy is archaeological, which means that it seeks not to make the truth present (to represent it), but, more modestly or at least more indefinitely, to brush some of the dust off the marks and monuments, which can only exist in the domain of the contemporary. His philosophy does not attempt to restore something but to write it and display its surfaces. What this ultimately involves is a production of a history of the present.[10] As it must always in many ways be, the interest in the past, which is a conspicuous element of this investigation of political representation, is necessarily part of and motivated by an interest in the present.

Foucault might call some of the general mechanisms that we aim to investigate "regularities"—productive, situated regularities—and he would emphasize the connection with "regulation," and make it explicit. This is not regulation with a definite source, simply invented and imposed from above (again, not the classical configuration of power as purely hierarchical and fundamentally coercive). He means regularity—regulation—as that which comprises and determines a system of practices and discourse and produces the identities, positions, and terms they contain. This definition seems to be an appropriate characterization of what I am going to be addressing here. This is representation, then, not as an inherently neutral instrument or tool in the hands of an independently existing creature who is its master but representation as coextensive with the creature itself, a sort of self-creation and creator, which articulates itself under the auspices of articulating what it must insist is already there. The interest in political representation is, finally, an interest in the political subject, and it is worth pondering some of the prominent, paradoxical meanings embodied in the following definitions: (1) the subject of the traditional, hierarchical variety, the identity of the vassal, subordinate to a ruler or governor of some kind and associated with hierarchical and repressive forms of power; (2) the subject as it has been linked in the modern period with the identity of consciousness, an identity that is associated with the autonomous, original power of free will, and so on; (3) the subject as something to be operated on, as in subject of an experiment, an identity associated with the productive power of formative techniques and dividing practices; and finally (4) the subject as in 'subject positions,' a presentation of the subject as differentially or relationally constituted (and therefore situated), a casting that both resonates off of and yet at the same time deviates from the others, a formulation that aims in part to emphasize the fluidity of effective identity.[11]

Fluid Unity

If there is unity in the history of Western thought, it must have something to do with the "perennial problem" of Unity, which has persisted in a variety of forms, among which is the problem of the One and the many. As a way of locating representation in Western philosophy and of circuitously foreshadowing the eighteenth-century (and onward) American discourse of a mixed government embodying the One, the few, and the many,[12] I begin with some observations about the One and the many made by Nietzsche.

The Nietzschean linkage of philosophy and metaphor—of philosophy and images of the truth—begins at the beginning. This beginning is not the originary source of Western philosophy, which is to say that it is not a wellspring—not a transcendental condition nor signifier—that would perpetually nourish, found, or, in a classical sense, determine the practice of philosophy in Western culture. Rather, the beginning is a specific, contingent, idiosyncratic signature in the Milesian region of our archive, the signature of Thales, the complex of marks bearing his name. Nietzsche's early address of Thales[13] culminates in the reading of a difference, the difference between Thales' special insight and the discourse that flows from it.

Through what Nietzsche calls a "mystic intuition" and, perhaps better, "the power of creative imagination," Thales grasped the unity of that which is, thereby transiting the gap between the One and the many. However, when he named the fluid gap circulating between the One and the many— when he gave voice to its identity and identified it—"he found himself talking about water!"[14]

It is clear that Nietzsche finds this articulation astonishing, intriguing, and even absurd.[15] It is absurd not so much because of what it names but because water marks the disruptive intervention of metaphor—of the image, of representation—into the truth. The articulation of truth necessarily involves an exchange, a substitution—a representation—even though it must also advance its images as literal in order to be counted as properly philosophical discourse. Thales means water when he announces "Water!" which in Nietzsche's reading is what makes him a philosopher and marks his break with the past. For Nietzsche, Thales' truth is in its expression, which means that the expression makes the truth and that it does not, in merely instrumental fashion, express or reflect the Real (the "really-real"), the One that holds the many together.

The point I wish to emphasize—a point I will stress in a variety of ways throughout this study, particularly in connection with the identity of the political subject—is not that Thales' identificative move distorts some prior, pristine, hierarchically privileged insight.[16] While it is important to keep sight of the deviant quality that Nietzsche associates so intimately with the utterance of truth ("truth as necessary error"), the question of difference here is not about the traditional gap posited between an independent reality (True) and words (false), between immediate insight and its necessarily errant expression, or between will (to truth) and its representation.

What I wish to stress instead about Nietzsche's Thales is that he names an *arche*—he gives it a specific identity— and that this name—this metaphor and image—is taken to be the truth. Once Thales utters "Water!" this unifying response floods the cosmos in all of its multiplicity while other possibilities remain apparently (and provisionally) excluded from the space circulating between the One and the many and from the discordant discourse of truth; coherence is established in the specificity of its totalizing utterance.

Like the extant texts of the Pre-Socratics, this point may seem fragmentary. However, Thales' water is the first sign of the truth I hope to cultivate here. More pertinent to the broader theme of this project, its intimate philosophical and historical association with the problem of the One and the many inscribes an initial connection between philosophy and the domain of political representation since the latter, too, is about truth and, in a unity or unitary system of expression, a configuration intimately tied to the problem of political expression and decision. More specifically, political representation has become the instrumental key to the general problem of bringing together the many voices of a society into the one body—ultimately, in the decisions and deployments—of its government (in legislative, executive, and juridical processes, in the apparatuses of bureaucracy, and in the general context of networked "communication"). Just as I want to avoid emphasizing that Thales' identification distorts some prior, pure, unarticulated insight, it is above all necessary to avoid assuming that political representation is a process that distorts some definite identity existing prior to it, founding it, and independent of it, the originally and finally autonomous political subject that has been posited in the background and as the foundation of the modern discourse of representation.

Water is the principle and ground of Thales' unity, and this observation is taken to be not poetry but the truth. Water is substance, the fundamental (not accidental) property, the Proper, not (from philosophy's perspective) a non-philosophical image nor a myth. What is true about Thales' water is that it is what the many share in common, what unites them and that naming it is an expression of this unity. Thales' water counters the threat of dispersing multiplicity and makes the incoherent coherent. In a way that is related, representation has come to be not only a mechanism—not just a neutral, accidental instrument—but a predominant principle and ground as well as a practical necessity for establishing the unity of the political organization of a society and for articulating and defining the republic. Political representation aims to approximate or takes as its ideal an exchange of unworkable (dangerous, anarchic) multiplicity—necessarily characterized by conflict and contest, marked by difference—for unitary order and univocal decision. The ideal of representation has come to be the true and unmanipulated realization of the political will, opinions, demands, or interests of the people made unified, realized in the One, the body politic, and the one of decision—the ideal, wild multiplicity domesticated and transformed into workable plurality through representation.

While the issue of representation in general and political representation in particular cannot be equated with or reduced to the classical problem of the One and the many (and we must be very careful not to push the analogy too far and not to take it too literally), the play between the One and the many may always be part of representation—part of what it is about. It may be useful to keep the classical aspect of this issue in mind during the ensuing investigation and not only when we get to the decisive, eighteenth-century discourse on mixed government. Insofar as it relates to problems such as that of the One and the many, the issue of political representation is a thoroughly and profoundly, if not entirely, classic philosophical issue. First, it indefinitely repeats the valorization of the One,[17] the metaphysical gesture par excellence, the figure inscribed and anticipated by Thales' water and tagged by Nietzsche. Unity, stability, and decision are what is at stake as a foundation[18] is established for coherent discourse—water or the United States—and as a space is constructed out of it, a space that enables a discourse and network of power to take shape, to institute itself, and to continue. As the one who is named (elected), the ideal representative is the condensed, mobilized substance of the electorate, of the representative's constituency, and of the political subject. Second, what Nietzsche's astonished reading draws attention to is Thales' substitution of water for the unity he is seeking. Representative government is a manufactured unity, a surrogate for an organic being that would be unworkably dispersed, indecisive, and inexpressible without the substitution provided for it by representation. Hobbes already offers a concise addition to this metaphysics of substitution in *Leviathan*:

> A multitude of men, are made one person, when they are by one man, or one person, represented; so that it be done with the consent of every one of that multitude in particular. For it is the unity of the represener, not the unity of the represented, that maketh the person one. And it is the represener that beareth the person, and but one person: and unity, cannot otherwise be understood in multitude.[19]

Unity cannot be understood in multiplicity—in the many—because it cannot be without the surrogate identity of the political representative. As water provides unity to Thales' cosmos, so representation provides unity to the political cosmos.

In short, while it would be a mistake to claim that representation feeds off of Thales' water, it would also be a mistake to overlook the relationship between the problem of the One and the many and representation. While it must be insisted that they are different problems and that the former is not just a more general version of the latter, it is also true that the newer one responds to some of the anxieties and complications that gave rise to the older one even if the concerns and stakes are very different for each. As a political discourse and practice, modern representation also reinscribes the metaphysical gestures of unification and order through substitution, as the artificial architecture of representative government is constructed as a dynamic stand-in for an autonomous and organic, but—without the mediation provided by representation—diverse and dispersed political subject.

The problem of the One and the many is an overtly philosophical problematic while political representation is a response to a practical, political range of possiblities; given the dispersal and disparity of a mass of particular subjects—of citizens—how do we pull their many wills, opinions, or diverse interests together into a general union? How do we effectively transform this multiplicity of individuals into a single, unified body politic? Plato's indefinite answer to the general philosophical form of the question of the One and the many—participation—is almost necessarily part of the first stage in answering the political form of this question, a question that might also be translated as, how do we set things up so that the many voices can participate in the (necessarily) univocal voice of the One, a voice that can choose and act, a voice that will not get lost in the cacophony? Differences, including the differences between the many political subjects, tend to generate indecision. A community and thus a government must decide. How, then, should differences get negotiated in the political sphere?

Representation offers or presents itself as a means—a tool—for making participation of the many (the voting citizens) in the One (their elected, governing body) both possible and practicable. The difference between the One and the many and political representation cannot be based upon the fundamentally philosophical profile of the One and the many and the fundamentally political, practical profile of political representation. Such a differentiation simply reinscribes the classical metaphysical opposition between theory and practice and revives the danger of such an opposition.[20] Both the problem of the One and the many and that of political representation hinge on the at least tacit but decisive assertion of a transcendental signified or condition, in the name of which a substitution is made. Consequently, both are equally metaphysical. That is one of the most interesting and crucial issues here. As Dick Howard has written:

> In politics, it is the danger of the One, the Prince or the Party who becomes the unification and incarnation of the Good Society. . . . In theory, the danger is also the One, the Truth or Being which is taken as the "really-real"[21]

Politics and theory are as inseparable from each other as practice and discourse and bear in common the same danger, deference to the One. So philosophy is not the only stronghold of metaphysics. (Philosophy may in fact be one of the more harmless forms of metaphysics.) This current project could be described as an investigation of the metaphysical dimensions of political representation. In its assumption of the "really-real"—of, for example, the original, willful political subject or, alternatively, of capital—the discourse and practice of political representation is as metaphysical as any philosophical resolution of the perennial problem of the One and the many. The danger here is not that of a dictatorial individual or party but of voting for the ontotheology of modern rationalism, which, despite all of its "pluralist" tolerances and its advocacy of "free" markets, may always be working toward unanimity, toward becoming a one-party system, a system of the Truth, that is, metaphysical closure, which is the end.

Chapter II

Representing England Twice

FROM THE GENERAL TO THE SPECIFIC

In his classic work on English Parliament, A. F. Pollard writes, "Representation is, moreover, an ambiguous word which needs to be defined before we can deal with its development."[1] Responding to this ambiguity, Helen M. Cam describes the apparently basic condition or simple scene from which representation arises: "If you want to get the opinion of a crowd, whether of children or of adults, you will in effect say, 'Don't all talk at once—who will speak for you?' If an agreement on action has been arrived at by a group of people, one man will naturally be empowered to act for them."[2] This primal scene of representation is an appealing image, particularly in conjunction with Cam's further comment that "these problems, you will note, arise when there is an active community upon which some external demand is made."[3] For her, this "community" is what is of most interest, and the key question in analyzing representation is, "what is the community that is represented?" The variable identity suggested and addressed by this question will determine the specific character and positive content of a given formation of representation.

While a critical investigation of representation cannot restrict itself to this question, it is this question more than any other that goes to the core of the problem of representation. As J. R. Pole states, "In any theory of representation, the question 'How?' is preceded logically by the question 'Who?' or perhaps, 'Whom?'"[4] However, while this observation indicates the most critical issue at stake, even this sequence of questions is preceded by having already answered what in a particular way, by determining that what is represented is in some self-evident sense a who. This is not a straightforward or self-evident conclusion. For one thing, there is always the danger of anachronism when we try to resolve this identity as it functioned in the past. Further, it may be impossible to answer how, who, or what on a general level. Nevertheless the general level does provide tempting access or orientation to the particular formation of representation.

M. V. Clarke's following observation remains on this more general level, contributing another dimension to the primal representation of representation offered by Cam:

> The principle itself, put in general terms, means that one or more persons stand or act on behalf of others and, at least for the purpose in hand, an identity of interests between them is assumed. The idea of representation in the widest sense is probably as old as the first primitive community which was aware of itself as a whole.[5]

The image of representation offered here emphasizes a transfer between persons, based on common identity (although, as we shall see later, identity need not be restricted to interests). Through this transfer, it could be argued that the simplest ambassador or spokesperson is and always was a representative, and there is an important truth to this observation. Clarke also repeats the link between representation and community and in this connection suggests that this transfer, translation, substitution, or exchange is an ancient one. Recognizing its long and complicated history in the community and seeing it as the condition or perhaps instrument of the possibility of univocity—of making a coherent voice or political decision possible and practicable—the antiquity of representation could also be associated with the antiquity of metaphysics since the complex gesture of unification and substitution through an identification of common interests (e.g., essential characteristics) is one of the gestures most characteristic of Western metaphysics.

At the same time—and this cannot be overemphasized— we cannot be talking about a persistent formation that simply reappears in different guises. Different formations of representation are different from each other. It is vital to take these differences seriously, to work from the general to the specific, an alternative to the more traditional philosophical route, which has tended to work in the opposite direction. It is vital to confront and take seriously the differences between the specific formations of substitutive exchange characteristic of representation since there is no representation apart from them. Clarifying these differences will be the primary task of the entirety of Part One of this project.

THE COMMUNITY OF REPRESENTATION IN MEDIEVAL ENGLAND

> The king to the sheriff of Norfolk and Suffolk greeting. Whereas on the part of the bishop of Worcester, the earl of Leicester, the earl of Gloucester, and certain other nobles of our realm, three knights have been summoned from each of our counties to be at St. Albans on the approaching feast of St. Matthew the Apostle, in order with them to treat about (*tractare*) the common affairs of our kingdom and whereas we and our nobles aforesaid shall come together on the same day at Windsor to treat concerning peace between between us and them; we command you on our part to give strict orders to those knights from your bailiwick, who have been summoned before those nobles on the aforesaid day, that avoiding all excuse they come to us at Windsor on the said day (and you are also strictly to prohibit them from going elsewhere on that day) to have a conference (*colloquium*) with us on the aforesaid matters; so that, as a consequence of this business, they may see and understand that we propose no undertaking but what we know to be for the honour and common benefit of our realm. By witness of the king at Windsor, September 11.
>
> —Writ Summoning Three Knights of the Shire to Parliament at Windsor (A.D. 1261)[6]

> Initially, representation is a representation *before* the Prince, before Power. . . .
>
> —Etienne Balibar[7]

> In dealing with medieval representation we have always to think in terms of feudal service rather than in those of democratic principle.
>
> —A. F. Pollard[8]

It is difficult to isolate the practice of representation in medieval politics, partly because representation was practiced first by various orders within the Church (the Dominicans are always cited).[9] In England, the formal political practice begins in the thirteenth century when representatives were summoned by Henry III (r. 1216-1272) on numerous separate occasions. Assembled representatives did not yet constitute an ongoing, regular representative assembly but were called in connection with always specific royal concerns during this period, probably usually with fiscal and also military concerns, which, as ever, inevitably overlapped.

The feudal orders (orderings) officially represented in medieval English government are the estates of the realm—the clergy, the baronage, and the commons—which together, united through their representation in Parliament and in conjunction with the privileged power of the throne, come to comprise or, perhaps more accurately, to represent the community of the realm.[10] The identity of the clergy was of course derived from the institutions of religion and included both the clerical baronage and the lower clergy. The identity of the baronage, however, was derived from estates granted directly by the Crown (or via hereditary inheritance of such royal grants). Coded territory is the obvious source of this identity. It is also the source of the identity of the commons, which is constituted in connection with the shires, towns, and boroughs.

The first record of representatives of the shires (of, specifically, knights) being summoned to the king, along with the other two estates (the clergy and baronage), was during the reign of John in 1213. Over the course of the thirteenth century, knights were periodically summoned as representives of the shires although Stubbs points out that the nature of "these assemblies is a matter of debate, and it cannot certainly be said that the knights of the shire were regarded as a necessary ingredient of parliament until 1294. Their regular and continuous summons dates from 1295."[11] From then on, the third estate, commons, was included in government—in Parliament proper or in various kinds of assembled councils—through the mechanism of representation. But it is important to ask that if it is the subjects of the community of the realm that are represented in Parliament, who or what are these subjects?

Formulated in terms of the estates, these subjects were not individual wills or even, perhaps, interests—we are not talking about a modern political subject here—but localities, classes, orders, and geographical divisions as well as networks of specific powers. That is, although every individual was a subject—the King's—a subject of the realm was not an individual. In short, the subject of feudal representation is the community, organized in terms of territory.[12]

> What is the community that is represented? . . . In English sources, the oldest unit to be represented is the vill, in 1110; the next is the shire and hundred, in 1166; the next is the cathedral chapter, in 1226; the next is the diocesan clergy, in 1254; the next is the 'community of the land'— otherwise the barons—in 1258; and the next, the borough in 1265.[13]

Extending this point and its ramifications for our understanding of medieval identity, Clarke writes:

> Perhaps this sense of place, this membership of a geographical hierarchy, is the part of the outlook of the medieval Englishman which is now most difficult for us to imagine, though all the evidence of the records goes to prove its existence. Either by the king at the centre or by

the ordinary man in his village, political geography was deemed to determine something essential. John Green was not only a freeman of the parish and vill of Cow Honeybourne, he was also a member of the hundred of Kiftsgate, and, through that membership, had his part in the county of Gloucester. Each form of membership had its corresponding activity in the courts of the vill, the hundred and the shire.[14]

This territorially articulated subject possesses several definite identities: as a juristic base (administration and organization of the law via organization of territory becomes a vital dimension of the organization of the community of the realm, or of the Kingdom itself); as a tax base (it does not represent but is a tax base); as a military base; and thus, more generally—all of these identities combined—as a power base. What is common about the third estate, then, is that it is comprised of communes, and what a commune is—the vill, the hundred, the shire, the county—does not include common people even if it assumes above all else the labor of their bodies. Common people are not representatives; they do not participate in the process of selecting representatives of the shires to which they belong—the communities in which they live and work—and common people are not what was represented in the assemblies. Even villeins, a class of serfs who were freemen in their legal relations,[15] did not participate in the process of selecting the knights who would represent the shires. The representatives, and those who belonged to the courts[16] that selected them, were mainly members of the nobility (the lesser nobility), whose own vassals, fiefdoms, and territories were what was at risk in every play of power, although already in the thirteenth century, yeomen (landholding freemen) were also allowed to represent the shires in parliament, if knights were unavailable.[17] This absence of common people from Commons was not an omission but a transformative affirmation of existing feudal hierarchies. As Pollard puts it, "Representation was not the offspring of democratic theory, but an incident of the feudal system."[18]

The power embodied in medieval English representation—the power of the community of the realm constituted by the combination of the monarch and the estates formally fused in representative assemblies—continued to be a rule of the classes and orders for whom the land was named (via royal grants) rather than a proto form or logical predecessor of popular sovereignty (which itself is not something self-evident, as we shall discuss later). Power was, above all, in the hands of the great magnates, who were in no sense political equals with the lesser landholders and middling classes—the knights and burgesses—who sat in the House of Commons (these last represented the bulk of tax resources), not to mention the vast majority of the population, whose labor made the entire machinery of medieval society possible. Commons may have represented the tax base of the community of the realm, but it did not represent common people, and landholders as a whole were the beneficiaries of the broadened participation in a centralized government that developed in the thirteenth and fourteenth centuries.

THE FORCE OF REPRESENTATION

Regardless of the sources of the ideas behind it, there are strong breaks in the history of representation, and the previous section on medieval representation is offered neither as part of a comprehensive history nor as a serpent's egg through the membrane of which might be seen the outline of the already formed creature within.[19] Instead, it is offered as a contrasting image to what follows in order to emphasize that the discourses and practices of representation change enormously and to serve as a precaution against assuming that we already know in advance what representation is. The following section on the discourse and practice of virtual representation serves a similar purpose except that the contrast developed here may be characterized as part of a more self-conscious, immediate conflict, which in one of its vectors culminated in an actual war, the American Revolution.

By the eighteenth century representation was neither a merely technical convenience nor an abstract issue but a driving force linked to other breaks in history. Representation was—and remains—a force as well as an idea, which is to say that it is above all a practice, a dynamic material configuration with practical effects. This image is one of its profiles, and one of its values. Representation does not exist because, for whatever reason, some group of people think that what they do is represent, because they intend to represent, or because they call or name what they do representation; the bottom line is that representation exists as a practical part of a given network of power and of the discourse that constitutes the terms and features of representation and the identities in play there. This preliminary observation may help clarify certain aspects of the following point about virtual representation.

The theory of virtual representation grew out of the practices that had begun back in the thirteenth century, as England was beginning to consolidate and unify itself as a nation. To subvert a Hegelian perspective here by means of Foucauldian laughter (i.e., by means of Nietzschean irony), this growth can be interpreted as an extension—better, a sort of graft[20]—of rationality. It is not a "rationality" associated with an expanding, developing Reason but rationality as a process of rationalization or legitimation,[21] something added on to that which it rationalizes, that which it makes rational or coherent (but which is in no way above, outside, nor even dialectically connecting it all together, nor grounding it). In short, the theory of virtual representation legitimated a predominant dimension of the existing political, economic, and social structures and the complex of power practices associated with them even as this complex was changing (the rationalization is perhaps an effect or reflection of this change). In an ironic sense, then, the advocates of the theory of virtual representation were right in believing that their theory described what representation is.

However, it must be emphasized that this legitimation is not necessarily a matter or process of "ideology." As shall be discussed in a later chapter, and as Foucault argues,[22] the metaphysical notion of "ideology" necessarily implies falsity (over against Truth) and plays on sentiments of suspicion, for instance, of an unseen agenda concealed behind a smoke screen of visible discourse. Regardless of the intentions of its advocates (which sometimes certainly did involve the deployment of smoke screens and other dodges, as usual), the theory of virtual representation did not hide anything so much as it more simply authorized the way things were and were becoming; it thus provided a strong conservative defense against challenges to both traditional and new institutions of representation and of English socio-economy and politics generally, challenges that acquired a threatening visage in the seventeenth century.

"The Politicians of Metaphysics"[23]
(and Virtual Representation)

> For everie Englishman is intended to bee there present, either in person or by procuration and attornies, of what preheminence, state, dignitie, or qualitie soever he be, from the Prince (be he King or Queene) to the lowest person of Englande. And the consent of the Parliament is taken to be everie mans consent.
>
> —Sir Thomas Smith (1583)[24]

During the period from the sixteenth century through the seventeenth—through the English Civil War and then the Glorious Revolution with the consequent adoption of the Bill of Rights in 1689—the Crown was losing power in bits and pieces, and Commons was picking it up. In the margins of politics, a discourse of popular sovereignty was making itself evident (e.g., the Levellers, who were part of an emerging discourse of natural law and natural rights). In other spheres, those of empire and trade, England was becoming a world power, and the great corporations devoted to the exploitation of faraway lands[25] had begun to contribute to the transformation of England's identity, largely through the correlative creation of a new class of wealthy merchants. One powerful ramification of this development was that the fundamental value of land began to float; wealth became something mobilized, commodified. The arboreal grounds of feudal value in the codes of bloodlines and soil were being displaced by the power of capital. These interlocking factors contributed decisively to the transformation of the conditions and the discourse of political representation in England.[26] One of the most prominent tendencies associated with this transformation was given voice by the theory of virtual representation, which in its conservatism paradoxically helped reinforce new socioeconomic realities.

While he did not invent what some writers call the "fiction" of virtual representation,[27] which had begun to develop some time earlier, the most well-known proponent of this theory is the eighteenth-century British statesman and political writer, Edmund Burke. As Pitkin observes,[28] his is by no means a consistent set of doctrines (sometimes there are even what to a modern eye may seem to be surprises[29]), and the intent here, then, is not to present Burke's philosophy, but, more simply and specifically, to use Burke as a vehicle (an actual or virtual representation?) of virtual representation, a theory that may seem simply to express the status quo but which could be viewed instead as one of its constituting elements. Here, the political subject—what is represented in Parliament—is no longer coded land but interest (which, it turns out, has strong associations with property, i.e., with capital).

One thing clear from the outset is that in its elaboration of the general interests of a nation, the notion of virtual representation is not as straightforward as it may sound at first. To begin with, a virtual representative does not represent or stand (in) for "the people." The political subject in play here is clearly not popular sovereignty. In fact, Burke is consistently, explicitly, and aggressively opposed to demands for representation on the basis of natural law or the natural rights of Man, demands that were, of course, heard continually at that time (he condemns them as "metaphysical" [cf. note 23]). For Burke, it is only through the institution of virtual representation that people can be "actually" represented. Perhaps the mixture of this position—ultimately, "actual" is made to depend on "virtual"—helps illustrate a point that should be emphasized both here and in this project as a whole, an emphasis that will become even more important in later chapters; what is meant by "actual" representation may be just as metaphysical and no more self-evident or self-identical than what is meant by "virtual."

In very concrete terms, Burke's canonized 1774 "Speech to the Electors of Bristol at the Conclusion of the Poll," provides the basic tenets of the doctrine—the theory, the description, the fiction, the discourse—of virtual representation, a doctrine which assumes a paradigmatic position in what Pitkin calls the "mandate-independence" controversy,[30] a position that affirms the independence of the representative and authorizes a representative unbound by—unobligated by, free of—instructions from his constituents.[31] The mandate-independence or delegate-trustee controversy seems to revolve not around what is represented but instead around the relationship between the terms of representation, which is the relationship between represented and representative. The way this relationship is taken up is through the identity of the representative.

Is the representative simply a delegate, an agent, an inherently neutral conduit or empty, merely instrumental (non)identity, charged with the task of pushing an agenda provided—spelled out—by those who have elected him? That is, does the representative simply mirror his constituency? Is the representative a trustee, someone truly special and wise, chosen because he[32] knows or is capable of coming to know what is good for the community and may be trusted to ascertain and pursue its genuine interests, independent of the particular, partial, and often misguided desires of those who have elected him, desires that may be better left ignored? It was these sorts of questions about this relationship that concerned politicians and political thinkers in the eighteenth century. Burke and the other proponents of the theory of virtual representation believed that the representative must be an independent

trustee and that only this identity could offer a representation that was "real," probably even more real than that provided by "actual" representation, an amazing convolution that
may become clear in what follows.

Here is how Burke presented the case to his constituents:

> Parliament is not a congress of ambassadors from differ-
> ent and hostile interests, which interests each must main-
> tain, as an agent and advocate, against other agents and
> advocates; but Parliament is a deliberative assembly of
> one nation, with one interest, that of the whole, where,
> not local purposes, not local prejudices ought to guide,
> but the general good, resulting from the general reason
> of the whole. You choose a member, indeed; but when
> you have chosen him he is not a member of Bristol, but
> he is a member of Parliament.[33]

I might begin commenting on the identity of the virtual representative suggested here by recalling remarks made earlier
about Nietzsche's astonished response to Thales' interest, and,
specifically, about the connection between the problem of the
One and the many and the tendencies of political representation, a connection embodied in the theme of unification.
There is "one" nation, asserts Burke, "one" interest, a unity
directly linked to and even coextensive with "the general"—
general good, general reason (general reason, not general
will)—and repeated by "the whole." All of these terms are
assembled together as members of a unitary network, an economy of national unity, which stands above mere local purposes; like the necessarily flawed and deficient particulars participating in Plato's Forms, local purposes have True (here,
truly political) significance only insofar as they participate in
the general interest of the nation. In some sense, Burke's unity
must be based historically upon the unity inscribed by the
notion of the community of the realm, and this massive, concrete-abstraction or instance of the "social imaginary"[34] is one
of the nodal points of the metaphysics of virtual representation. At the same time, this unity is also an effect or instance

of (the return of) the general economy of Western metaphysics, which is an economy of the truth.

What is self-evident for Burke from the outset—what any educated, cultivated, practical, and wise gentleman would see—is (1) that the nation is a unity, one formulated in terms of general, objective "interest," and (2) that this unity takes clear precedence over the (subjective) particularity of local life and over all of the diversity (and conflict) that local life, multiplied throughout all of Great Britain, embodies. "The general good" rather than "local purposes" constitutes the meaning and aim of representation, and the hierarchized relation between these oppositional terms bears an enormous amount of metaphysical value.

The *good* here revolves around the interests of the nation. That it should be general is another eventual, perhaps meaningless[35] consequence of the notion of the community of the realm, which may not have led to but nevertheless helped pave the way for the development of the British nation-state and for the network of political and economic practices and exchanges that constitute its material(-symbolic) reality. At the same time, it is important to mention the obvious fact that in the history of Western metaphysics—in philosophy since Plato—the Good has always been general. Knowledge— the object, aim, and product of the exercise of "general reason"—has always taken precedence over mere opinion (local purpose, particular perspective). Such opinion is so inclined to be false—to miss its Truth, or True interests—and tends to be shaped by the short view, the narrow view, in contrast with the absolute, genuinely philosophical (i.e., ontotheological) view—"the big picture"—which is determined by and oriented toward totality, toward the One, which is also the Good.

In fact, however, as a working politician, it is not as if Burke himself neglected or overlooked local purposes, since in everyday politics truly doing so would encourage dissent and possibly lead to revolution. Thus, he has his own framework, applicable on the practical level, within which a True and legitimate local purpose may be determined for the practical tasks faced by a representative assembly. More specifically,

Burke turns Proper local interests into something general, by relocating—dislocating—them, by fitting and absorbing them into categories, such as agricultural, manufacturing, trade, and religious interests, bootstrapped up to and in all individual cases unified under the aegis of the collective interests of the nation. As the canon repeats, Birmingham may have no actual spokesman in Parliament, but its trading interests are virtually (and therefore effectively, competently, even better than "actually") represented there by Bristol's representative, since Bristol's interest,[36] too, is trade. If Irish Catholics are neither actually nor virtually represented in Parliament, it is because Catholics are not represented, and this is a general interest that has been omitted from and should be incorporated into the institution of representation, not a particular one. That is to say, the particular interest is a legitimate or politically recognizable interest only insofar as it is one of those really quite few, objectively determinable ones that concern the nation as a unified whole.[37]

What is represented, then, are interests, but what is an interest? What constitutes one? In order to address the material that the representative has to work with, we must investigate what it is that is represented under the auspices of interests, especially since, as has already been suggested, this variable identity is what determines the configuration of a particular formation of representation.

An entire ground of value was upset when, with the emergence of a wealthy merchant class—with the emergence of capitalism—land became a mobilized commodity. Until then, in feudal times, land had been the ground in all senses, the stable foundation of social hierarchy and of order, the order of power; the order of feudalism was written on the land. With the commodification of land that accompanied the rise of a new, wealthy, commercial class, anyone with enough money could purchase land, and the special, foundational status of real property, while by no means lost, became less positive, less clear although something clearly different from what it was before. What had been simple, beyond question, was now a complicated, confusing affair. What had been unambiguously real and stable began to float a bit, in a way perhaps metaphorically related to Baudrillard's nightmare world of floating signifiers.[38] What had been stable began to move; being became becoming, and thus becoming became being. What had been the source of (and ground) of identity and assurance, of wealth and power, now became a source of conflict and convolution, as it finally reached the point where boroughs and eventually seats in Parliament were actually put up for sale.[39]

Still, land continued to be (or perhaps became) a concern central enough that land requirements for representatives to Parliament were officially established in 1710 (and were not abolished until 1858).[40] Some historians see the continued talk about and obsession with land as something on the order of mere lip service to outmoded ideals—traditional feudal ideals—or as nostalgia. (This may be true although "anxiety about" might be a more fitting phrase than "lip service.") However, such an observation is no longer pertinent if the focus is shifted from land to, more generally, property. Whether the understanding of property and the overt importance and priority given to it at the end of the seventeenth century by, for example, John Locke,[41] was one of the causes of discursive conditions and events, or an effect,[42] the fact is that there is a great deal of attention being paid to the issue of property during this period.[43] Writing a hundred years after Locke—Rousseau having obsessed with it more recently—Burke returns again and again to the issue of property in *Reflections on the Revolution in France*, upset perhaps above all by the various seizures of property, particularly ecclesiastic property, carried out in France in the name of revolution, of Liberty, Equality, and Fraternity.[44]

Coextensive with the fact that anyone with the money could now simply buy land, it is no longer land that is represented in Commons. What is represented for Burke and for the theory of virtual representation is "interests," which may be a permutation of the earlier representation of land, refracted through the development of commerce and an economy connected increasingly to areas outside of the British Isles by trade and exploitation. This permutation is not a blend (of land plus developing socioeconomic factors), but is, rather, something truly new in history, a genuine hybrid. The hybrid produced by this permutation and socioeconomic development is property, and it is property—capital—that constitutes the bulk of "interests." While it would be a mistake to reduce Burke's interests to property alone—religion will be the persistent exception— most of the things that count as legitimate interests for him are forms of property, which are also forms of capital.

Let us move back from the level of general interests to the local and to the relationship between national interests and particular interests. Bristol and Manchester and Cambridge have particular, local interests, which must be served, but it is precisely these local interests which prevent individual communities—which prevent the atoms that make up the body of the nation—from grasping the broad interests of the nation as a whole. On the local level, the all too clear outlines of the trees make perception of the forest impossible. Apprehension of the particular obscures the general. The subjectivism of local self-knowledge conflicts with the objectivity that accompanies a vision of the nation as a whole as it fits into the world (i.e., as heart of the new world market and the world distribution of power).

These concepts are all utterly metaphysical. Given the context, so, too, is the observation that particular interests must be served in order for national interests also to be served. We have mentioned how this is accomplished; the particular is recognized and served by being absorbed into general categories of interest. This absorption is possible for Burke because the vision or determination of interests is an objective process and because the interests themselves are objective, positive, and self-identical.

However, although they may be objective, positive, and self-identical, these interests are not obvious, not, that is, obvious in the way that subjective interests—desires, wishes, opinions, and products of the will—are obvious in their expression. For Burke and for the discourse of virtual representation, the representation of objective interests is simply not synonymous with, even if it often coincides with, the representation of the will or wishes of his constituency. Once again, what is represented virtually is not people. As Pitkin puts it, "he who represents a person must act in accord with that person's wishes; he who represents an interest must act in accord with that interest."[45] Thus it is not and cannot be wishes with which representatives act in accordance, not if they are doing their job properly. "For Burke, then, the representative has no obligation to consult his constituent. . . . Burke's position on this issue is related to . . . his view of government and politics as matters of knowledge and reason, not of opinion or will; to the idea that political questions have right answers which can be found."[46] If political questions have true, definitive answers and if objective interests are not obvious in the way that subjective interests (i.e., expressions of the people's will) are obvious, how are they determined? "How" here means "who" (Nietzsche). Who, then, determines them? The representatives do, of course. But who are the representatives?

"A true natural aristocracy is not a separate interest in the state, or separable from it," says Burke.[47] Whatever its socioeconomic relationship to the rest of the community and all that is implied in it, the outstanding attribute of the fortunate members of this aristocracy is a finely honed, practical wisdom, a general wisdom, which provides the special talent required to participate in the deliberation about and articulation of these interests and in the decisions about how to serve them well. An elite corps—practically speaking, a club—of gentlemen deliberate, formulate, and decide together, each a particular instance of reason, the body together constituting that general reason needed to determine the general good of the nation and of the whole.

As an individual, each representative does represent the interests of his consituency, although, as has been described, those interests are defined not in their own terms but in terms of the way they dovetail into the interests of the whole. The representative must actively, independently pursue this (objective) interest rather than transmit or carry out the constituency's wishes or any kind of mandate provided by the constituency—this is crucial—formulated outside of the unique, rational, objective context of parliamentary deliberation, the deliberation in which Parliament's true natural aristocracy is engaged (interest and will remain and must remain separate and decisively different from each other). Everything important is formulated within the exclusive, truth seeking world of Parliament, a world in which parts and wholes must be brought together seamlessly. Each part represents something particular (i.e., a particular as determined in relation to the whole), and each and all together represent the whole. Ultimately, then, legitimate particulars cannot really be in conflict with the whole, or, if they are, it will always be possible to determine a reasonable resolution. The scene of representation is not one of conflict, and the end is not multiplicity but unity, univocity, cohesion, agreement, and reason; that is the telos that makes it all make sense.

One interesting, practical feature of Burke's conception of representation is that the number of representatives for a given interest does not matter[48] although this is really not so curious when one considers his view of the nature of the representative body and its tasks and activities. As Burke periodically asserts,[49] good government is not a matter of mathematics. This means not only that it is not a matter of applying formulas (anyone could perform such a mechanical activity) but also that it is not a matter of quantities (e.g., how many are for or against an issue). Instead it is a matter of quality: quality of debate, quality of the deliberative process, and quality of reasoning that goes into determining how to formulate and respond to an issue. Good representation is not a rote process of calculating how many desire some particular state of affairs but of wisely determining how that state of affairs should be best and objectively served. The representative process should never succumb to the subjective perspective of desire but should always remain within the sphere of objectivity, a sphere guaranteed by the very quality and independence of the members of the representative body, a body whose view is always ultimately to the general good. Because of its objectivity and the quality of its members, the representative assembly is and must remain truly independent; its judgments are open to reevaluation and change (by it) but are basically beyond question. In the final analysis, it remains beyond accountability, and the only practical check on it is its own collective wisdom.

Burke's representative assembly, then, is an elite group of cultured, well-educated, generally wealthy gentlemen (who else could be "independent"?).[50] Jeremy Benthem offered a graphic illustration of this elite club when he sarcastically proposed, "Why do not the Oligarchy, form themselves into a Grand Eating Club, to eat for the whole nation, and then tell the starving people they are virtually fed."[51] The scepticism and sarcasm inscribed by this image was one that was shared on the other side of the Atlantic by many of the American colonists.

Finally, as a moment of transit between Bristol and America where we will dwell for more or less the remainder of this phase of the investigation, let me break the fragment of Burke's 1774 speech out of its current discursive isolation and note one element in it that crosses the ocean. "Parliament is not a congress," insists Burke, quite conceivably aware that, as Pole points out, "the word Congress was being used at that time for the meeting of delegations from the different American colonies in Philadelphia."[52] If he was a reformer, then—one of his traditional identities—Burke, despite his aggressive and sarcastic polemic against metaphysics, was not a metaphysical reformer. He continued to grant privilege to gentlemanly deliberation about the Unitary interests of the nation rather than step down and open the door to the kind of conflictual space constituted with such uncertainty by the Continental Congress, which, after the representative assembly of Parliament instituted the Intolerable Acts,[53] officially convened for the first time from September 5 through October 26, 1774 (this meeting culminated in a ban on British products). Burke delivered his speech to Bristol on November 3, thereby constituting an emblematic intersection of conflicting views, a conflict perhaps open to productive debate within a congress but theoretically excluded as conflict from the unitary general reason at work in the institution described by Burke.

It was not congress nor conflict that Burke wanted, but unity. While it might be a mistake to push this claim too far (and while its meaning may change when applied to the period following the Revolution), the American revolutionaries were a little more metaphysically adventurous (as well as politically rebellious) than Burke,[54] since they could not help but generate an institution of conflict. The Boston Tea Party, which provoked four of the five laws constituting the Intolerable Acts, enacted a subversive metaphysical drama about representation as the 'Indians' tossed the archetypally English tea[55] into the harbor in protest of taxation without representation, virtual, actual, or otherwise. "Otherwise" was what America would breed, as its wild invention and development broke with traditional political discourse, including the categories derived ultimately from Plato and Aristotle, even as it was affirming and reinscribing them in the mixed government it succeeded in instituting.

Chapter III

Common Sense[1] and the Constitution of Representation

ACTUALLY IN AMERICA

Edmund Burke was by no means the only eighteenth-century proponent of the theory of virtual representation,[2] which was also an institutional practice and an analysis or legitimating explanation that was widely applied at the time. A dramatic example of such an application (or deployment) was the response elicited from the British by American opposition to the Stamp Act, a 1765 revenue law requiring colonial publications and legal documents to bear a tax stamp. This act infuriated the colonists, who were increasingly threatened, disturbed, and angered by instances of "taxation without representation."

The official English defense of the Stamp Act centered around the notion that the colonies were virtually represented in Parliament. It was argued that even though the American colonies did not vote and had no actual representatives in Parliament, they were nevertheless virtually represented there since, "'every Member of Parliament sits in the House not as representative of his own constitutents but as one of that august assembly by which all the commons of Great Britain are represented.'"[3] That is, the colonies were part of Commons, just like those English towns and districts that had no actual representatives. Since, it was argued, representation is fundamentally virtual—that is what real representation is—the colonies (and thus the colonists) were on a par with the rest of Great Britain and were represented no less than any other legitimate sector of the empire. It was argued further and significantly that this should not be confused with the issue of elections, "'for the right of election is annexed to certain species of property, to peculiar franchises, and to inhabitancy in some particular places.'"[4] Although only a few have the right to vote, every English citizen is represented; representation and election are separate issues and should not be conflated (later, of course, the Americans were to develop an intimate connection between elections and political representation). In the background of all of this rhetoric, supporting it all—and, again, this is the metaphysical pattern emphasized in the previous section—"what made this conception of virtual representation intelligible, what gave it its force in English thought, was the assumption that the English people, despite great degrees of rank and property, despite even the separation of some by three thousand miles of ocean, were essentially a unitary homogeneous order with a fundamental common interest."[5]

On one level, then, the Americans questioned the notion that they were, in fact, virtually represented the same way that a town like Manchester was, and their response to this analogy with English towns tended toward skepticism (radicals went even further, arguing that English towns like Manchester should have representatives too). On a more basic level, however, many of them were expressing their ambivalence about the notion of unitary order and common, objective interest[6] and were, thus, questioning the very basis of the theory of virtual representation (even though the republican images of unitary order and common interest would be repeated in important ways after the Revolution). With an argument for virtual representation based upon the notion of common interest, one could just "'as well prove,'" mocked James Otis, "'that the British House of Commons in fact represent all the people of the globe as those in America.'" It was a notion, wrote Arthur Lee, that "'would, in the days of superstition, have been called witchcraft'" for what it means is that while

> our privileges are all virtual, our sufferings are real. . . . We
> might have flattered ourselves that a virtual obedience

would have exactly corresponded with a virtual representation, but it is the ineffable wisdom of Mr. Grenville to reconcile what, to our feeble comprehensions, appeared to be contradictions, and therefore a real obedience is required to this virtual power.[7]

Thus, while some argued that America was not virtually represented in Parliament, others argued more radically that this conception of representation was nothing but an attempt to legitimate the exercise of English power over the colonies. In general, the colonists swallowed neither the taxes nor the rationalizations offered by Parliament. Through this scepticism and this questioning, they were taking steps from which would soon emerge truly new political configurations, new configurations of power, which would be coextensive with new configurations of representation. At the same time and on this same basic level, American scepticism about the official justification for a tax that was in no way chosen by them may be linked to what would become a conviction about the vital role played by voting in the process of representation in America.[8] From the standpoint of the colonists, the members of Parliament had no clue regarding the interests of Americans and could not have had without American consent,[9] without, that is, the actual representation of America via the direct involvement of elected American delegates (and even then . . .).

The debate about the nature of representation was already in full swing in the colonies. It was a practical debate, too. There were many debates, a point emphasizing that the inhabitants of the colonies were not a homogeneous or cohesive unity even if the popular tendency may be to read them that way.[10] The different colonies were different from each other in more than name alone—in interests, in historical ties to England, and in political organization—and significant differences within each colony helped make for a diversity that would confound the notion of a fundamental unity or cohesion (even though, at the same time, certain institutional patterns seemed to develop across many of these differences).[11] In the long run, these realities helped determine the kind of representation that would get instituted in America and the way that it would get organized.[12]

At the same time, though, representation was more than just the subject of a debate, more than just talk (discourse is practice, and—more than just instrumental—organization is a form of production). For one thing, while the bodies of laws and the formal political structures governing the various colonies and thus determining representation seem to have been based largely upon English law, representation was already undergoing mutation. In 1769, for instance, the Georgia legislature refused to tax four new parishes which had been denied representation by the Royal governor;[13] this gesture deviated from the English model by aggressively and unambiguously affirming the practical link between one authorized identity for a specific locality—the locality identified as a tax unit—and that locality's direct representation. Another example is that residence requirements were generally actively required for voters and their representatives in the colonies,[14] but, back in England, residency for voting and for officeholding was a dead issue in the corrupt domain of Parliamentary politics[15] (despite a residence qualification still in effect by a neglected statute instituted all the way back in 1413 [so much for conservative invocations of the hallowed English parliamentary tradition[16]]). While these pre-Revolutionary examples, particularly the latter, and the importance generally attached by the Americans to the practice of instructing representatives, might seem like merely technical matters, they signal a very concrete American affirmation of a direct (rather than virtual) link between the specific constituency and its representative, between a place[17] and the identity standing in for it in the various representative assemblies of the colonies; they thus mark an important break from English representative practices. Other general differences from English practice also affirm this more direct link, such as "constituency payments, frequent elections, elections of many officers, the doctrine of instructions, the banning of placeholding by representatives, and the decline in the prestige of the real-property qualification for the vote. . . ."[18] While it would be a distortion to reduce the American break in representation to a turn away from virtual to direct representation, mechanisms that emphasized the local and tended toward "direct" representation and clearly away from virtual representation nevertheless became part of everyday colonial political discourse-practice fairly early on, even well before the tumultuous, formative atmosphere of the 1760s and 1780s. So, for instance, while the representatives of the prosperous eastern counties protested against English taxation without colonial representation, the inhabitants of the western frontier districts demanded of the easterners that they be allowed their own representatives—that they be actually represented—since the concerns of the powerful, commercial eastern counties, which dominated the political apparatus, were very different from those of the pioneering farmers in the west, who felt underrepresented, if represented at all.[19] This example illustrates just one of the many, simultaneous material logics at work in the colonies. While the British, in an apparently logical extension of practices at home, tended to insist on officially incorporating new townships in the colonies without granting them representation (which in some short-term senses might have worked to the advantage of the commercial interests of the eastern counties), the westerners of the more sparsely populated interior continued to clamor for representation with a wary eye not so much on the English as on their eastern neighbors. Directly connected to this east/west (and urban/rural) difference—a difference which probably had a strong political aspect in all of the original thirteen colonies—the officially authorized right to wide-based representation in Massachusetts was not secured until the Act of August of 1775 (just weeks after the Battle of Bunker Hill), which granted one representative to every town or district of thirty or more qualified voters and two representatives to towns of 120 or more voters.[20] This act did not resolve the conflict in Massachusetts, however, because the commercial, heavily populated eastern counties argued that it did not equalize representation, particularly since they paid more (an unequal portion of) taxes. Thus, the original act was transformed the following April when a new act was passed at the end of a session of the Assembly when many of the western representatives had already left for home; now, every town of 220 freeholders was to get three representatives on top of which every extra 100 freeholders would qualify that district for one more representative. Some furor followed the passage of this act, and Pole points out the remarkable fact that in the very season of the Declaration of Independence, nothing was inscribed in one of the major documents in this Massachusetts debate about grievances against England but only about potential grievances of property (i.e., the eastern cosmopolites) against the representation of the countryside.[21] Here, again, it is not just America against England but also important developments and relationships within America that contribute to the new formation of representation, a representation that embodied conflict. The generative effects of contestation are at work not only in the relationship between old and new but also within the different, evolving segments of the new, which necessarily contain strong traces of the old,[22] from which they both find orientation and deviate at the same time.

The broad desire for local representatives, an emphasis on residency requirements, and the practice of instructing representatives—tendencies and techniques found within the various colonies—contributed to the development of differences from English political practice and thus from tradition. This development even acquired architectural embodiments (more than just cosmetic flourishes), such as in 1766 when the Massachusetts House of Representatives decided to build a public gallery, "to enable anyone to see that nothing was passed which was not to the real benefit and advantage of the constituents. . . . By exposing its debates to the public, the Assembly offered itself to the people as an agent of public opinion far more direct and immediate than could have normally been the case before."[23] What this architectural change is about is the transformation of the relationship between the terms of representation, between the representative and what is represented. It is thus also a transformation in the dyadic

identities at work in representation, a transformation occur-
ring within the workings of the colonial governments themselves apart from the connection with England. The image
and possibility of the Massachusetts House of Representatives'
new public gallery stood in marked, material contrast to the
image of the exclusive London club—Parliament—of which
Edmund Burke was a member since the public could now keep
a direct eye on the work of their representatives and be
exposed to the all-important deliberations, which previously
had been the predominantly private domain of those privileged to participate in the upper regions of representation.
Returning to the differences between different colonial and
then state governments, this public gallery can also and less
dramatically be contrasted with the situation in Pennsylvania
where outsiders were not admitted to hear debates until
1770—and even then only qualified electors were allowed in—
and where newspapers did not report legislative debates until
1776. Alternatively, it can also be contrasted with the out-
ward "appearance of almost monolithic authority" of the lead-
ership of revolutionary Virginia,[24] an appearance which concealed internal conflicts, the kinds of conflicts that would
have been more publicly visible in other colonies particularly
as witnessed from the public gallery in Massachusetts.
Another significant, material difference between practices of
representation in Massachusetts and Virginia was that the burden for remuneration of representatives fell directly on the
towns in Massachusetts—which, in the case of small towns
unable to afford it, sometimes resulted in the absence of representation—while the new Commonwealth of Virginia paid
all of its representatives uniformly, in set weights of tobacco
(which would be converted into cash at going market rates),
plus extra tobacco for mileage[25] (since the Middle Ages, trav-
eling has been one of the necessary practices and repeatedly
noted inconveniences associated with representation).
Differences abounded, all feeding into the development of new
forms of representation.

The distance from England contributed a significant
dimension to this development. More specifically, it made

possible a marked tendency or desire toward self-legislation if not autonomy and independence. Kammen cites a number of instances of seventeenth-century offensive maneuvers, challenges, and resistances to royal power by representative assemblies in Virginia, Massachusetts, Barbados, Antigua, Jamaica, South Carolina, east New Jersey, West Jersey, Pennsylvania, and New Hampshire.[26] As diplomatically worded as a communication addressed to his Sovereign Majesty might be, these challenges tended to be fairly direct, and many revolved around issues of not only approval but also actual initiation of legislation; beginning very early on, the colonists did not want things imposed upon them by the royal government but wanted to formulate and to choose for themselves. For our purposes here, it may be better to emphasize not the issue of how immediately effective this move toward independence was but simply to note that this American assertion of power against the English tendency to impose and demand ended up contributing to the shape of American representation. While they may have been citizens of Great Britain, the Americans were a long way from London, and they knew it and used that distance. The tension between England and America began developing long before the Stamp Act; from the standpoint of the Americans, this conflict appeared to be the tension between "power" and "liberty."[27]

POWERING DISCOURSE, LOCKING IN TO CONSENT

On the one hand, there is the question of the obvious colonial power dynamics between England and America and the way these dynamics inform the development of representation in America. On the other hand—and this is where philosophy would traditionally tend to focus—there is also the question of the intellectual influences of Europe on the New World. While this kind of distinction, which is a version of the distinction between the play of power and the play of ideas—between, ultimately, practice and theory—may be philosophically problematic, it nevertheless remains useful, particularly if the play associated with these two regions is not seen as belonging to different orders.

One of Foucault's important contributions to our current intellectual milieu is not a private, authorial insight but one pervasive in much postmodern discourse even if it is by no means uniformly distributed and even if its every instantiation marks a difference as it is repeated. This is the insight that the formative aspects of discourse are less the products of specific authors, of individual geniuses, than they are the constitutive and reinforcing elements of, effects of, and contributors to regimes of discourse and practice. These formative aspects are the historically specific "truths," rules, or determinants of discourse, which become broadly dispersed and insinuate themselves everywhere with a range of practical effects. A simpler or certainly more down-to-earth, perhaps just more American, way of putting this is that some ideas are just "in the air,"[28] such as the idea of natural rights, which is so pervasive and productive from the late seventeenth century on through at least the early nineteenth. The "laws" associated with specific discursive formations belong to and issue from no one in particular but emerge from and are dispersed as naturalized[29] throughout the community in which they appear.

American thinking was organized around the following kinds of naturalized metaphysical divisions: liberty vs. power (a version of right vs. might); natural rights (freedom) under siege (by coercive, monarchic power); and natural rights (natural freedom) necessarily situated in, struggling in, sometimes pitted against an unnatural state of affairs (in this case, tyranny). The origin of all government has an artificial aspect from the standpoint of the discourse of natural rights—all government involves if not a fall from at least a break with a state of nature—but hereditary monarchy is more than unnatural (it is an abomination) since its institution aggressively contradicts natural rights, which some advocates would claim to be God given while others would shift the stress to the natural.[30] So, a hereditary monarch and a nonrepresentative Parliament produce a relationship of arbitrary power against liberty, of tyrannical coercion, oblivious to consent, aiming to cancel out freedom as power tends naturally to do. This is a powerful discourse (and a discourse of power); it is also a state of practical affairs.

What was most conspicuously absent from England's colonial policy was American consent, which was the vehicle for the expression of rights as well as an instance of those rights. From the American standpoint, consent could not be represented virtually but only actually—expressly, directly[31]— and their exclusion from the political process angered and alienated the Americans.

What Americans were alienated, though? Who counted? Whose consent counted as directly rather than virtually countable? Was it the consent of all Americans—of old, young, rich, poor, men, women, free, indentured, and slave Americans? Did it include white, black, native, and the always growing contingency of mixed-race Americans? Was the overt consent of all of these different kinds of people at stake? Were they all Americans, that is, all to be considered active or direct participants in the processes of "consent," and citizens possessed of natural rights?[32] Were they all taken to be part of the process of instituting representation? That the concept of consent did not extend to and include everyone was not obvious to everyone,[33] but it was obvious from the standpoint of many influential figures, many of those whose stature significantly helped shape the debate and draw it to a conclusion. Who counted in the account of the representation of consent had a lot to do with who was doing the counting and with who was constructing the accounts. It was not Reason at work here, but, rather, reason, which is to say the reasoning(/maneuvering) of specific "individuals," of mostly well-to-do, white males. This observation is in alliance with the general Nietzschean point that it is important to know who is doing the talking (cf. Foucault; in a given complex of discourse-practice, who is authorized or in a position to make certain, specific types of statements?). "Who" here refers less to a subject whose prioritized attribute is a discrete consciousness than to a subject position or identity in a network of power, which is always a relational position. The people who were

writing about consent and about the people were not themselves the people, even if they stood in for them, spoke for
them, and represented them. The people doing the talking
were themselves specific people, points in a power discourse,
not the imaginary, potentially univocal universal in the name
of whom they purported to speak.

The seams of this discourse lead us into the American
embodiment(s) of the idea that people have natural rights.
This is not a simple, unitary embodiment, particularly because
of the differences between radical democrats, who tended to
push for the egalitarianism prescribed by one logic of natural
rights philosophy, and conservatives, who tended to articulate representative processes in terms of interests, which of
course by and large translated fairly directly (often without a
moment of mediation), as they still tend to do, into the interests of property and commerce. It is difficult to corner the
eighteenth-century American concept of consent because
there was not a consensus regarding its definition and thus
truly not an essence of the meaning of that concept (nor of
representation) except in a negative sense (i.e., contra Great
Britain) before the Declaration of Independence. At that
moment practically every American who was not a Tory
seems at least to have agreed that English policy was indiffer-
ent to American consent, and that this, for the moment, was
what really mattered, however "consent" might be construed.
Some general remarks can nevertheless be made regarding
consent, remarks that begin to suggest some of the relationships between the fledgling United States and America today
and between some of the metaphysical repetitions that bind
them.

Generally speaking, consent is the element of mediation
between two political agents, one of which—and here I sum-
mon the specter of a generalized, amalgamated contract theory—is the original (natural and naturally rights endowed)
agent, the other of which is that agent's substitute, a political
(artificial) agent.[34] Consent is the unit of exchange between, in
this case, public opinion ("will") and government—between
society and state—between what is represented and what rep-

resents it, between the choice of a naturally existing, naturally free subject and that which stands (artificially) in its place. It is that expression by means of which the two can be in mutual alignment, or mutual self-reflection ("scene and mirror"[35]). Consent is the coin of representation, the expression and correlative recognition of which ensures the actualization of democratic or republican[36] value.

However, consent is not just a general identity. In order to highlight some of its potential tendencies, it must be located somewhere, in some specific discourse. As soon as reference is made to an exemplar, though, positions and differences begin assuming shape. Here, John Locke, whose name floated so visibly in the revolutionary air of America, suggests some interesting specific possibilities in this regard, possibilities which appear in America one hundred years later. In the canonic chapter "Of Property" in Locke's *Second Treatise* and in the context not of a discussion of America but of what appears to be a quasi-historical discussion of the origins of property (that exposition of original conditions and of a state of nature, the primal scene of the covenant, so essential to social contract philosophy), Locke writes that

> Since gold and silver, being little useful to the life of man, in proportion to food, raiment, and carriage, has its value only from the consent of men, whereof labor yet makes in great part the measure, it is plain that the consent of men have agreed to a disproportionate and unequal possession of the earth, I mean out of the bounds of society and compact; for in governments the laws regulate it; they having, by consent, found out and agreed in a way how a man may rightfully, and without injury, possess more than he himself can make use of. . . .[37]

What is included by "men" in this consensual Ur-scenario here—"consent of men"—is not entirely clear especially since Locke asserts that this particular consensus is established before society and the social contract, that is, in a state of nature. However, Locke's decisive discussion of property[38] provides a basis for determining whose consent this involves; the men who consent to the existence and unequal distribution of private property are most likely the same souls who already "possess" it. They are those who are not only industrious (and thus respectful of the will of God) but also modest in their desires since "what portion a man carved to himself was easily seen; and it was useless as well as dishonest to carve himself too much, or take more than he needed." This portrait seems to be a representation of the subject of consent—the primal property owner as rational, restrained, and "civilized," i.e., European. Struggling against the intrinsic violence suggested by Hobbes' version of the state of Nature, Locke's state of Nature seems more like a polite English garden, whose lawn and roses might get trampled by brutish outsiders inclined to transgress the law of nature, which is the law of Reason given us by God, who commands us to work hard. It is clear here that for Locke, "men" and the legitimate consent associated with this formation has a restricted meaning, an observation perhaps evidenced further by his personal investments in the Royal Africa Company, whose business was the slave trade. Locke's is one specific conception of consent in the air at the time: consent is linked to or its legitimacy exhibited in the holding of property.

The version emphasizing property is only one prominent form of consent articulated by Locke. Locke's concept of "tacit consent,"[39] for instance, could support quite a range of scenarios. For one, it could be seen as a description of a passive social compact; as long as the political subject does not protest or simply leave, he, like Socrates,[40] has implicitly agreed to be governed by the laws and power of the given regime under whose authority he lives. Or it could be seen as legitimating an active exclusion of those who are not part of the processes of overt or express consent, those who are automatically (articulated as) included in the general processes of consent just by virtue of their presence out there (tacit consent, tacit presence [and let it be noted that presence is always tacit, i.e., that it is always something assumed, as well as virtual and "actual"]). The notion of "tacit consent" is important and interesting because it opens up or recognizes (i.e., legitimates) a breach in the meaning of consent that will make many things possible for republican democracy. On one level, it could reinforce the apparently benign, apparently obvious, "commonsensical" notion that if the electorate is unhappy with a representative, it can simply wait until the next election and vote the representative out of office (this seemingly concrete remedy has a curiously abstract aspect, which will be discussed later in Chapter VI). On another level, the notion of tacit consent could be used to invoke the silent majority as the political identity that legitimates extreme political action. A higher public good (a republican ideal) is easily linked to and legitimated by tacit consent, assuming, that is, that *good* is what government is for or about.

Locke seems inconsistent in regard to his position on what government is about although it might be a mistake to see this inconsistency—this textual tension—as a contradiction. On the one hand, he writes that "government has no other end but the preservation of property . . . ,"[41] and that "the great and chief end therefore, of men's uniting into commonwealths, and putting themselves under government, is the preservation of their property. . . ."[42] On the other hand, he writes, "For the end of government being the good of the community . . . ,"[43] and, further, "The end of government is the good of mankind. . . ."[44] Here is a point at which it would be too easy to accuse Locke of contradiction, to make a charge that would miss the point altogether. One reading might find Locke to be alternatively unclear or undecided about what government is for. Is it for the preservation of property or for some public "good" that is irreducible to the preservation of property? Locke could be seen as snagged here, flip flopping in the face of decision. A more aggressive reading, however, would indicate that, far from being either contradictory or confused, the public "good," for Locke, is synonymous or— slightly less aggressively—coextensive with the preservation of property, which he identifies so closely with human labor, the result of compliance with the wishes of God, who has endowed us with reason and natural rights as well as with the setting in which they get lived out. The ground of the good could be ground permeated by the legal (legitimating) discourses and economic practices which transform it into property.[45] But who are we, as readers, to impose a decision on Locke? Locke was establishing links between the ends of government and property, but his interests were not confined by the boundaries of property.

Prompted in some respects by Bailyn, as well as by more general observations regarding history, I have already suggested that it may be a case of following the wrong trail, or at any rate a relatively unproductive trail—an idealist trail—to seek some origin for the American Revolution and, more specifically, for American representation, in philosophy, and in ideas; philosophy may be a relatively important thread, but it is just one thread among many here (the others would be equally uncontainable—a wild complex of wild variables—and would have to include such diverse phenomena as the obvious tax issue, the tobacco market, the fur market, the Protestant ethic, the material distance from Europe, competition between different European powers, the relations between Europeans and Native Americans, etc.). The point in citing Locke, then, is not to divine the source but to exhibit—to put on exhibit[46]—the kinds of tensions embodied in the texts of natural rights. These tensions, oppositions, contestations, mixtures, impurities and indecisions were characteristics evident in the political discourse of America then. Americans—who, within inevitable limits, were quite aware of the unprecedented historical import of their acts—were trying to decide what it was that they were doing. The question was less what it "meant," perhaps, than how it should all be organized (a problem complicated by the differences between the general government—first constituted by the Articles of Confederation, later by the Constitution—and each of the new states). Insofar as they were building new forms of government and establishing new governmental practices, it is clear that the confusion was not just about ideas. That Locke could have been quoted and used to support arguments on all sides, including those of Tories as well as revolutionaries, provides a strong metaphor not only for the malleability of ideas but also for the mixed American atmosphere, which entailed the absence of consensus about new political values, priorities, and realities.

There is something significant in Paine's claim that he had never read Locke. In noting this, I am not attempting to replace the influence of Locke with the influence of Paine, to argue that it was intellectuals in America rather than intellectuals in Europe who were the source of the revolution. I am not trying to Americanize the Revolution in this sense (Paine was English anyway) although there is no question that American intellectuals played an important and more immediate part in it. It may be more helpful to broaden rather than pinpoint the "sources" of representation. For one thing an expansion of this sort allows for more than just the generative effects of intellectual leaders (who in some important respects, again, were riding ideas and discourses that were widely distributed, just in the air, and uncornered by anyone even though all players, including George III, were trying to corner them).

Nevertheless, both despite and because of the tensions within his text, Locke did mark out a particular perspective on consent and its context. It was a perspective, it might be argued, that was less determinative than determined and very much part of the discursive atmosphere—part of what was in the air—in a way that might have been not just influential in a traditional sense but part of a broad historical milieu comprised of many factors. "Consent" was a medium that linked government (representative) with the natural political subject, and it had something to do with rights and will, with affirmation and with agreement. However, one of its central features was that the identity of this consensual subject was not definite but wide open to debate. If Locke's discourse is a mixed one, one that recognizes both equality and hierarchy (with equality necessarily subordinate to hierarchy and the common side of the hierarchy naturally subordinate to its superior), then this mixture prefigures and, more importantly, embodies the tense mixture of Revolutionary discourse, the diversity of opinion, the confusion about issues such as mixed government (the legacy of Aristotle and England), the problem of the representation of property, and the relationship between the concepts of republic and democracy. These particular issues provide productive points of access to what it is that gets represented in America (even if that 'what' cannot be expected to stabilize or acquire a final form).

MIXING REPRESENTATION: A HOUSE DIVIDED

The notion of mixed government was derived from the familiar Greek division of government into three types, each of which corresponded to the metaphysical categories, the one (monarchy), the few (aristocracy), and the many (democracy).[47] The notion of mixed government—of government composed of a balanced combination of the three essential forms—was not, however, Greek; this innovation was above all an English one. Given the self-destructive pitfalls traditionally associated with each of these three types in their pure forms (as well as insights derived from a reading of Montesquieu's, *The Spirit of the Laws*, which addresses these different classical types), and benefiting from the tradition of their legalistic English heritage, some of the Americans embraced the model of balance embodied in the structure of English government. This model included all three classical eidoi, as it mixed monarchy (the Crown) with aristocracy (the House of Lords) and democracy (the House of Commons). These three types kept the excesses of the others in check and only together constituted a complete representation of society, which is why it is especially worth bringing up here. As Wood has written, the concept of mixed government ". . . had significance because the mixed government was not an institutional abstraction set apart from the society but indeed was the very embodiment of society."[48] This organic view makes sense given the image of England as a unified whole, a coherent collective with common, objective interests, an ultimately single, univocal body—the body politic. Here, "embodiment" is one way of saying representation. In England, the contents of mixed government stood in for the contents of society by representing the one, the few, and the many in the form of the three estates: the Crown, the nobles (lords spiritual and temporal), and the commoners.[49]

So, on the one hand, the revolution in America resulted in distinctively new political formations. On the other hand, however, this revolution turned to tradition for—or simply inherited from it—some key conceptual and practical clues or established points of orientation regarding the constitution of good government. As Wood suggests, what is important about this turn to tradition is that the traditional English conception of good, balanced government implies a tripartite vision of society as a whole, a vision in which each of the three estates of (organic) society corresponds directly to each of the three classical (artificial) political entities. From the standpoint of this model, then, the view is that there is something natural about mixed government and the equilibrium that it institutionalizes, a borrowed naturalness derived from the given "natural" existence of three social orders.

While the obvious decisive dimension of the new American political institutions is the sheer break from the formally authorized estates represented by the monarchy and the blood aristocracy, what is also significant is the American devotion to the tradition of mixed government, which, practically speaking, supported and was up to a certain point even synonymous with the interest in and adoption of a bicameral model for legislative assemblies.[50] From the standpoint of many Americans, what was wrong with English mixed government was not the English idea of mixture but the English execution of it (the classical theory/practice division gets repeated here once again). Meanwhile, for their own part, while the Americans in general were aggressively faithful to the rights of man and to the cause of liberty during the actual revolutionary period, less critical attention was paid to the practical issue of achieving and preserving these goals. This issue soon presented itself in all of its necessity to the states, both independently of each other and united, as they faced the immense task of constructing constitutions following the

Declaration of Independence. Considering the activity during this period, it is startlingly clear that while a constitution is a thoroughly textual matter, it is not just a written document but a process of organization, of, truly, *constituting*, of the building of social identities, political practices, and institutions. It is also clear that the Americans did not constitute themselves from scratch.

The (naturaliz*ed*) naturalness of mixed government contributed a great deal to the constitutive processes of organization that occurred in the fledgling states. At this point, it was a question of balanced arrangement. How, for instance, should power be distributed amongst the different elements—the one, the few, and the many—making up the republican government? The executive power was by no means an unproblematic issue—how to insure that it would not become monarchic?—but it nevertheless assumed the position of the one, the position traditionally held by the monarch (the One). The position of the many—the position of democracy—would be represented in the legislative assembly. However, these placeholders were not the only problems to solve since the main goal (the justification for the conceptual schema) of mixed government is that of a balance, a balance in the representation of the given divisions of society and a balance of power. While displacement of a traditional aristocracy accompanied the revolutionary displacement of the Crown, it was nevertheless widely believed that in order to achieve this balance, the "ablest" or "wisest" part of the citizenry (the few) should be represented in a separate legislative chamber, an upper house or a senate. These desires were fulfilled in nearly all of the new states as well as in the legislative structure established by the Constitution. But ability and wisdom were not the only requirements for the upper chambers, which were to be more independent of the electorate than the lower chambers (here, the notion of independence cast in terms of being beyond outside influence is an important concern). For the upper houses, all but two states (Virginia and Delaware)[51] established property qualifications exceeding those required for candidacy for the lower houses. As Wood has written,

"Although wisdom and integrity were difficult to measure, property was not."[52] The development of such upper houses was not a new idea in America, a brand new way of redeploying mixed government, which just appeared from out of the blue in 1776. An extreme precedent, one draft of Pennsylvania's first constitution from the 1680s, actually proposed an explicitly hereditary upper house of representatives based on the ownership of 5,000 acres or more.[53] The notion of a higher representative body was thus already well-established not only in England but also on the continent of North America.

Later, during the period of the Revolution, some Americans questioned and condemned the schism represented by the notion of an upper house, a schism between the egalitarian type of society associated with the discourse of the Revolution and the elitist and thus more traditional overtones inherent in the notion of an upper house. Others, on the other hand, worried that the two legislative houses—the duality of which, again, was supposed to help provide the alleged balance characteristic of mixed government—would not be different enough from each other if they were chosen by the same electorate. In Massachusetts (in the Essex Result and in public assemblies), it was argued that the senate would not be independent enough even if it were chosen by the lower house (rather than "the public"), which was one obvious alternative for selecting this elite, who would fill out the distribution of representation and balance the power of the one (the executive) and the many (the lower house).[54] Thus, its 1780 constitution, which raises property qualifications for voting and holding office above their prerevolutionary levels,[55] bases representation in the upper house on the proportion of taxes paid out by the different electoral districts and formally codifies and declares this direct association between property and representation in the upper house by noting that "the House of Representatives is intended as the Representatives of the Persons, and the Senate of the property of the Common Wealth."[56] That was in Massachusetts, but it was widely argued throughout the new states that the characteristics required of the senatorial body would be most prevalent among people with education and money, particularly the latter. Increasingly, property became the criterion for determining who was qualified not only to serve in but also to vote for those serving in the upper chambers.

The representation of persons and the representation of property are two different representations for two different entities, for two different configurations of the political subject.[57] Many influential people, including the democratically inclined Jefferson, seemed convinced of the necessity of representing these two networks independently of each other since it was thought that only such separation could provide the balance of power made possible by a mixed government.

What was represented in the bicameral legislatures, then, was a mixture, a doublet (a division), certainly nothing as fundamentally (or apparently) simple or unitary as "the people" or "the public thing." Here—not just any old example—slaves presented a real, concrete problem, being sometimes considered as people and sometimes as property in the eyes of the law and the bureaucracy, a serious difficulty when confronted with a practical issue such as apportionment of representatives and how many congressional legislators a given, particularly Southern district or state might be allotted; the Southerners, of course, wanted the noses of their property to be counted in the calculation of the population base that would determine the number of federal legislators. Here, it is worth moving momentarily from the level of the individual states to that of the nation, since Madison grapples with this particular issue in *Federalist 54* and with the relationship between censuses and the representation of persons, on the one hand, and taxes and property, on the other.

Madison's argument is extremely revealing in connection with what he believes is to be represented in the government sketched out by the new constitution. In an equally productive fashion, it could be seen as nonrevealing, insofar as it keeps this *what* vague, strategically (not surreptitiously) vague insofar as certain arbitrary decisions get elevated to the level of political science and serve to legitimate hierarchy in the midst of—rising over, defining, and partially determining—republican equality. The argument begins by noting that "it is agreed on all sides that numbers are the best scale of wealth and taxation, as they are the only proper scale of representation." Madison's argument thus opens by invoking a consensus about an objective standard—numbers. How does this standard relate to the problem of factoring slaves into the machinery of representation? What is the basis for including slaves as persons, as part of a census, or as part of the representative base rather than simply as property to be counted for taxes? To begin with, since slaves do have a dual identity (for instance, they are persons insofar as they are punishable for violence committed against others), it would be inconsistent to count the slaves as part of the tax base, to subject slaves-as-property to numbers but not to include them—slaves-as-persons—in the censuses used to determine the number of representatives (Madison never actually provides an argument explaining why it would be inconsistent but only suggests that it would). Here, in concluding that slaves should be included in the censuses used to determine the base of representation, Madison argues that it is irrelevant that states do not allow slaves to vote because the proposed federal Constitution does not instruct states on how to determine who is eligible to vote. (Madison points out that probably no two states determine the right to suffrage the same way, a rhetorical ploy which functions to reduce the exclusion of slaves to just another difference among differences between the ways different states determine qualifications for the vote, a ploy that for one thing glides right over the fact that the one voting practice all the slave states held in common was the exclusion of slaves from suffrage.) On the basis of censuses, the federal government will determine the number of representatives each state will be allowed, but it will not tell them how to choose those representatives, how to count their own inhabitants in this phase of the representative process.[58] Consequently, concludes Madison, "Let the compromising expedient of the Constitution be mutually adopted, which regards them as inhabitants, but as debased by servitude below the equal level of free inhabitants, which regards the *slave* as divested of two fifth of *man"* (a direct reference to Article I, Section 2 of the Constitution[59]). Therefore, according to the Constitution of the United States, a slave counted as three-fifths of a man. While the mathematical principle behind this fraction remains mysterious, Madison is not engaged in philosophy or logic here but in the Federalists' effort to persuade Americans ("the People of the State of New York") to adopt the Constitution. What amounts to an argued plea to accept the solution to the problem of the unity of the states suggested or made possible by the terms of the Constitution is followed by a very different sort of argument, an argument that covers the other side of slavery, the property angle.

The line of Madison's argument just described argues that slaves should be counted as (semi-)persons for the purposes of determining numbers of representatives. The second line, which uses the issue of slaves to defend the representation of property, is worth quoting in full:

> We have hitherto proceeded on the idea that representation related to persons only, and not at all to property. But is it a just idea? Government is instituted no less for protection of the property, than of the persons of individuals. The one as well as the other, therefore may be considered to be represented by those who are charged with the government. Upon this principle it is, that in several of the States, and particularly in the State of New-York, one branch of the government is intended more especially to be the guardian of property, and is accordingly elected by that part of the society which is most interested in this object of government. In the Federal Constitution, this policy does not prevail. The rights of property are committed into the same hands with the personal rights. Some attention ought therefore to be paid to property in the choice of those hands.

While the representation of property was not formally incorporated into the text of the federal Constitution, this quotation from James Madison provides a glimpse of his original, author-itative intent here.[60] What is implicitly included in "We the People," apparently, is property, which refers to the large prop-erty interests which the Federalists themselves were con-cerned with preserving. A buttressing argument in favor of allowing slaves to help determine the apportionment of rep-resentation, then, has nothing to do with their being people but with their being property, and Madison is in effect arguing that the owners of this particular kind of property (or, really, by extension, of any kind of property) should be represented more than others and should have a stronger vote (i.e., more representation) than those without property.

While it is, of course, highly significant that the Constitution does not formally admit the representation of property, it is also significant that powerful political networks, such as the Federalists, did admit it and that there was much debate about formalizing the distinction between representa-tion of persons and representation of property at the Philadelphia Convention, where the Federal Constitution was hammered out: "Behind the Virginia Plan," which initiated the convention, "lay the formal scheme of persons and prop-erty, each represented in a separate chamber."[61] While this issue did not survive the drafting process—again, the Constitution leaves qualifications for the right to vote up to the states—it is significant that it was so much part of the debate.

With the exceptions of Pennsylvania, Georgia, and Vermont, the new state constitutions established bicameral legislative assemblies with the upper houses (the senates) embodying, more or less, the gentry and property and the lower houses embodying "the people."[62] One important factor contributing to this development—this was a critical element in the image of balance (of power)—was a concern about the majority tyrannizing the minority or overrunning their rights; the minority in question here was a specific one, not an ethnic or religious minority but above all the tiniest, perennially supreme minority, the wealthy, propertied class. The concern was that without distinct and independent representation, the

many—the hoi polloi or the people—represented in the legislature, would usurp the rights of this minority. Here the terrifying image of mob rule is a factor, an image reinforced by the
recent past, when Tory property had been outright seized by
some of the new states and by other threatening signs emerging from "the people." Connected to this concern, the wealthy
became committed to establishing a strong, federal republic in
the years following the Revolution to protect them from local
instabilities such as Shays' Rebellion, the 1786-87 farmer's
rebellion in western Massachusetts.[63] Shays' Rebellion in particular appeared as the instantiation of mob rule that the
Western tradition, beginning with Plato, had articulated as
the outcome of democracy.[64] Thus, the fortunate members of
the wealthy minority desired institutions—organized powers—that would recognize the threat posed to property by the
people, check that threat, and preserve minority rights. As
Alexander Hamilton argued, "Give therefore to the first class
(of the rich and well born) a distinct, permanent share in the
government. . . . Can a democratic assembly, who annually
revolve in the mass of the people, be supposed steadily to pursue the public good? Nothing but a permanent body can check
the imprudence of democracy."[65]

Madison reinforces this discourse further in *Federalist
63*, where he argues that an upper house may act "as a defense
to the people against their own temporary errors and delusions." Here, he echoes the discourse of virtual representation, implicitly assuming something like objective interests. In
the same essay, he prefigures a familiar, more contemporary
analysis[66] arguing that "liberty may be endangered by the
abuses of liberty as well as by the abuses of power. . . ." True
liberty requires the limitation of empirical liberty (true republican democracy requires the limitation of democracy). Such a
limitation—a check, a formal balance—might reside in an
institutionalized representative body, a senate, situated at a
further distance from the people than the more directly representative lower house

Once dominant opinion[67] in America determined that the organizational model of mixed government would provide the key to solving the central political problem—the balance of power in a postmonarchic political structure—these two possible realms of representation, people and property, were considered to be distinct from each other (although in another sense they blended together again in the discourse surrounding the federal Constitution since property was not excluded from that discourse). Possibilities other than mixed government seemed to evaporate. However, at the same time, as Wood concludes:

> Because republicanism depended so thoroughly on a unity of interests in the society, some Americans as early as 1776 had questioned the possibility of accommodating republican principles with the existence of upper houses—any kind of upper houses, whether embodying property or simply the wisdom of the society—and had moved to challenge directly the applicability of the entire theory of mixed government for the new American states. Such a challenge represented a glaring departure from the eighteenth-century English, even the radical Whig, tradition of political thought and a return to theories of government that had not been seen in England since the days of Lilburne and the Levellers. The denial of bicameralism in any form and the advocacy of an "unmixed" democracy, a government solely by the people expressed in fact the most politically radical impulse of the American Revolution.[68]

While it was not this impulse that ended up determining the formal shape of American representative government, at least not on the most obvious level, the unrealized possibility of an "unmixed" democracy connects us to the American grasp of "democracy" and "republic," a grasp which Shoemaker has argued was not firm or definite ("their understandings were generally quite hazy") and about which there simply was not a general consensus. As is clear from his argument, only by moving to a quite general level can Shoemaker claim that "Representation was much more often associated with republicanism than with democracy and thus serves as a legitimate criterion to distinguish between the two" (although this generalization immediately excludes radical democrats who also advocated representation, such as Paine). Shoemaker concludes that "briefly put . . . the difference between a democracy and a republic is the difference between the Articles of Confederation and the Constitution."[69] This observation is helpful insofar as it suggests the more republican than democratic leaning represented by the Constitution, but the general clarity provided by this exegesis helps us less than the real American confusion between the terms, a confusion that survives today. Through the multiple, confused grasp of the distinction and relationship between democracy and republic, through the struggle between wealthy conservatives and fields of resistance to them, and through certain developing dimensions of the American organization of mixed government, a picture emerges of what it is that was getting represented in American politics, what sort of political subject or object (which was never and has not become something closed).

"I draw my idea of the form of government," Paine writes in *Common Sense*, "from a principle in nature which no art can overturn, viz., that the more simple anything is, the less liable it is to be disordered and the easier repaired when disordered; and with this maxim in view I offer a few remarks on the so much boasted constitution of England."[70] Paine then proceeds to argue that this constitution is not simple at all—it is "exceedingly complex"—and that this is because it is articulated as a union of three separate components, the three estates, two of which are the "monarchical tyranny" and the "aristocratical tyranny," the two real sources of an intrinsically tyrannical form of government, mixed government. Paine promptly attacks this form's most oft-cited virtue, namely, the notion that mixed government provides a balance by means of checks that its three component parts place on each other. As he objects;

To say that the Commons is a check upon the king presupposes two things: First, that the king is not to be
trusted without being looked after, or, in other words,
that a thirst for absolute power is the natural disease of
monarchy. Secondly, that the Commons, by being
appointed for that purpose are either wiser or more worthy of confidence than the crown. . . . Some writers have
explained the English constitution thus: the king, they
say, is one, the people another; the peers are a house in
behalf of the king, the Commons in behalf of the people;
but this has all the distinctions of a house divided against
itself, and though the expressions be pleasantly arranged,
yet when examined they appear idle and ambiguous. . . .[71]

Thus, from Paine's democratic standpoint, mixed government
works against the unitary possibilities of the states united and
against the representation of the public good.

In the following year, 1777, the far from radical Alexander
Hamilton, despite his reservations regarding popular government (and his later more extreme conservatism), said that
"compound governments, though they be harmonious in the
beginning, will introduce distinct interests; and these interests
will clash, throw the state into convulsion and produce a
change or dissolution."[72] A senate—an upper chamber—would
degenerate into an elite hierarchy, an aristocracy, on the one
hand; on the other hand—another extreme—direct democracy
was too chaotic to be practicable. However, thought Hamilton
at this early date, a simple, popular, representative legislature
would provide the most effective, stable form of government
in the long run. Radical Pennsylvania (the only state to abolish
property qualifications in its new constitution) and then
Georgia and Vermont affirmed this kind of thinking in their
new state constitutions, a kind of thinking in which democracy and republicanism were being identified as interchange-
able. No mixed govenment could secure a republic since they
would draw clear lines of conflict and since some of the components would always dominate others (would dominate the
democratic branch and therefore the people, as Paine had

argued). Thus, democracy was not just one of the elements in a republic comprised of formally different interests; only a purely democratic republic was a true republic, a republic genuinely embodying the public good and the will of the people, which would not be hierarchically differentiated in the political sphere. "To say, there ought to be two houses, because there are two sorts of interests," argued one Pennsylvanian in 1776, "is the very reason why there ought to be but one, and *that one* to consist of every sort."[73]

In this last phrase "*that one* to consist of every sort," is the argument that perceives republicanism as constituted by full, unmixed democracy, then, just another metaphysical return of the One over the many, the many subordinate to the One? Perhaps it is not; from a reading of this simple but loaded phrase, it could be argued that these democratic republicans were deliberately trying to overcome that traditional metaphysical drama, the political drama of the One (with which the few are fused as One) over the many. There is one interest in a republic, an interest to be obtained only through a democratic political process and that interest is the (in some sense) preservation or recognition of every sort of interest and of (this translates into) the equal representation of every one, and this is the meaning of republicanism. While the divisions accompanying mixed government codify or generate definite sorts of identities in their divisions (property formally distinguished from persons) the one that consists of every sort leaves the question of the identity of what is being represented fundamentally open, indefinite, and in the following sense, totally democratic; its oneness could be associated not with completion, closure or the lines of inclusion or exclusion but with incompletion (the democratic and representative processes are always developing), indefinite openness, and (democracy as a form of theater) entrances and exits of different political subjects (in contrast with stable Presence). If this image of democracy is a metaphysical image—a debatable point even if democracy is a dream from the past as well as the future—it could be argued that it is a deviant metaphysics insofar as it is a discourse which devotes itself to the recognition and defense of difference (rather than the polarity determined by the property/people opposition). In the discourse of "unmixed" democracy, what could mistakenly be seen as a simple repetition of the notion of unity of national interest and the correlative univocity of representative government (both are traits embodied also in virtual representation) turns out to be a very different story altogether since the people are not an entity but a diversity.[74]

However, many people, at least many politically active people, were not thinking this way (were not thinking of the subject-object of representation as diverse). The arguments of those who opposed unmixed government took many forms, which ranged from an insistence that a second legislative chamber did not represent anything different from the first assembly (the problem faced by this argument was justifying the need for a second one, then) to the argument that the senate would embody the "naturally" finest men (who were the best by merit rather than bloodline, but this still smelled elitist) and even to arguments that senates would, indeed, represent property. The more consistently compelling reason, one that grabbed people's attention, was the argument that a unicameral legislature had nothing checking it, nothing counterbalancing its power and that it therefore had a very practical potential for becoming tyrannical. Only a "double representation," then— only a two-chambered legislature—could ensure a truly republican democracy and a democratic republic. Meanwhile, the Pennsylvania constitutionalists argued that a single legislature did have a check and that the check was the people of the state as a whole. However, although formally incorporated into Pennsylvania's constitution, this argument was starting to sound abstract since it seemed utterly unwieldy and impracticable. Despite its proponents' intentions, the impracticability of this reference to "the people" may effectively have helped legitimate double representation. Once this kind of argument in favor of double representation had acquired visibility and the justification for a senate could be posited without reference to any sort of elite, the movement supporting mixed government in the states had acquired new fuel.

Now it was possible to argue that the upper chamber was in no way a hierarchical elite, a potential aristocracy, since both legislative chambers drew their power from the same source, from the people.[75] The justification for two houses of representation was a practical rather than classist one about the control of power. Each chamber would keep a check on the other, which was not a check on different interests since the interests (of the people) were one and the same (here the affirmation of unitary interests necessary for republicanism); instead, it was a check on the possibility of misrepresentation (or nonrepresentation) of the public good. In fact, it was argued by some that a unicameral rather than doubled assembly was the form with the true potential for becoming an elite. Two houses were a necessary check of that potential, then. One interest and one republic required multiple representation, double representation of the public good. By 1788, Madison was able to write in *Federalist 62*, that

> a senate, as a second branch of the legislative assembly, distinct from, and dividing the power with, a first, must be in all cases a salutary check on the government. It doubles the security to the people, by requiring the concurrence of two distinct bodies in schemes of usurpation or perfidy, where the ambition or corruption of one, would otherwise be sufficient. This is a precaution founded on such clear principles, and now so well understood in the United States, that it would be more than superfluous to enlarge on it.

It is the last sentence, which offers firm and aggressive support for the ideas preceding it, to which attention should be directed here. Whether Madison's statement is true or not is both unverifiable and in some respects irrelevant; what is significant is the simple, positive fact that by 1788 he was able to make such a statement, to assume that his audience did not need further defense of this particular justification for double representation. Interestingly enough, in affirming the general Anti-Federalist concern that the balance of power be ensured by the formal inclusion of a plethora of checks, James Winthrop (writing under the pseudonym *Agrippa*) could be at least generally repeating the Federalist Madison's confidence when he says that "it is now generally understood that it is for the security of the people that the powers of the government be lodged in different branches."[76]

While Madison went on to extend his justifications for a bicameral legislature, he perceived that his audience did not require further persuasion on the point of security (of maintaining a check on the potential tyranny or misgovernment of a single legislature) since they "well understood" the "clear principles" upon which the notion of the double security of double representation was based. It is impossible to say how large was the audience who understood these clear principles—which, given the issue, must be principles regarding the nature of power—but Madison was effectively right, at least insofar as the Constitution was ratified, and the idea of double security through double representation was realized and legitimated on the federal level.[77]

REPRESENTATION DISTRIBUTED

Like the theory of representation itself—like so many of the basic assumptions or determinants of American political discourse—the theory of mixed government (one surface of the organization of representation) may have come from England, but it was being genuinely transformed through America's articulation. It is true that old threads, such as the elite visage of the upper chamber (with its roots in the House of Lords) and the notion of the implicit representation of property, remained indefinitely embedded in the discourse and practice of American mixed government and that the effects of these traces lay by no means dormant but beyond calculation. Not very long before—practically just yesterday—these old threads had been the content associated with the form of bicameral representation, a form that had found new content (double security by means of the double representation of the people) in order to become legitimated on the federal level while the representation of property in state governments (calculated on the basis of taxes) remained as vestiges of the formally recognized representation of property in the upper chamber of the original bicameral model.[78]

Nevertheless, the transformation was very real, and it would be too limiting to claim that the reality of the transformation of political discourse was the simple result of any particular group's intentions or of a process of manipulation controlled by some definite sphere of interests even though there were plenty of vested interests doing their most to control the constitution of the new Constitution.[79]

While a number of issues could be cited to reinforce the reality of the transformation and the impossibility of controlling this process, the most spectacular textual reference here would have to be to the Bill of Rights, a document which stands as a monument to the power of difference, in this case, democratic difference from conservative Federalists, whose recent efforts had culminated in the ratification of a Constitution that did not include a Bill of Rights. The Constitution and the Bill of Rights amended to it are not a seamless whole in history,[80] the latter some sort of logical, organic, or necessary extension of the former. Not the effects of a single difference, the two documents, which together constitute "one" document, the Constitution, stand as a monument to divided discourse—which was not just a matter of two opposing sides—and to discourse kept open, that is, to democratic discourse (no single participant has a corner on this developing discourse, although that may be precisely what every active participant tends to seek). The political process was not a unified affair. That is one side of the story.

Another important side, however, is suggested by the less spectacular characteristics shared in common by different sides (this is one reason why the difference invoked here is not formed just in terms of simple opposition). Here, Kenyon's work on the Anti-Federalists and Wood's more broad-scoped historical analysis, for example, affirm a generally Foucauldian reading of the political discourse after the Revolution. These analyses, while not glossing over the important differences between different positions—such active conflict[81] could be neither overlooked nor underestimated—at the same time do not obscure common determinative features dispersed throughout the range of positions in this political discourse-practice.

One common discursive determinant shared by all sides was a profound and unquestioned faith (if faith is the right word) in the necessity of a text, specifically, of a written constitution, a faith or insistence that we cannot get around today—we cannot think or talk politics without it—even though it has undergone significant transmutation in the last two hundred years. This faith in a written constitution is not as mundane (natural?) or obvious as it may seem, a point that acquires clarity when directly contrasted with the unwritten covenant, the original covenant, which is the condition of the possibility of a written covenant that is part of seventeenth and eighteenth-century social contract philosophy. In America, the concept of constitution continues to be a matter that is not only textual but thoroughly inscriptural.[82]

However, it would be a mistake to derive from this the assertion that once the Constitution of the United States had been signed, the basic apparatus of American representation was in place. Such a view would grant priority to theory and to writing and would look for modifications rather than transformations and transvaluations. Such a view, that is, would affirm an essence nailed down in writing and might underestimate the real change that accompanies or is generated by discourse and practice; it might also deny the fact that representation truly is a process.

Here is an appropriate place for affirming the completely political aspect of textuality, which in one of its tangents develops into political positions regarding the nature and status of texts. If the conservatives had really won the formative battles at the inception of the organization of our government, the Constitution might have been a self-contained, theoretically impermeable, archival and isolated text—a book, The Book—an absolute, exhaustive point of reference for all time eternal, kept perhaps up-to-date but fundamentally unchanged by the procedures for amendment provided in Article V (like the yearly volumes added to the *Encyclopedia Britannica*).[83] But no text ever has or ever could embody such characteristics regardless of intention. In this respect the conservatives did not win, and more democratic factions or forces won the battle for the Bill of Rights in 1791,[84] which with its hasty, formal initiation of the process and practice of amendment—the Bill of Rights was itself an amendment—transformed the Constitution from its (hypothetically) potential status as The Book into a constitutional text and a textual constitution defined and kept open-ended by the possibility of supplementation.

The current battle for representation borne by, for instance, the Equal Rights Amendment is a concrete case in point and helps illustrate the claims being made here. In addition to the specific issue of equal rights for women and the logics of current pro and con positions on the E.R.A., it only makes sense, then, that conservatives continue to fight the supplementary dimension of the constitution since each amendment only reinforces the constitutional or constitutive logic of textual open-endedness. Such is the deviant logic of a law[85] that gets more definite in its development. In so doing it ambiguously affirms its own transgression, its own incompleteness and vulnerability as well as its inconclusion, its openness to further process and supplementation, the factical truth that its writing is a rewriting, and its final truth that its truth is not immutable but always open to modification and never final.[86] In its faith in what it thinks of as the self-identity of the past, the logic of conservatism is a logic of fixity, of closure.[87] While one dream-telos is an end to the need for further supplementation (left-thinking, too, advances its closures), which would be synonymous with the written guarantee of representation (how could a written guarantee ever guarantee anything?[88]), the Constitution remains not only unfinished but also unfinishable. Another, simpler way of saying this is to state that the Constitution does not stand outside of a given social, economic, or historical context, that it is not only not impermeable to but is actively constituted by contextual contingencies.

At any rate, regardless of explicit positions about what the Constitution should be and of implicit positions about the status of books and texts, a common axiom of political discourse in the America of the late eighteenth century was faith in a written constitution. This faith, too, was part of an English heritage, at least insofar as it derived much of its power from a tradition of written contracts.

Another shared discursive determinant, one with more particular but nevertheless not completely determinable sorts of effects for American democracy, was a widely distributed certainty that representation was the key to a democratic republic, to overcoming the geopolitical problem outlined by Montesquieu, which was the notion that a republic would never work in an extended territory, particularly in a place as staggeringly enormous as America.[89] While not everyone supported it as the state and then the federal governments were being organized, representation was an aspect of democratic or republican political organization that had to be confronted by the entire spectrum of political activists, from the radical democrats (whose wild models of unmixed democracy incorporated perhaps minimal but nevertheless unavoidable representative aspects) to the Anti-Federalists (with their deep and perhaps not entirely unfounded suspicion that representation would not work on the federal but only on the state level) to conservative republicans with their utterly self-interested desires for the explicit representation of property (and if explicit would not work, well then, they would just have to rely on implicit [unwritten or unauthorized] representation). Here, in connection with this discursive political condition—the condition represented by representation—what is most striking in a selective juxtaposition of the relatively radical Paine and the Federalist Madison is less their obvious, predictable, and important opposition than their common conviction that representation is what American government is all about.

In classic, natural rights style, the following passage about representation from Paine's *The Rights of Man* opens with a contrasting reference to a simpler state of affairs. "Simple democracy," writes Paine, "was society governing itself without the aid of secondary means." As was obvious to any European, though, and particularly to anyone who had traveled in America and had a grasp of its diversity and immensity (as well as to anyone who had come in contact with the ideas of Montesquieu), this simple state was inscribed in eighteenth-century discourse as a present impossibility. Things were too complicated now. Simple democracy was not viable anymore. Representation, then, constitutes the condition of the possibility of a more complicated state of affairs, a network of states, the unity of a multiplicity, the United States of America. Paine proudly marvels:

> By ingrafting representation upon democracy, we arrive at a system of government capable of embracing and confederating all the various interests and every extent of territory and population. . . . It is on this system that the American government is founded. It is representation ingrafted upon democracy. . . . What Athens was in miniature, America will be in magnitude.[90]

Paine marvels, and we must marvel at his well-founded marvel and follow up on only a couple of the many threads running through these few words. One is the implicit notion that original, simple democracy was coextensive with society, in some sense identical with it (with the community), and not an extraneous, secondary affair nor instrument. Neither was it just a technique nor a (political) process or institution at an ontological distance from the community. Representation, however, is now understood as a technique, one grafted on to the tree of democracy. Although everyone—particularly the French intelligentsia but also very much including the Americans—saw the entire enterprise as a kind of experiment, this graft was not undertaken simply in the spirit of experiment but was added on to original democracy as that decisive supplement which would make democracy continue to be possible in a populous age, in an age when government and a diverse, dispersed society were no longer directly identifiable with each other. The production of the identification of government and society would have to be an indirect affair, i.e., would have to rely on representation.

By ingrafting, embracing, and confederating, representation would bring the whole society together, would make it one, and would make possible that one consisting of every sort, that one interest—the people—that is synonymous with a democratic republic. Could it be that the unity of the people, which had been met by the Americans with such scepticism when it was one of the linchpins of the English discourse and practice of virtual representation, had returned via representation to this new democratic republic? Indeed, it had, only with a difference. From the standpoint of democrats like Paine, the difference was that the unity would not simply purport to include the people but would be the people, albeit indirectly, through the instrumental possibilities provided by representation.

Is one of the limitations of Paine's vision his inevitable inability to recognize the way that the original, arboreal trunk of democracy—of an imagined democracy—would become critically transformed when representation was grafted onto it as the condition of the continued possibility of its being? While he was aware of and welcomed the transformation represented by the ingrafting of representation onto democracy, what may (or may not) have been out of his reach was a grasp of the indefiniteness of the subject-object of representation, of what was going to be represented here. To democrats like Paine, it may have seemed self-evident that it would be "the people," but what could not have been completely evident was what this term might cover (e.g., capital), as well as cover over or hide (e.g., women of every color). Perhaps less obvious and more important, what also could not have been completely evident was the productive rather than "representative" possibilities of representation (to which Part Two of this project will address itself).

While Madison belonged to a political species clearly to the right of Paine's, he too shared the conviction that what was going to distinguish American politics and make an American republic possible was the implementation of representation. The following passage from *Federalist 10* requires more contextual elaboration than the fragment from *The Rights of Man*. *Federalist 10* begins with a discussion of the problem of factions in politics, a discussion which admits that "the most common and durable source of factions, has been the various and unequal distribution of property":[91]

> Those who hold, and those who are without property, have ever formed distinct interests in society. Those who are creditors, and those who are debtors, fall under a like discrimination. A landed interest, a manufacturing interest, a mercantile interest, a monied interest, with many lesser interests, grow up of necessity in civilized nations, and divide them into different classes, actuated by different sentiments and views.

It is possible, apparently, that "lesser interests" includes the interests of "the people" amongst all of these ("of necessity") other greater, natural interests, but at any rate, "the regulation of these various and interfering interests forms the principal task of modern legislation, and involves the spirit of party and faction in the necessary and ordinary operations of Government." In other words, "factions" are inevitable in a civilized nation, and, therefore, in its government. The real problem with factions arises when a majority faction (possibly these lesser interests?) holds sway, thus potentially threatening "the public good, and private rights," and this is the problem that Madison proposes to solve here.[92]

Pure democracy, Madison argues, cannot solve this problem, and he resurrects the traditional, Platonic image of democracy as a somewhat chaotic, violently dangerous institution, afterwards concluding that "theoretic politicians, who have patronized this species of Government, have erroneously supposed, that by reducing mankind to a perfect equality in their political rights, they would, at the same time, be perfectly equalized and assimilated in their possessions, their opinions, and their passions." So much for theoretic politicians, who may not have been so starry-eyed about the effects of "leveling" as the theoretic Madison is asserting here (his charge actively and probably willfully misses the point about equality, as does every discourse which levels democracy by leveling the charge of leveling at it). Madison continues:

> But in contrast with a democracy . . . A Republic, by which I mean a Government in which the scheme of representation takes place, opens a different prospect, and promises the cure for which we were seeking. . . . The two great points of difference between a Democracy and a Republic are, first, the delegation of the Government, in the latter, to a small number of citizens elected by the rest: secondly, the greater number of citizens, and greater sphere of country, over which the latter may be extended.

Representatives of the people—not the people themselves—will be able to discern true interest and to pursue justice, and "will be least likely to sacrifice it to temporary or partial considerations." Directly addressing the problem posed by Montesquieu (the great worry of the Anti-Federalists), representation makes for a republican system that is especially appropriate for a large, populous country like America since a larger population will provide a wider range of choices of men to serve as representatives and will thus be more likely to field the best candidates and to choose—to elect—the most worthy men (the cream will rise to the top, where, in fact, it has probably been all along). While the larger the territory, the less familiar the representatives will be with what it is they represent, this potential problem is solved in advance in America, where, as laid out by the federal Constitution, particular interests will be served in the local and state representative assemblies, and the "great and aggregate interests" will be representatively serviced by the national legislature. Going back to the original problem—the problem of factions—Madison asserts that all of the various positive aspects of representative government in a large republic will work against the development of dangerous "factious combinations."

Here we see an amazing juxtaposition. While Paine writes with praise of ingrafting representation upon democracy, Madison explicitly argues a republic over a democracy, the distinction for him being the practice of representation. While Paine, regardless of his expectations about the effects of leveling, is interested above all in equality and equal representation, Madison expresses worry about temporary, impartial interests—a majority—trampling the nation's true, great interests (e.g., land, manufacturing, mercantile, money, etc.).[93]

But the one thing that both Paine and Madison were sure of was that it was the institution of representation that would make an American democracy and an American Republic[94] possible. Representation was the one thing that they both believed would secure an American political organization. This very organization would secure each of their conflicting desires, which were the conflicting desires of a young, hopeful, worried, and anxious United States.

It is this convergence rather than their obvious differences that might be emphasized here since in the convergence it becomes clear that representation functions as something akin to one of Foucault's discursive determinants, a productive "idea"—a rule—that makes possible an entire field of new American political discourse and practice and is something in which this discourse finds the logic and orientation toward which it aims.

Representation, then, seems to have a certain independence from any political position (truly, no one controls it), which means that it seems to be wide open, its outlines colored in—red, white, or blue—and its terms given meaning (content) according to the positions taken in the discourse that deploys it. This question should be posed here: Is representation really so neutral or open? Is it really such a self-contained idea, just a tool that can be used by any position or does representation have certain kinds of productive rather than instrumental effects, effects having to do most importantly with the production of its terms in itself? This possibility will be explored in the next section of this project.

Thus, further pursuit of the subject of representation will have to carry into Part Two since it has already been in our hands several times and slipped right through our fingers. It changes shape according to the political context and "uses" to which it is being put. Seldom completely definite or univocal, it is usually an unclear "idea" in the discourses and practices in which it appears, its logic at any rate always a logic of indirectness, of x standing in the place of—exchanged for, substituting for or translated into—y. "Public opinion" or the identity of "the people" were not formulated clearly or univocally in eighteenth-century America, and it is already obvious that "public interests" include, for example, the interests of capital, along with the welfare and natural rights of citizens, two examples that are sometimes separate and sometimes the same.

The question of what is represented continues to be one of the most critical questions about representation. The fact that the terms of representation are extremely pliable and capable of going in a range of directions[95] and that representation is characterized by this pliability rather than some stable identity highlights the importance of this question. One way of describing why is to refer back to the natural rights philosophy that intersected the massive political transformations of the late seventeenth and the eighteenth centuries where rights are written not only as inherent in "the people" but also and simultaneously as implicit in the specifications of the law.

Rights, that is, are written. If representation is seen as a feature of the law, it does not just neutrally embody and display rights, but, in its own inscription, it constitutes those rights and, later, those interests. Representation constitutes, that is, the subject of representation.

As I temporarily retreat from the task of determining the identity of the subject of representation, it is important to repeat that while whatever else was going on with the discourse and practice of representation in America, Indians, black slaves, women, and white indentured servants were not capable of voting for, much less being, representatives. It is not even clear that they are part of "We the people" except as bodies to be counted in censuses that would determine the apportionment of representation. Within a more traditional critical framework, this status could be interpreted in terms of "exclusion" from the processes of representation. However, with at least equal force it could be associated with very effective mechanisms of "inclusion." That is, native Americans, blacks, women, and indentured white servants had very specific positions in the constitution of "the people," positions which disqualified them from voting or holding office but which in that very disqualification kept them in very particular positions in the socioeconomic life of early America, performing very specific sorts of functions and contributing toward *the constitution of the people.* In this vital respect, only one side of the story is told if these kinds of people are described as "excluded" from the processes of representation and thereby excluded from the legitimate political subject, "the people."

To offer a concrete example, one might argue here that slaves were certainly not excluded from America—they played a vital role in socio-economy—and one might ponder further the paradox that the more slaves counted in the census of a given state and thus the more national legislative representatives that state was granted, the less those slaves would be represented as people and the more they would be represented as property. That is how they are included in representation, an inclusion based upon an inscribed identity, an identity articulated not only in words but in practice.

Women are not even mentioned in the Constitution; amongst all the masculine references in the Constitution, there is not a single feminine inscription. Nor did any women sign it.[96] This conspicuous lack of inscription consigns them not to oblivion but to a position of very clear, well-policed subordination in the domestic, agricultural, and industrial socio-labor force.[97] "Indians" ("merciless Indian savages," they are called in the Declaration of Independence) are mentioned several times, thus further defining not only their space in the white discourse but also their practical identities. White, indentured servants, who formed a significant portion of the population in the eighteenth century,[98] are mentioned indirectly in Article I of the Constitution between free persons and untaxed Indians, and are added into the calculus of apportionment used to compute the number of representatives. All of these identities get included in specific ways in the notion, "the people," but not in a fashion that renders this concept seamless or universal.

Eighteenth-century America provides an investigation of representation with a number of images and possibilities to ingest, including the peculiar political subject that gets represented in early American institutions of representation, a peculiarity characterized by all sorts of differences and transformations. Whatever is included in or designated by "the people"—whatever, that is, "the people" represents—and whatever the informal status of property, it is clear that the people were determined to be what is sovereign in America and that they remain so. What, then, are "the people"?

A diverse range of historians have described the term "the people" as a fiction.[99] Edmund S. Morgan, who suggests that this fiction was the concoction of elites who used it to mollify the masses—"the people" as the opiate of the masses?—makes this anxious point: "I have been troubled by the perjorative [sic] connotations attached to the word, but I have been unable to find a better one to describe the different phenomena to which I have applied it."[100] The trouble will remain, but the term *fiction* provides a useful and suggestive way to begin describing the subject of political representation, particularly if this fiction is not opposed to the Truth and is viewed as the productive and inclusive architecture of effective reality or of what Machiavelli calls *effectual truth*.

Part Two

Putting Some Pieces Together
(and Taking Them Apart Again)

Chapter IV

Achieving Ends:
The Service of Representation

GETTING LOST IN TRANSLATION

Revolving as they do around different political subjects, the theories of virtual and actual representation seem to constitute two polar and paradigmatic models, the embodiment of something like archetypes or of an archetypal confrontation. While it may be difficult not to favor the possibilities of one of these discourses of representation over the possibilities of the other—while it may be difficult not to vote here—it is also important not to lose sight of the fact that neither of these two discourses indicate what is 'really real'—both are thoroughly metaphysical[1]—and that they share assumptions which are similar not in content but in gesture. The most conspicuous assumption common to both discourses is that both take political representation to be a possibility comprised of two fundamentally distinct, theoretically separable terms, a tool of translative exchange in the hands of (political) reason or consciousness. The second term, the representative, substitutes or "stands for"[2]—stands in the name of—an original, autonomous first term (the subject represented, e.g., objective interests, national interests, property, subjective desires, the will of the people, etc.). This second term, the term of substitution—the representative, the representation—is considered to ultimately reflect, embody, and derive its value from the original term.

The "directness" or "literality" of direct representation suggests that what is to be represented is self-evident. It seems that there would not be so much confusion and overt conflict regarding direct representation if this species of representation really were as self-evident as its name indicates. Commonsensical, the name also sounds almost empirical (it belongs to an empiricist language-game). However, empirically speaking, what does "direct" representation look like? Can it be represented or articulated by a two-party system (e.g., by a system that represents only democrats and republicans)? Is proportional representation a more direct strain of directness? If proportional representation is more direct, what about the inevitable compromise and confusion created by the working necessity of coalitions, and what about the ultimate, unambiguous, univocal duality—yes/no—marked by the final tally of a given vote? The line of practical questions begged by the suggestion of "directness" and "literality" continues: Can both single member and at large electoral configurations be direct, or is one of them more direct than the other? More simply, is one of them direct and the other not direct? There are no direct answers to these kinds of questions.

A similar although more obvious indirectness holds for what is "virtual," too, since it must with the same necessity also declare its subject or object to be self-evident. However, the virtual is then burdened with the apparently further need to pinpoint the identities of objective interests. This burden looms large for philosophers, who tend to linger too long on the track of truth, but the burden may not be so distressing for those powerful gentlemen whose positions in life have granted them the privilege required to really know what is real, what is true, what is really and truly of value, and to be familiar with the contents of the issues and to have appropriated and incorporated the cartographic axioms of debate and decision.

"Virtual" representation is clearly metaphysical in its assertion of a transcendental signified. The same can be said for "actual" representation, which in getting down-to-earth has not left the realm of high-altitude metaphysics, or, again, of "fiction" or of truth as necessary error.[3] Both formations of re-presentation are translations, neither offering the possibility of presenting nor of distilling out the pristine political subjects upon which they depend but which must be deferred. Whatever "actual" means, it cannot really mean "direct" when associated with representation.

An everyday way of illustrating this point might be to say that if representation is translation, then something invariably gets lost in the translation. However, while true, this way of putting it too simply repeats the givenness of, in particular, the original term, of the self-identity of the subject of representation. It is the assumption of the givenness or independence of this identity that helps determine what representation is and the ways that it is thought about. Coextensive with this assumption is the move to translate—transfer and transform—that self-identity into another sort of identity, a practicable governmental identity, a deciding, decisive, and decideable identity, an identity of rule and law, of effective decision, a substitute identity, a stand-in. A faithful translation—a translation that does not betray its subject—would seem to be one that is as literal as possible (remember again John Adams' famous and elegantly simple image of representative government as "in miniature an exact portrait of the people at large"). Clearly, in order to affirm the translation or transfer—in order to support a representative political system—one must first affirm the identity of that which is to be translated and represented even if it is evident that not everything associated with this identity will carry over in the translation effected by representation. What warrants such an affirmation, such an assumption?

The emphasis on the metaphysical character of "direct" or "actual" representation, with which I open this chapter, is another instance of not taking sides, of not voting (not yet). Here, I want to emphasize what, apparently, "virtual" and "actual" representation have in common with literal representation which is just as immersed in the deviant, substitutive possibilities of translation as its political opponent, virtual representation. The metaphor of standing for or acting for—of representing—is itself embedded in metaphor, one that pivots around the image of an independent subject rather than one constituted by a particular discourse and practice of representa-

tion itself.[4] On a more specific practical level, what these two
political opponents share in common is this instrumental
notion of translation or transfer, one of them putting this tool in
the service of objective interests, the other in the service of that
vast and willful multiplicity, the people, who would remain
indefinite, inarticulate, and ineffectual without the instrument
of representation. Both representations, that is, emerge as instruments developed and institutionalized in order to achieve ends
(ends perhaps not confined to the domain of politics), in order to
realize (to make real) what on its own would not come to be,
would not count, and could not surface (become effective) in
the univocity of decision and political action. Without the
instrument of representation, the political subject would be
fragmented and scattered. It would remain without order, without reason, lost, perhaps, in Hobbes's version of a state of nature,
hovering perilously on the verge of a state of war.

In short, the logic of substitution embodied in representation is an instrumental logic. That, at any rate, is the way that
representation is generally and implicitly thought of. While
few philosophers or political theorists today would be so naive
as to believe in the ontological independence of an entity such
as "the people"—probably few believe in a transcendental ref-
erent or source for representation—political representation nevertheless continues to be conceptualized within the framework
of an instrumental logic, and it is thus not belief that requires
critical questioning here but the discursive conditions which
shape modern and contemporary thoughts about representation. If the general discursive condition is instrumentalism,
the next move is to look at some of the important things that
this instrument achieves and to look at its reasons.

THE LEGITIMATION AND RATIONALIZATION OF
FORMATIONS OF POWER AND DISCOURSE

> In the representative system, the reason for every-
> thing must publicly appear.
>
> —Tom Paine[5]

All regimes obtain legitimacy by being in some
degree representative or at least convincing their
subjects that they are.

—J. Roland Pennock[6]

What is controversial is the relation of legitimation
to truth.

—Jürgen Habermas[7]

The political question is not error, illusion, alienated consciousness or ideology; it is truth itself.

—Michel Foucault[8]

Power is tolerable only on condition that it mask a
substantial part of itself.

—Michel Foucault[9]

In Chapter II, near the beginning of the discussion of the
eighteenth-century English discourse of virtual representation, a brief historical observation was made regarding the
rationalization of the roots of this particular configuration of
representation. There, I remarked on the rationality of virtual
representation but noted that "rationality" in this context
should be equated not with the progress of developing Reason
(or, in conjunction with this, with the expansion of freedom as
such) but with processes of rationalization and legitimation,
processes always contingent upon the specific contexts[10] in
which they occur. It is time to pursue this set of possibilities
further and to explore the forms of rationality and legitimacy—approached here strategically in terms of rationalization and legitimation—generally associated with political representation.

Following through with the logic of that earlier passage, it
must be emphasized that some persistently particular rationality does not gradually emerge through the developing historical process of political representation, eventually express-

ing itself, for example, in the theory of virtual representation. That is to say, the medieval representation of feudal geoeconomic divisions and the estates, which rested on a discursive and ontological allegiance to specific territory—here, the synonymy of name and place—did not lead with logical necessity to the later discourse of virtual representation, which was situated in a political field intimately associated with the emergence of a world market, i.e., with capitalism. This was a very different field of logic that, in contrast with the underpinnings of medieval representation, tended away from the allegiance to specificity so vital to medieval systems of organization and exchange. Virtual representation operates in a field that levels down, that absorbs or appropriates rather than reinforces or exalts specific difference, and this was part of an architecture appropriate for the reinforcement and enhanced rationalization of a new capitalist socioeconomic structure.

What does this mean? To begin with—it is important to emphasize this from the outset—this observation is not the product of a theory of ideology, which would emphasize definite forces operating more or less independently of, yet behind, the rationalization or legitimation. Following Foucault, and as I have tried to suggest elsewhere, legitimation cannot be confined by the notion of ideology, at least not so long as ideology is articulated as an organized system of what, in essence, must be lies—from planned or unplanned (logically spawned) ideas to transmitted images—generated in order to conceal reality, which in its true, pure, or nonideologized form would be too ugly to tolerate. Alternatively, discourse fabricates identities in its very articulation and in so doing covers itself up; in a sense, it is invisible, a "pure" cover, with which all of the identities it establishes and authorizes work in complicity.[11]

Here, it is vital to note that this argument is not a denial that falsehoods are deliberately disseminated through manipulated (or unmanipulated) ideological channels or that lies and covers (e.g., cover-ups) are a prominent part of political discourse. The gesture here is not one of denial but of a change in focus, a shift in emphasis. The shift is from looking at the discourse of legitimation as, primarily, a malign curtain over and

causal effect of Reality to focusing on the productive and determinative character of "legitimative" discourse. While also not
a consensual ground, the discourse of legitimation, then, is
not a concealment of reality but the armature of effective reality. For example, the reality that the discourse and practice of
virtual representation legitimates is certainly real—effectively
real—but it does not exist independently of or beneath this
discourse. Through this discourse and its associated practices,
objective interests are fabricated and articulated, and they are
also objectively and materially made real (even while in competition with other "objective" realities, such as the conflicting historical reality established by the discourse of popular vs.
virtual representation). Virtual representation provided a
strong conservative defense—not just a legitimative but a practical and effective (i.e., both reinforcing and co-constitutive)
defense—against challenges to what at least seemed to be the
traditional institution of representation and of English politics generally, challenges that acquired a new and threatening visage in the seventeenth and eighteenth centuries.

Virtual representation, then, covers up but does not, fundamentally, lie. Rather, representation is a productive articulation of the truth and of the terms—the players or identities—authorized by the truth it establishes. While Marx, for
example, assumes the independent, positive existence of the
objective, "material" source of ideology (the organization of
the system of production), Claude Lefort's approach seems
more helpful:

> We clearly break with Marx's conception in so far as we
> do not treat ideology as a reflection, but seek to uncover
> its processes and to think of formation and transforma-
> tion together, that is, to attribute to it the ability to artic-
> ulate and rearticulate itself, not only in response to the
> supposed "real," but in face of the effects of its own dis-
> simulation of the real.[12]

Here we begin to move into some of the more positive possibilities regarding the legitimacy of legitimation and the ratio-

nality of rationalization. Some of the positive alternatives to more traditional linkages between legitimation and ideology posed by Lefort are offered in the form of questions: "What change in the principles of legitimacy, what reshaping in the system of beliefs, in the way of apprehending reality, enabled such a representation of power to emerge?"[13] Lefort's list of conditions of emergence mentions only things that would traditionally be considered functions of the subject pole—principles, beliefs and apprehensions—and so to it I would add some more ambiguous and elusive material dimensions. For example, what technologies (e.g., the technologies of speed and communication) enable particular representations of power to emerge?

In Lefort's language, formations of power invariably inscribe "models,"[14] and are embodied in them since the models are coextensive with (although are not the reductive source of) the identity of a given formation. These models are not Plato's ideas nor any other transcendental source outside of specific configurations of power (rather, they are the inseparable architecture of those configurations). Nor are they mere images, mere reflections. Lefort's general statement here can be appropriated and pushed into an even stronger position, then, by approaching the discourse of legitimation as a powerful, political articulation and (co-)constitution of effective reality and of the truth; the truth is always something specific and practical and always something that is articulated, which means voiced but also visible. Truth has a visibility that is neither complete nor expressive in any traditional sense.[15]

The processes of rationalization or legitimation I am affirming here may be associated with what Castoriadis calls the "institution of the social imaginary," which is the gesture of self-creation or self-founding, the institution of society.[16] Again, the imaginary is not the origin of reality (reality is made up of many materials) but, along with other factors—other material—is one of its necessary and constitutive dimensions. As Dick Howard describes Lefort's thoughts, "To be, the political must articulate itself."[17] In other words, formations of power must generate "models," which are self-models or self-images or self-identities.

Foucault approaches this matter from a related but importantly different perspective. By investigating the terms and specific determinations of legitimation and rationalization—i.e., of representations of power—what Foucault seeks, finds, and analyzes—what he dissects—is the truth, which is always located in specific institutions:

> The important thing here, I believe, is that truth isn't outside power, or lacking in power. . . . Truth is a thing of this world: it is produced only by virtue of multiple forms of constraint, . . . a "regime" of truth. This regime is not merely ideological or superstructural; it was a condition of the formation and development of capitalism. And it's this same regime which, subject to certain modifications, operates in the socialist countries. . . . The political question, to sum up, is not error, illusion, alienated consciousness or ideology; it is truth itself.[18]

The point here is not to reduce reality to language—to its representations—but to emphasize that discourse, too, is real and effective, practical and interwoven with practice, not just reflective, not just words, true or false, pure or corrupt, and not just the explicit or implicit universalization of norms.

Part of the truth is that the relation between the different formations of representation that we have already addressed and their respective subjects and objects is one of legitimation—legitimation *is* truth—legitimation of all of the terms of representation, including interests and rights, property and people, as well as those who represent them. While coextensive with particular formations of power, legitimation is rational but only insofar as it provides a logic and "meaning" for a given network of power, i.e., produces sense and produces what count for and are counted as subjects and objects. It produces, that is, a system of truth. Rationalization is a creative process, which is to say that it helps bring an object or reality into being, not as ideas or forms of consciousness but as an effective dimension of the politics coextensive with specific forms of socioeconomics,[19] and with specific configurations of power.

To stay with the example already in play, in the articulation of its subject or object—interests—virtual representation purports to describe a real state of affairs existing outside of itself. In so doing, what it also does in the same stroke is organize that subject or object, found itself, and account for the complex of practices with which it is associated. What it does, then, is institute itself, bring itself into being, legitimate itself, make that kind of representation *be*, e.g., legitimate a way of doing political business that could not come into being or exist without the rationalizing, reinforcing architecture provided by the discourse of virtual representation. That is, the discourse of virtual representation legitimated, rationalized— or 'author-ized'—the existing political structure and the complex of power practices associated with it even as this complex was changing (the rationalization is an effect and reflection as well as a constitutive element of this change). In an ironic sense, then, its advocates were right in believing that their theory described what representation is because they—that is, their discourse—had made representation virtual, had produced that particular form of representation. So, for instance, Burke "sees interest"—the subject or object of virtual representation—"very much as we today see scientific fact: it is completely independent of wishes or opinion, of whether we like it or not; it just is so."[20] Is "interest" what all of the things covered by that term intrinsically or fundamentally really are in some objective sense? Is "interest" a way of rendering them, thereby producing a general system of values determinative of socioeconomics (and thus of representative politics) as a whole? Are interests what is actually (or virtually) fundamental to the sphere of representative politics? Are they in themselves what counts and what is effective?

The discourse of virtual representation legitimates interests and all of its other terms not in the sense that a fake passport provides an identity to a smuggler but in the sense that this discourse authorizes an entire complex of practices, that it organizes, constitutes, and grants it its very existence. What proves the truth of virtual representation is its effective establishment, its "hegemony," and its very visibility. The rule and visibility of a discourse and a practice is its proof even as its rule is contested and in conflict with other contenders (which may or may not be made visible by the dominant discourse-practice). Within the effective sphere codetermined by the discourse of virtual representation—within the ground it wins and provisionally holds—"interests" is the subject and is what counts. It is what counts because it is what is counted, just as, alternatively, other subjects and objects—people and public opinion—are counted in a discursive system constructed around a different, perhaps ultimately conjoint political subject, one in which a broad suffrage provides the material for what is counted (literally, votes).

The competition between the discourses of "virtual" and "actual" political representation may indicate a major shortcoming on the part of Foucault, whose articulation of regimes of truth may seem a bit too formal sometimes and a little too neat since the neatness often misleadingly suggests a self-contained unity or apparently monolithic character of regimes of discourse, as he breaks them up into clearly defined periods and coherent, discrete formations. What is often underemphasized or remains unthematized in Foucault's analyses is the competition between concurrent, conflicting discourses. However, there are good reasons for this strategic underemphasis; rather than looking at different discourses as radically different from each other, or, alternatively, rather than accounting for conflicting discourses by means of, for instance, dialectical logic (which also neatens up and even resolves conflict), Foucault is interested in the determinative features that different, perhaps even opposed, discourses have in common with each other. He is interested in tracking regularities distributed throughout different sectors of a given discursive regime, which might often contain different positions or make possible the emergence of positions at odds with each other. That is, Foucault tries not to let ideological differences obscure other, broadly dispersed regularities. However, competing discursive formations are also often in genuine conflict with each other even as they depend on common determinants.

While differences do confront each other in discourse—e.g., the differences between national interests and local ones and between the interests of capital and those of the people, which do not necessarily coincide—and while discourse tends to be divided, not monolithic, these differences cannot be associated with invention in the hands of consciousness, of independent identities. Instead, they develop anonymously, impersonally, as contributing, legitimating features of broad configurations of power, generated in differential relation to each other: the power of "the people" congealing against the power of "objective interests"; "objective interests" and property entrenching themselves against the threatening configuration of power embodied in the people. Further, these conflicting political discourses are all discourses of identity, which means that they are discourses of definition and the forces of certainty; the same self-fabricating logic is at work simultaneously in multiple, competing discourses, providing the force that rules the terms of each discourse and practice and consolidates multiplicity. In part, this is the force that binds, which is what makes it the force of "understanding." I will explore the phenomenon of conflict as such more directly in Chapter VI, but for now this reference to definition or certainty of identity leads to Foucault's emphasis on regularities. More specifically, this reference gives rise to the following question: What, in their certainties, do different forms of modern political representation—forms that might be in overt conflict with each other—have in common? Although the question broaches a range of complexities, it intersects the closely related issue of instrumental discourse, which is a discourse of autonomous consciousness.

One of the key elements associated with the legitimating processes of modern political representation in general is its self-presentation as mere instrument in the hands of a definite,

autonomous political subject. Political representation is articulated as an inherently neutral means to an end. While it may
continually get derailed, perverted, and distorted, it is in itself
only a means to a republic, to a democracy, or even to a democratic republic; it is a means to a harmonious (unified) society,
a society in which all are able to express and fulfill themselves, either at the top or somewhere else and even down
where the benefits or crumbs of fulfilled interest eventually
trickle. Maybe the end or aim of politics is self-expression in a
popular government, a self-expression made possible by means
of representation. However, is political representation fundamentally just an instrument, a means of achieving something
other than itself?

INSTRUMENTING REPRESENTATION

> Democratic impulse can actually produce demo-
> cratic government only when appropriate institu-
> tions exist for making possession of power a public
> trust. . . . All institutions are instrumental in nature,
> and some training is necessary before representative
> institutions can be used to advantage.
>
> —Henry Ford[21]

This passage from another Ford's 1924 book,
Representative Government, is saturated with dense but traditional and familiar words. Such density gives rise to a number of questions linked to the issue of instrumentality. To
begin with, what is the meaning of this key phrase, "democratic impulse"? What fuels this impulse? Is it reason or biol-
ogy? (Is it Eros, Thanatos, or some sort of struggle of desire
[democratic impulse vs. fascistic reflex]?) Is this impulse fundamental and universal, or accidental and episodic? Many of
the traditional metaphysical alternatives arise here, and many
modern decisions are repeated in Ford's words.

If the impulse that is assumed to use and thus be behind
representation remains unclear, it is in any event self-evident

what representation is, at least as such (i.e., in its isolated, instrumental essence) since what it is on its own is really not much, practically nothing at all. In itself it is 'no thing,' just a tool, and essentially neutral, as all instruments are, at least in themselves. According to this familiar discourse, representation is just *an* institution, a structural or organizational device, a mere means to an end, or a means to serve a purpose that exists ultimately independent of and prior to the techniques it utilizes to actualize, realize, or achieve itself. Although the end is the real essence of democracy—an essence to be contrasted with mere instrumentality—that end is not completely definite and really could not be unless it was represented Properly. What the end does, though, is use representation, at least theoretically. In practice, however, a great deal of development is necessary in order to make the practice match the theory, the tool match the intent, in order to get the means and ends in alignment with each other. To begin with appropriate institutions are necessary and training is a prerequisite for the proper use of any tool. It always takes awhile to use a tool to advantage, to get the hang of it, especially if training means self-training (which is inevitably the case with democracy's use of representation since the manual of democracy has not and never will have been written in advance).

The concept of representation as a tool continues to be one of the basic ideas dominating the diverse discourses of representation; as a practice, representation is a means to an end, an instrument of, generally, democracy. Implicitly and explicitly, this technological understanding of representation is at work on all sides of representation. However, even if it is correct that representation is an instrument, this does not mean that it is true (a Heideggerian distinction). Ford's statement is intended to be a description of representation, but it makes more sense to read it as symptomatic of the instrumental perspective on representation, a perspective that renders representation as in itself neutral, which is to say that it neutralizes representation in the workshop of democratic discourse. Ford's discourse sets itself apart from its subject matter, discussing representation as if it were a self-evident and masterable object (at least theoretically), one that may not have had all of the bugs worked out of it yet but which is potentially and in itself transparent and neutral. However, no descriptive discourse is apart from the discourse and practice that it selects and thematizes, and no discourse is either transparent, self-evident, or "merely" instrumental.

Castoriadis begins "Technique," by drawing a line:

> To the Greek idea of man, *zoon logon echon*—a living being possessed of logos, or speech-thought—modern thinkers have juxtaposed, and even opposed, the idea of *homo faber*, man defined by the fabrication of instruments, therefore the possession of tools. Anthropological evidence seemed, for a time, to support their case, but this was no more than an appearance: flint instruments survive, whereas only indirect inference is possible concerning speech preceding the written word. Progress in anthropology has put us now in a position considerably to qualify this contrast. . . .[22]

Initiating his discussion of technology by providing definitions of a human being, Castoriadis points to the contingency of the problem of instrumentality (to the contingency of its dominating insistence), thereby destabilizing or putting into question the modern privilege granted to the critical link (or to a particular determination of it) between human beings and tools. The destabilization is the result of the contrast between this privileged link and a different range of possibilities. Castoriadis begins his discussion of technology or instrumentality, then, with an assertion of difference. This assertion does not advocate a definite side so much as suggest that there are alternatives to instrumental understandings. The movement here is not to a vote but to a different dimension of the democratic process, an opening up of philosophical possibilities and a suggestion of alternatives. It looks to the cultivation of something different from *homo faber* but also informed by the figure *zoon logon echon*, the being possessed of speech-thought or of what Foucault calls "discourse."

As a construct, representation in particular is more than just a system of political expression; it is the self-made body of the political subject, the semi-direct (and sometimes virtual) extension of a sovereign self, a sign of and a manipulable and controlled substitution for consciousness and rationality. It is through this self-made body that "we get things done," and that "we realize our political ideas." Regarding instrumentality more generally, Castoriadis notes that for the modern period (including Marx) "technique is creation insofar as it is the unfolding of rationality,"[23] which is embodied in but cannot be confused with its diverse and transient products (occasionally, these products are defective [e.g., representation that does not seem to represent]). This is a creation, then, that is restricted and even neutralized by, subservient to, and defined sheerly in terms of the instrumental service it performs for the controlling ends that exist outside of and prior to it. Thus, Castoriadis continues, "Technique becomes the instrument which mediates between two fixed points: a rational nature which can be tamed and fashioned, and human needs which define the towards-what and the for-what of this domination."[24]

However, in its division of ends and means (and theory and practice, etc.), the instrumental casting of *techne* contains and thus obscures the truly creative dimension of human productions and discourse-practice. This is not the only possible casting of *techne*, which Castoriadis alternatively translates as making/doing; on a general level, technique can accomplish "what nature is not capable of accomplishing."[25] Thus, Castoriadis talks about absolute creations; "Brute reality is not fixed, but bears within it immense interstices which allow of movement, assembling, alteration, division; . . . man is able to insert himself as a real cause in the flux of reality."[26]

If man is a cause and if the motivation that causes things to come into being (e.g., to develop technology) is human needs, the very needs that determine technique are themselves as perdurably fluid as the river of Heraclitus. As Castoriadis writes, "There exist no problem or problems of man which have been defined once for all, so that he can meet them, in the course of time, by 'obligatory' or progressively improved solutions; human 'needs' are defined by no fixed point."[27] Putting a Foucauldian spin on these observations, one of the powerfully creative features of discourse-practice, then, is its articulation of human "needs," which consolidate the constitution of subject identities and function as nodal points in the projection of what Castoriadis calls the "social imaginary."

Castoriadis continues: "Industry is not just 'the open book of the essential powers of man,' it is also the endlessly continuing text of the impossible translation of desire into realisable intention."[28] Recalling the discussion of translation in an earlier section of this chapter and pushing one facet of this last observation further—connecting it directly to the problem at hand—it can be argued, then, that (the always specific) formations of the discourse and practice of political representation create the (also always specific) configurations of "intention" associated with the political subject and that they create these from indefinite but always (materially and historically) situated "desire." In other words, discourse-practice is the product of the always fluid and specific circumstances of "desire."[29] As Castoriadis writes elsewhere:

> Man is not this need which contains its "proper object" as its complement, a lock with its key (to be found or made). Man can exist only by defining himself in each case as an ensemble of needs and corresponding objects, but he always outstrips these definitions—and, if he outstrips them . . . this is because they spring out of him, because he invents them (not arbitrarily, to be sure, for there is always nature, the minimum of coherence required by rationality, and previous history), and hence because he makes them by making things and by making himself. . . .[30]

I will return to the issue of sovereignty in the final chapter, but Castoriadis helps make it possible to move for the time being away from the sovereign, instrumental subject, away from what Heidegger calls "the lord of the earth,"[31] master of language and all other instruments of the will, to—I press in with Foucault's perspective—a subject that is the product or effect as well as a participant in and perpetuator of discourse and practice. That is, Castoriadis helps take us from the definite, sovereign identity—the one that manipulates all identities—to an identity generated, organized, shaped, and determined within a given discourse and practice. Again, discourse shapes its subjects as it shapes its objects, not from a distance—it is not removed, not transcendental—but as coextensive with them (i.e., discourse is itself no more sovereign than the subjects and objects and other bodies that it organizes and that engage in it). At the level of its most important processes, it is not merely a tool of sovereign consciousness to shape things; no body is ultimately in control, no matter how much some try to control it. Discourse is productive in all of its terms. The identity of what is represented is effectively constituted by the social imaginary of representation, an instrument that is more than a fundamentally neutral instrument or a means to the end that governs it. One instance of this is the formal institution of political representation.

A critical analysis of instrumentality necessarily encounters, generates, or takes up a positive tack. This is a productive move anticipated in certain respects by Marx, one that will lead through and to further critical analysis and finally to political representation and the instrumentation of "communication." Insofar as it expands the background of instrumentality, a brief glance at Marx may help throw light on representation.

Precisely at the point where he misses the mark by remaining within instrumentality and the hierarchical foundation provided by his dialecticized idea of "materialism," Marx offers some profound insight into the productive rather than simply instrumental side of technology and anticipates some alternatives to the rationalist means/end hierarchy of the instrumental perspective. This is a materialist insight, and, as such, can be seen as contributing to our grasp of the forces of creation rather than committing that grasp to a solid, transcendental ground (which is what materiality must return to for Marx). In a moment, I will address the sense in which Marx loses hold of his insight by pushing one of its aspects too far. Meanwhile, it is of note and, I would argue, not accidental that the ground of transformation he uses in his example here is, quite literally, the field of battle.

In "Wage Labour and Capital," Marx writes that

> With the invention of a new instrument of warfare, firearms, the whole internal organisation of the army necessarily changed; the relationships within which individuals can constitute an army and act as an army were transformed and the relations of different armies to one another also changed.[32]

Here is an image of the power of socio-material production that could be reduced to the infrastructure/superstructure hierarchy emphasized in Althusser's understanding of ideology (the hierarchy established by the absolute privilege Marx grants to the organization of forces of production, the privilege that is the necessary basis of scientific materialism). What is more interesting is that Marx is also addressing a profoundly creative kind of transformation, one disrupting the limitations of the instrumental perspective.

To begin with, Marx is saying that the firearm is not simply an enhanced version of the club, spear, lance, sword, bow, pike, or crossbow, which is to say that it is not just a new means for accomplishing an old end, a better tool for doing the same thing, or an improved application of an in itself stable, self-identical idea (killing people, winning a war, or enhancing or reinforcing power). While it is not wrong, that view of the firearm remains strictly within the confines of an instrumental, rationalist understanding and consequently misses the transformative and socially productive effects of a

new technology. Instrumentalism is certainly not what Marx
is stressing here.

What Marx seems to be emphasizing with this example
is that far from being neutral instruments in the service of
ontologically independent intentions—things over which
humans are in sovereign control—tools influence the very
nature of both their use and their users, which is to say that
objects help bring into being—create—the identities of the
subjects who use them by determining the range of possibilities available to these subjects (on the most general level,
technology creates the needs it serves). The introduction of
the firearm is simultaneously the introduction of a different
kind of soldier, a different kind of army, and a different kind
of war. That is, the firearm is an ontological as well as a material object, which contributes to the transformation of the
context into which it emerges and helps change what the
other elements of that context—soldiers, armies, battles, and
wars—are; a new system of production generates a different
set of possibilities, of social relations,[33] and thus a different
kind of subject.

If, then, to use a Heideggerian distinction,[34] it is correct
(but not necessarily "true") that political representation is an
instrument, what kind of instrument is it? That is, if representation is taken as a method for ordering political power—as
a technique, a set of procedures, a tool—how might it be characterized? Earlier in this chapter, I talked about representation as a tool of translation, a system of exchange. One could
also approach the general characteristic that allows for all of
these binarily-ordered descriptives by articulating political
representation as an instrument of or formal set of procedures
for "communication." Representation is the tool by which
the political subject communicates its needs, interests, and
wishes and offers its consent. That is, representation is the
apparatus by means of which consensus is communicated and
expressed, formally inscribed and authorized. As such a

means, the communicative possibility offered by representation functions as both a conduit and a guarantee. It is a conduit of consent—and thus, ideally, of consensus—and a guarantee of a rational politics, a politics that represents rather than dominates. What if "communication" does not (implicitly or explicitly) depend upon, advance, and safeguard the claims and possibilities of independent reason? Further, what if "communication" has recently mutated into something different from what it might have been before, a mutation that is central to the hi-tech culture of the "information" age? Alternatively, what might it mean to paraphrase a provocative Derridean gesture and to assert that "there never was 'communication'"?[35] What would this do to the integrity of the political subject, of political reason, and thus to the politics of representation which is derived from this subject, who participates in it via the medium of consent? Would the denial of "communication" be synonymous with the denial of "the people" and of democratic representation? If it did, we would all be in trouble.

However, there is an alternative way to unfold the assertion that "there never was 'communication,'" which is to insist that communication never was what it is usually and implicitly thought to be. That is, that it never was an instrumental conduit governed by the telos of a clear (distortion-free) channel of exchange, operating, ultimately, according to the simple, digital model of lines of transmission/reception. This explanation has become especially clear in this communications culture and information age, a period in which "informing the subject" has come to mean something different from a mere transfer of, for instance, data (knowledge or propaganda) from point A (the source) to point B (the subject). Informing the subject is more than just this sort of neutral (or distortive!) transfer since what the political subject is is not independent of the various networks of "information" and "communication," but is to a large and very real extent produced by it. Practices of communication are forms of production, and this in particular points to forms of production of the political subject.

Never neutral—and this partly means never independent of the medium of communication—information informs the subject, by which I mean more than just that it provides an autonomous subject with resources or tools. By keeping us filled in, information helps fill out what the subject is.

Chapter V

Counting Images
of the Political Subject

Power can be transmitted, but not will.

—J. J. Rousseau[1]

Modern ideas of representation assume that the representative is bound by the will of the represented, but the will of the people is a modern fact which largely partakes of fiction.

—A. F. Pollard[2]

"We the People" tell the Government what to do, it doesn't tell us. "We the People" are the driver— the Government is the car. And we decide where it should go, and by what route, and how fast. Almost all the world's constitutions are documents in which governments tell the people what their privileges are. Our Constitution is a document in which "We the People" tell the Government what it is allowed to do. "We the People" are free.

—Ronald Reagan[3]

DRIVING FORCES

One fascinating feature of this printed excerpt from President Reagan's 1989 "Farewell Address" is the open transformation of democratic Government into a proper noun, which is conjoined here with the possibly conflicting claim

117

that in America, the only real proper term or name of the political subject is "We the People." The quotation marks around this latter phrase inscribe a formal reference to the Preamble of the American Constitution, a reference full of dense resonances, resonances which grant Reagan's speechwriter's text a certain power and authority, despite the clumsy and purely instrumental car/driver analogy. Through this canonized phrase, the President's speechwriter's text taps parasitically into the textual power of the Constitution, the very root and hallowed source of American democracy.

However, these quotation marks also inadvertently perform a kind of mundane *epoché*. Suspending the phrase midtext—"_____"—they suggest a disinvestment of belief in that which stands between them, which does not necessarily fictionalize the content but nevertheless grants it a kind of irreality (turns it into a phantom, perhaps the palimpsest of the last several hundred years of the discourse of popular sovereignty). Made irreal by this *epoché*, the phrase "We the People" serves very appropriately as part of the final official address delivered specifically to an audience—to "We the People"—by a president who, in the context of politics, had himself always been irreal and had even acknowledged this as early as 1966 when he asserted that "politics is just like show business."[4] Reagan was certainly not the first American President whose political identity was largely the product of the radio and television, but he was the first who seemed utterly inseparable from it. The Reagan identity was so firmly embedded in the "communications" media that the President even survived massive, multifronted, public scandals virtually unscathed; that is, other aspects of reality[5] did not damage the identity. It was such a successful identity that the People (i.e., the audience numbered in the sampling polls) continued to support him even though at the same time polls indicated that he was widely perceived as a liar and that a high percentage of the people did not agree with his policies. This apparent contradiction may not have been possible had Reagan been someone "real." As if to literalize the language of Hobbes for the first time, the artificial, irreal identity of the executive representative was quite literally that of an actor.

The discourse and practice of political representation seems to be undergoing a mutation that is associated to a large extent (but not only) with the development of a "communications" culture. "Communication" is itself a historically specific formation and transformation of discourse, and one of its effects has been to grant all the terms and identities of representation a new sort of irreality. By calling it this, I mean nothing technical, fixed, or definite, which is precisely the point. "We the People" are or is (plural, singular?) clearly there—present—in the substitution inscribed by Reagan's speechwriter's text, but it is not very clear how or what this presence might mean. This distinct lack of distinctness is shorthand for the subject of this chapter, which is the political subject, the subject of representation.

The bulk of debate about political representation continues to revolve around binary configurations from the past, particularly those configurations and values that emerged so dramatically in the eighteenth century.[6] Often, these binary configurations are constituted in outright oppositional forms. One by now familiar example is the opposition between actual and virtual representation, and another is the related one between direct and indirect representation. Another still is the also related difference between a representative seen as a delegate and a representative seen as a trustee; the difference between these two antagonistic, practical-discursive identities is one way of laying out the "mandate-independence controversy," which is the phrase used by Pitkin for the theme of the major debate about representation.[7] What all of these different, conflicting identities have in common is another binary configuration, one that is split and hierarchical in nature although not necessarily oppositionalized; regardless of the side taken in the debate, it is the relation between the represented and its representative that tends to receive the dominant emphasis. As Eulau has written, "Whatever the scheme of representation, the core problem involved in representation is the relationship that exists between representative and represented."[8]

It is true that the relation between these poles provides a key access point to the problem of representation and that it is usually taken to be the core problem, regardless of the particular scheme of representation or the positions marked out and taken by those engaged in the debate. However, the relation between the representative and the represented is not such a straightforward problem since it has tended to be considered primarily—almost exclusively—in terms of the identity of the representative. The most general form of this favored consideration would be manifested in the following sort of question: What are the tasks, limits, and attributes of a representative government or of the citizens' representatives? A more specific question might address a representative's obligations to its constituency: Should the representative's main job be simply to carry out instructions and to implement the bidding of the people? Are representatives to be entrusted to do what is best for their particular constituency and/or for the nation as a whole based upon a specialized knowledge derived from acquaintance with working government and with the interests of the electorate (whatever form those interests take)? By concentrating on the representative's identity, this approach to the relation implicitly takes the identity of what is represented as not only self-evident and determinable but also as ultimately independent, whether that identity is associated with public good, public interests, public will, public opinion, etc. Thus, both representational poles function in the discourse of which they are part as relatively (or potentially) clear identities, certainly as distinct from each other. Even if the relation between them remains open to debate, everyone knows that one is the electorate and the other is the elected, one is the original source of the power and the other its instrument and that one is a natural identity and the other is artificial—a surrogate, an actor, merely a representative. By focusing on and debating about issues such as, in particular, a representative's obligations to its[9] constituency, the energy of analysis is diverted away from what is quietly assumed in the background, namely, the independent identity of what is represented. The existence—interests or will, etc., of the represented—is assumed to be something prior and semi-objective (e.g., "natural"), something given, something that unobtrusively but clearly justifies or "grounds" representation, i.e., which functions as representation's source and as the source of its legitimacy.

If it is clear that the identities of the representative and the represented are fundamentally distinct from each other and that the former needs to be addressed as dependent upon the latter, this is the sort of clarity that obscures its own assumptions (this is the sort of light that blinds). More specifically, the clarity of the hierarchizing division between, for instance, representative government and the people (from whom legitimate government draws its power) obscures the powerful coproductivity of their relation, a practical relation not isolated from other complexes and complex factors, such as economics, history, and the development of "communications" technology and the networks it produces.

I will continue the tradition of approaching the problem of representation in terms of the relation between what is represented and its representative, but I want to shift the emphasis and try to further consider what it is that gets represented. More to the point, I will focus on what it is that representation is about or has come to be about.

HIERARCHIES OF DIFFERENCE:
RETURN OF THE ONE AND THE MANY

Popular government is also described as self-government or self-rule. The idea here is that what is sovereign is the people and that, once again, the government is in essence only an organization, reflection, and expression of that sovereignty; it is a substitution, whose power is fundamentally derivative, as it transforms the semi-organic people into the People, the originary multitudes into a public and one plane of society

into the state. The people are the pure spring from which legitimate power flows. Whereas powers of the past flowed down—
down from the largest warrior or down from the throne—
power flows up and then out now (this is one of the dominant
conceptions of power accompanying modern democracy); the
pyramid has been inverted (the model for power remains pyra-
midal). In the (pre Enlightenment) days of monarchy, the government had been the head of everything and what was
sovereign was the royal will residing (eventually) in the King's
two bodies (the individual's royal body, which functioned as
the substratum for the other body, the body politic). In contrast, a popular government is only an instrumental body, an
ideal Cartesian body. This form of government provides the
possibility for putting many heads together as or as if one,
making practical decisions and political motility possible.
Locke, for example, writes that "'Tis in their legislative that
the members of a commonwealth are united and combined
together into one coherent living body." Here they are one
body, coherent, mobile, and alive. Also, though, they are one
soul, unity of will, which means political will. "For the
essence and union of the society consisting in having one will,
the legislative, when once established by the majority has the
declaring and, as it were, keeping of that will."[10] Locke's use of
the word "keeping" is significant here. In a sense, the will
rendered by the practice of representation is on loan to the
legislature. Keeping does not necessarily mean safekeeping,
though, so Locke leaves the system open; "every one is the dis-
posure of his own will, when those who had, by the delegation
of the society, the declaring of the public will, are excluded
from it, and others usurp the place who have no such authority
or delegation."[11] Images of conflict and division appear here.
While the government provides society as a whole with a
body, the public will is something from which it is possible to
be excluded when government and people divide or when
power overrides or excludes consent. That is, the atomic unit
of the political subject, individual will, does not necessarily
coincide with public will, which is located in the governmental body. When it does not coincide, will becomes fragmented

as if returning to what it is originally without government, disembodied. At this point, it is possible for society and state to be truly and unworkably split and for the semi-organic (but not natural) bond between them (the product of consent) to dissolve. Political unity then vanishes. In its most extreme form this split would be synonymous with the disappearance of the common body, the body politic. It would be synonymous, that is, with the collapse of government.

However, this whole way of talking—this kind of logic— entails a certain tension. In order for the possibility of political unity offered by representation to exist—in order for there to be representation, whose alternative would seem to be conflict, possibly chaos—there must necessarily be a difference between the terms of representation. The people are unified by but not identical with their government. If there is not this difference and if this difference is not determined by consent—if the difference becomes a "real" difference and not a delegated ("artificial") difference—the legitimacy of the government deteriorates. That is, the government ceases to represent. So, a position such as Locke's (which in at least this respect is typical) requires difference between the terms of representation, but it is a difference that must be determined, monitored, and controlled by only one of the two differentiated terms—the will of the people who are to be represented—and not by the other term. That is, this is difference, but it is an instrumental, mastered, hierarchical difference (difference but governed by Identity (because the Truth is One ["nation, under God, indivisible"]). For Locke and, more generally, for the dominant Enlightenment or modern conceptualization of political representation, the term that represents must remain subservient to the sovereign term, to that which is represented.

In a more strictly contemporary context, one alternative to this fixed hierarchy of difference—to this casting of the relationship between representative and represented—is the totalitarian possibility, in which the difference between the terms of representation collapses or is made to collapse, which in practical terms translates into the insinuation of the state into all dimensions of society, a process granted legitimacy by Lenin under the auspices of "the withering away of the state."[12] Totalitarianism is one of the outside limits of the collapse between the two terms of representation, in which the value differential necessary for substitutive practice (i.e., real/artificial) breaks free of any practical sense of source or foundation, any sense of what is really primary. For the discourse and practice of modern, democratic representation in general—which counterposes itself against the totalitarian loss of distinction or leveling[13] of value—the real power is with the people (however their identity is to be determined, which varies according to who is doing the talking and who is saying who or what counts[14]). Following Locke, we continue to insist that the power of the government is only borrowed. When it is not borrowed but seized or otherwise appropriated, then that government is neither representative nor democratic.

Let us take a practical turn here and confront the first of two alternative ways of viewing this relationship between the terms of representation, between, more specifically, democratic government and the people. This first alternative is a strategic, transitory move rather than a fixed position, which refuses to acknowledge difference between the representative and the represented but in a very particular, practical, and in some ways obvious manner. Often, there simply is no will to constitute the represented, and the only subject position in play is that of the representative, who in such cases is as much will as substitutive body, which itself may be more substance than it is substitute. As Pitkin points out, "The fact is that, at least in political representation, the represented have no will on most issues."[15] They have no consciousness of problems, decisions, or the terms of decision and thus no will. Will often simply does not exist when it comes to the esoteric issues facing working representative government. How could there be representation if there is nothing—no position, no subject other than the representative—to be represented? Yet there is "representation."

This gap might get covered on the theoretical level by talking about consent as something general, but this would be a curious cover if general consent (to be governed?, in the passive?) is taken to be the expression of an active, conscious, decisive, and ultimately autonomous and individual political subject; consent construed this way would seem to be as much a surrender of power as a trust. A similar problem holds for that remarkable, persistent, and passive image of tacit consent. Would such a general transfer of power be characteristic of an active, autonomous, free, and decision-making political subject? This substitution is more than a straightforward transfer, and popular sovereignty seems to lose some of its value in the exchange. Nevertheless, the traditional understanding continues here, insisting on the priority of an independent political subject. If the representative does not do what the people represented want, then she will not be reelected. However, this line is less Yankee-practical and more abstract than it sounds; above all, it assumes that people possess desires formulated independently of the machinery of representation (desires that also embody some consistency, some stance, some backbone, and some position [outside of representation]). But what would such "independence" look like? Where is this representation-free subject position? If it is a place purged or purified of the machinery of representation, it must lack even a portable black-and-white television (but no news equals no opinion and consequently no political subject), a radio, or a copy of *USA Today* (America's most conspicuous, omnipresent printed source of simulated information).

Everything is not a simulacrum and not reducible to simulation, and it is important to be explicit here. Of course "the people" do have desires (and at the same time there is such a thing as a sphere of public interests and public opinion). I am not suggesting that there is no public opinion, only that there is no public opinion formulated independently of the multifaceted machinery of representation, which, again, is not just instrumental; it is itself connected to history, economy, and technology, particularly the "technology of speed,"[16] at the multiple heart of which is the service economy and the technology of "communication" and "information." This is a fairly obvious and mundane point, but one that might provide

an effective way to begin seriously questioning the now oscillating image of an autonomous political subject. If what is
represented is, fundamentally, public opinion (a.k.a. the people
or even objective public interests [whose objectivity is always
the first question]), is this what it is that ultimately determines the representative, i.e., that determines representation?
On the other hand, what is the value of public opinion? As
an initial index of its precious value, consider how useful
"public opinion" is for the politicians of representation, who
read it (via samplings) to inform their election and reelection
strategies.

Tradition has it that the prospect of reelection provides a
check on wayward representatives and keeps political power
ultimately in the hands of the voting public. The abstractness
of this apparently practical conviction is appreciated in a
rather different way by Samuel Huntington in *The Crisis of
Democracy: Report on the Governability of Democracies to
the Trilateral Commission* (1975), in which he, optimistically
echoing Rousseau's pessimism about English representative
government, clearly devalues the meaning or power of an independent political subject and of a mandate delivered by means
of elections. He writes that

> Indeed, once he is elected president, the president's elec-
> toral coalition has, in a sense, served its purpose. The day
> after his election the size of his majority is almost—if
> not entirely—irrelevant to his ability to govern the coun-
> try. What counts then is his ability to govern the country.
> What counts then is his ability to mobilize support from
> the leaders of the key institutions in society and govern-
> ment. . . . The governing coalition need have little rela-
> tion to the electoral coalition.[17]

Is this passage a description or prescription? Emphasizing
the latter would provide the condition for a comfortable and
obvious (i.e., simplistic) critique of the neo-"Machiavellian"
perspective and agenda woven into this report. However,
Machiavelli's advice to the Prince was by no means only a

prescription, since, he insists, it was comprised to a large extent of selective observation of the operations of power. (Machiavelli writes, "I have thought it proper to represent things as they are in real truth, rather than as they are imagined . . . leaving aside imaginary things, and referring only to those which truly exist.")[18] Surely, Huntington's words do not constitute something like a neutral or objective perspective (a more general point is that observation, perspective, and prescription are not so disjointed from each other).[19] Further, Huntington's analysis does not entirely mesh with another central theme in his section of the triadic report (which is that too much democracy threatens Democracy in the United States). This casting of the issue seems to short-circuit the value of support from the people altogether (except for the election day ritual)[20] and perhaps, even, to render the whole notion of representation meaningless. Nevertheless, Huntington's observation does not seem untrue. When he asserts elsewhere in the report that "'who governs?' is obviously one of the most important questions to ask concerning any political system," it is no surprise that his answer does not even consider the civics textbook prospect that it is the people who ultimately govern American representative democracy.[21] When he follows with, "Even more important, however, may be the question: 'Does anybody govern?',", he does not mean to point to some fundamental anonymity of the liberal democratic space, filled by no one, open to the power and voice of all. His perspective becomes more clear when he continues:

> To the extent that the United States was governed by anyone during the decades after World War II, it was governed by the president acting with the support and cooperation of key individuals and groups in the Executive Office, the federal bureaucracy, Congress, and the more important businesses, banks, law firms, foundations, and media, which constitute the private establishment.

While the possibility of support from the people is necessary in order to realize representation through the periodic ritual of election,[22] ongoing, practical support for modern government—effective support, support associated with action—seems to come from somewhere else. Does all of this really render the notions of popular sovereignty and representation meaningless? As an alternative to pushing this possibility, the rest of this final chapter will argue that the nature, value, or power of support from the people is connected instead to a transformation in the meaning and processes of representation and of what informs, communicates, and counts in representative democracies these days. Meanwhile, whether perusing the more everyday, workaday world through Pitkin's ordinary language analysis or peering down from imperial heights with the Trilateral Commission, it is generally clear that will or consent is not always an issue in representative government; there is no mediation between two terms if one of the terms (will) and thus the conduit between the terms (consent) simply does not exist. That is, there is no question of mediated unity or substitution of will, because the only will in play in many cases is the will of the representative (i.e., of the government). It might not be going too far to say that in many cases the only real political subject is the representative, particularly if the term can be broadened to include the vast bureaucracy that constitutes such a substantial part of contemporary government and also to include "the more important businesses" (e.g., the armaments industry, the transportation industry, the energy industry), "banks, law firms, foundations, and media."

The Trilateral Commission's analysis, which operates within a predominantly traditional paradigm of power, seems to suggest that contemporary democratic government is fairly independent of the people, although this suggestion is not connected to an assertion of the primacy of independent public opinion. In contrast to this independence—whether the emphasis grants priority to the independence of the people or to the government—the totalitarian possibility consists of the claim that there is no independence of either of the two poles of the political sphere because the state is not, or should not be, separate from society. Quite possibly, the separation of state and society would fundamentally be an expression of domination and alienation, a negation which itself needs to be—must be and will be—negated in order to produce a positive human unity and a resolution to conflict (and difference). The leading image and telos here seems to be that of a perfectly harmonious and even homogeneous society, one so well coordinated that the state is not distinct from society itself; here is a society for which representation—which necessarily implies a division between representative and represented—is no longer necessary. Regardless of possible claims to the contrary, here is a society that has gone beyond representation, perhaps into something like a material order of pure reason or reasonableness. (Turning things around, an order "beyond representation" would be a totalitarian order.)

It can be argued that society is not fundamentally separate from the state and yet assert a possibility very different from the particular collapse of difference associated with the logic of totalitarianism. This would be another alternative to the dominant modern understanding of the relationship between representative and represented. It might begin with the observation that society (the people) is no more fundamentally separate from the state (the government) than it is from, for example, the economy or the possibilities (e.g., "communicative" possibilities) associated with technology (none of which, as discussed before, are mastered or masterable). However, the key difference between this assertion and the totalitarian reading is that this by no means implies a uniform, monolithic, homogeneous, or harmonious architecture. I hope to show that my perspective, which will emphasize differences (and warfare) rather than a telos of unity (and consensus), focuses on something critically different from the isomorphizing conflation of state and civil society associated with the totalitarian possibility. Here, to abandon the fundamental separation of the two poles of representation is not to deny or conflate their differences but to emphasize the mutually productive and coextensive rather than expressive, reflective, or "communicative" side of representation, which is never either neutral or isolable from all of the other dimen-

sions of society. Such denial also refuses to see power as orig-
inating from just one sovereign source. Here, the question of
the relationship between the terms of representation is not
oriented around something like the problem of unity/disunity
or the dialectical conflict of identity/alienation but emphasizes instead processes of positive constitution or social production and at the same time the interplay of differences. This
latter is not the play between the natural and the artificial
but the conflict that characterizes contemporary political reality.[23] "Diversity" is the dispersion and flexibility of identity
and definition that occurs in all dimensions of a society. This
multiplicity, which is not woven into a single harmony, has
become one of the marks of democracy even if the working
conception of a republic, which tends to emphasize together-
ness and unity, seems to work against it.

The discourse and practice of political representation is
never a monolithic one, by which I mean specifically that
the identities in play are not of an equalizing nature, that
there are other forms of representation and other forces and
practices that it actively intersects, and that there are divisions other than the one inscribed by the represented and the
representative that feed into it. For instance, there are divisions between more than just those expressed or constituted
by competing political parties. These include differences
between government and the people, between social classes,
between different occupations, between the public and private sectors, between different orders of issues and interests,
between rural and urban, and civilian and military, etc. They
also include the differences between the overtly representative domain of government (i.e. the realm of elected officials),
the different but connected bureaucratic domains, and the
lobbies, think tanks, and political action committees which
provide so many political ideas, policies, and possibilities for
the modern working democratic republic. But are all of these
divisions ultimately discrete identities, which "communicate" with each other, perhaps through or across the apparatuses of political representation? Do they fall outside of representation? What are they (in relation to political

representation)? What are they in relation to the political subject? Are they part of it? Are they part of what makes the political subject be what it is?

Even for Hobbes, consent is a necessary element of political representation; this is part of the central meaning of the covenant, which is a contract, an agreement (among whom?).[24] However, there are other sides to the consensual story. A common one is marked by Ford's observation that "in actual practice the people have never been allowed complete freedom of choice in selecting their representatives."[25] While based upon the standard metaphysical divisions between theory/practice and idea/reality, this traditionally formulated observation is true. For one thing, every specific (and not only formal) mechanism of the machinery of representation informs the process of selection and substitution and therefore informs "freedom of choice." In not any particular sequence or order, this includes: voter registration requirements (who can vote?); voting procedures (how is voting organized?); the party system ("choices"?); apportionment of representatives (relative quantity of representation); the electoral district (at-large?, single-member? What do its boundaries tend to produce?); the political appointment (the extension of representation); the judiciary (always "activist"[26]); the electoral college (mediating representation or doubling mediation); the informative involvement of "communications" technology and the news media; the analysis and formulation of policy by specialist organizations and think tanks; the active interventions of both governmental and private ("outside") lobbies; the organization of labor; the enormous power and influence of the massive underground economies and black markets (e.g., the international drug market); the cutting edge of the National Security Council; the Internal Revenue Service; public events which occur outside of formal political processes and institutions, etc. All of the core and marginal features and elements of the discourse and practice of representation serve not only to influence but, more constructively, to articulate, define, circumscribe, confine, and reinforce the meaning (i.e., range of possibilities) of "freedom of choice."

Recognizing possible implications of this circumscription and of the trade-off in the substitution, though, there is a position much stronger than Ford's. Ford's position only detects or selects images of compromising distortions, detects, that is, loss and dilution of the proper political subject, but not of its disappearance. However, the stronger position sees annihilation rather than just compromise. It is exemplified by Rousseau's insistence that "the moment a People begins to act through its representatives, it has ceased to be free. It no longer exists."[27] Representation ruins everything for Rousseau. Representation does not make for a bad translation but for no translation because will cannot be translated. "The English people think that they are free, but in this belief they are profoundly wrong. They are free only when they are electing members of Parliament. Once the election has been completed, they revert to a condition of slavery: they are nothing."[28]

Either way, and connected to the fact that they are based upon similar assumptions or foundational terms, whether the transfer of consent effected by representation is said to distort the political subject or to destroy it, it has been widely articulated in a broad range of discursive contexts that "freedom of choice" does not get expressed in complete form (original, integral, fully actual, etc.) in representation. This is especially true if the primary term—the sovereign term—is taken ultimately to be the people as such, who necessarily get lost in the translation into an electorate and, in America, lost further with the simultaneous or subsequent, multi phased translation from electorate into electoral college into elected.

This is one cause for concern about political representation. Representation does not do what it is supposed to do, which is to say that it does not represent—stand for—the will of the people in anything approaching a straightforward way. Representation deviates from representation. Furthermore, according to Rousseau's strong perspective, representation is utterly deviant.

However, this observation of incompleteness or even omission of the will of the people in political representation also misses the point, the ground zero, which is the assumption that there is a complete, complex being associated with position, decision, and the source of consensual expression. It makes the assumption that there is an independent, individual political subject. On this point, Foucault approaches things very differently:

> The individual is no doubt the fictitious atom of an "ideological" representation of society; but he is also a reality fabricated by this specific technology of power that I have called "discipline." We must cease once and for all to describe the effects of power in negative terms: it "excludes," it "represses," it "censors," it "abstracts," it "masks," it "conceals." In fact, power produces; it produces reality; it produces domains of objects and rituals of truth. The individual and the knowledge that may be gained of him belong to this production.[29]

This individual, produced in one of its vital profiles by the diverse and yet interconnected apparatuses of representative democracy, is articulated as the atomic, autonomous political subject, the source of the consent and consensus that is both what counts and what is counted in the constitution of its government. Ideally, then, government is itself actually the political formulation or manifestation of knowledge of this individual, the acknowledgement or exposure of who this individual is, where it stands, what its interests are, and what it believes in; representative government is the political subject turned inside out, the private constituted as public. This is what the story suggests. It is also and in some ironic senses the truth.

The addition of Foucault's general observation to the image of the distortion or destruction of consent makes a double point here. First, the discourse and practice of selecting

representatives renders "freedom of choice" and thus consensual possibilities in a particular way (i.e., produces the consent
of individual political subjects rather than provides a neutral
conduit for its expression); in the timid terms of classic liberalism—Ford, here—this means that the People do not get fully
or accurately represented in popular representative government. However, second, to view this as an inhibitive, distortive, or otherwise essentially negative influence is to operate within a traditional conception of power as sovereign
rather than productively pervasive (there is not outside of
power) and to miss the constitutive activity here in favor of
instrumentality and a telos of reason. Once again, political
representation—which is not just either a theory or a formal
system but a vast network of diverse elements and practices—
constitutes and determines all of its terms, all of its subjects
and objects. Representation fills in the blank spaces of possibility reserved for representatives, but it also fills in what gets
represented. Representative power—which is better characterized as dispersed rather than as fundamentally hierarchical (this includes the inverted hierarchy of democratic power,
the pyramid turned upside down)—incorporates and constitutes itself through a multiplicity of processes of dissemination. Processes such as the dissemination of information fill
the voter the in, which is something more productive than
communicative, if, that is, communication is viewed the traditional way, i.e., as a reciprocal exchange between different,
self-identical, essentially (rather than relationally) positioned,
ultimately discrete subjects.[30]

Working "our" side, the people's side: *The media fill us in
on what is going on. Information helps the voter decide.*
Working the other side, the representative's and the system's:
*The politicians of representation build and rebuild consen-
sus. The discourse and practice of political representation
forms and reforms—it* **shapes** *or* **forges***-public opinion.* These
everyday kinds of phrases reveal a great deal about contemporary politics (as do electoral laws and procedures, including
those that pertain to campaign funding and product promo-
tion [e.g., consider the currently powerful and controversial

role of PAC money]). Where they all intersect is in the determination of what counts in representative democracy, which is a determination that may never be masterable, and never beyond conflict. What counts is not only what is doing the counting and what is counted but also the powers and procedures constituted by representative politics, which is to say the discourse and practice of a specific network of counting and being counted.

WHAT COUNTS

> My findings are significant.
>
> —anonymous quantitative social scientist

> The number becomes a subject.
>
> —Deleuze & Guattari[31]

What is counted above all in modern representative democracy is votes, which are "expressions of opinion," and opinions, which have come to closely resemble votes. There are many other subjects represented in politics, which should be recognized and highlighted and not ignored or undervalued, but votes are the dynamic, open subject of representative government—the subject at the heart of the rituals of representation. The power and value of the vote[32] simply cannot be confined by or comprehended fundamentally under the auspices of the increasingly archaic concept of *expression of consent*. This does not suggest that the notion of *expression of consent* can be excluded from an articulation of the vote or of political representation; it clearly cannot. My point is not at all that there is no such thing as a political subject, opinion, expression, or consent, just that these are different from the autonomous identity that has generally been associated with them in the modern period, the period in which one key player has been the independent, conscious individual (I am I; persuade me) and another key player has been the development

and dispersion of representative democratic politics, of which
there are as many varieties as there are instances. What matters most in the processes traditionally seen as properly representative is not expressing (and thus not communicating in
any traditional sense of the term) but marking and counting.
This statement seems true in at least two of the dominant
senses of counting.

First, what is it that counts? In addition to the obvious
and vital question, "Who is doing the counting?" (who is it
that enunciates this value? [cf. Nietzsche's *Genealogy of
Morals*]), this question touches on the general topic of subject
positions and identities and translates into the question of
what it is that is counted or included as part of the political
subject and thus who it is that makes legitimate marks in the
tally, what identity is authorized to vote. This identity has
had many forms in both the history of representation and
that of democracy. For instance, the seventeenth-century
English Levelers are sometimes remembered as radical advocates of popular sovereignty, yet the electoral franchise they
supported excluded not only women, delinquents, and criminals but also wage earners (servants) and alms takers (beggars). In practical terms, the healthy (and unhealthy) majority
of England's residents were not to be counted by these radicals as part of the active, participating political subject of
popular sovereignty. Instead, they were not just passed right
over but included in representation in writing, constituted in
representation, taken care of, and possibly virtually represented. This was an important inclusion for the Levelers,
who expressed concern that "the poor" would be able to out-
vote "the people."[33] American women were not counted as
part of the active political subject until 1920; this development was the consequence of the addition of the 19th
Amendment to the Bill of Rights. This is an obvious point
but one worth mentioning, partly in order to emphasize the
unfinished, supplemental character of the Constitution,
which contributes its share to the transforming identity of
the political subject, a share that is never self-evident (the
determination of the subject constituted by the Constitution

is never simply given but always advanced and invariably the consequence of a variety of forms of struggle). Since they were continually viewed as an impedance to Progress and thus in the way of the manifest destiny of the development of the American political subject, Native Americans—the continent's original inhabitants—were not formally counted as part of the political subject until 1924; this development was the consequence of legislation, the passage of the Indian Citizenship Act,[34] as were the practical values established by the Voting Rights Act of 1965. As a final example, there was a significant increase in the size of the (potential) electorate when voting requirements were changed, lowering the voting age from twenty-one to eighteen (numbers enter in again, including body counts from Viet Nam). This last example is worth mentioning because it does not lend itself as easily as the others to nineteenth-century style logics, which might emphasize as seminatural the correlation between an expanded, ever-inclusive electoral franchise and the expansion of Reason, a.k.a. Freedom. The fluctuating age threshold is too obviously conventionalized and tied to traditional divisions (child/adult, potential/actual) and too connected to a particular historical context (here, it is Viet Nam; "if they're old enough to die for their country, they're old enough to vote") to fit within this model; yet it is safe to predict that despite a growing, multidimensional children's rights movement, it is unlikely that the voting age will ever be lowered to twelve or to eight. This last example of determining what counts in the identity of the political subject may seem trivial, but the point is that those who are under eighteen are part of the public—are people—too and that the precise cutoff age is no more well-founded or natural than any other inclusion and no less part of a specific coding and formation of power. What counts as part of the political subject has never been self-evident but always rendered—constituted—by the complex specificities of the discourse and practice of political representation. What counts, that is, has always been the product of the particular practice of counting that is authorized, available, and deployed at a given time.

The second kind of counting that is part of representation has to do with the accumulation and tracking of numbers, whether these are numbers marked by votes and counted in an election or statistics "collected"[35] in a poll of public opinion, the former being the immediate source of the representative's position, the latter being the monitor perpetually on the pulse of the political subject, with neither set of numbers ever far apart from each other. Whether an election tally or an opinion poll, what is represented are numbers, and numbers are what effectively constitutes rather than in any straightforward sense reflects "public opinion." Plugging into this reality, Baudrillard has claimed that "'public opinion' is . . . a fantastic hyperreality that lives only off of montage and test-manipulation."[36] Baudrillard's bold and absolutist slant skews things in just one direction, but his claim nevertheless expresses an important part of the truth of public opinion, which is the power of fluctuating numbers in the constitution of the subject of political representation.

The numbers counted never simply express definite, autonomous choices, opinions, decisions, or will; they are never so neutral, mediatory, or disconnected from productive political processes. For instance, themselves the product of numbers of votes, "good" representatives remain responsive to their electorate—to public opinion—but this cannot be taken to mean that they carry out their constituency's wishes in any simply translative terms; above all, in this context good means effective, which begins with the ability to get into office and to stay there. Around election time, politicians tend to modulate their images in response to their readings of ever-fluctuating opinion polls.[37] Out of these readings, they attempt to project representative identities, sometimes instantaneously (e.g., environmentalist), and often quite effectively (i.e., they win the election). They do this despite frequent conflict between a new identity and the past record. (Much of this record is itself formulated in terms of numbers, as statistics increasingly dominate the story, thereby transforming and displacing more traditional narrative forms and historical frameworks for public discourse and attenuating the strong sense of context—of place—these older forms involve [e.g., an environmental record rating would be established primarily in terms of quantitative patterns of votes and initiatives].) Being itself partially a response to poll readings but not other than some 'real thing'—some genuine identity—the representative identity-image continually monitors the polls, checking its ratings, making ongoing modifications when it is strategically efficacious to do so. Oftentimes it just hangs in there, trying to work the ratings, asserting itself, and insisting on itself. So this is not just a private reading machine with some wizard inside of it, because it writes, too. It introduces possibilities—primarily various kinds of public relations or media possibilities—and it aims to persuade, to make the numbers add up right because the numbers are the formal source of power. Constantly writing itself in its every action, the representative identity monitors the effects of its own offensive maneuvers, which are never really under its control once transmitted, because of the uncontainable diversity and many planes of social reality in the field of their deployment. (For example, consider a tactical attempt to shift public focus from ethical conflict to perception of ethical conflict; the attempt is offered as a contribution to some more general strategy, which will always operate against resistance since it is formulated in relation to differences and so must continue to monitor the ratings. It must track and reinforce the effort's effects in order to try to make the strategy attain its aims.)

Image has always been important on the side of the representative (well before but explicitly codified in Machiavelli), but the form and nature of image has changed as what Meyrowitz calls the "communication environment"[38] has changed. The image of the representative no longer stands glimpsed at a mostly mute distance, as was the tall, strong, imposing figure of George Washington, who never had a movie camera pushed into his sweating pores or a microphone jammed into his wooden dentures. Things are different now. Now, the politicians of representation are trailed by the media in a variety of ways (the public image is an ongoing media event). The microscoped image they provide is something very close to the televised simulacrum that Baudrillard associates with hyperreality; the reality of this image, which even while sometimes irreal is as real as its effects—i.e., very real— revolves around counting and accumulating numbers and pushing them around into a support network as much as is possible. Counting has come to be what counts. Numbers are what the battles of democracy are over; all active players aim to accumulate the fetishized numbers, to stack them up in order to have effects.

If the numbers of the discourse and practice of representation are viewed, as they must be now, as not merely expressive, mediatory, or instrumental, it becomes clearer that the political subject is also not derived from either of the two poles of representation (at least one of which, the represented, is generally assumed to be an identity fundamentally independent of representation) but instead gets constituted in the apparent conduit of consent presented by representation, i.e., in the very practice of representation, which is so well-informed these days (it is often overwhelmed with "information"). This is not the way that the tradition has tended to see things, and it has not because of its assumptions about the nature of the identities in play in representation. President James Garfield repeated those traditional assumptions in 1881 when he asserted that "real political issues cannot be manufactured by the leaders of political parties. The real political issues of the day declare themselves, and come out of the depths of that deep—which we call public opinion."[39] Pointing out that this remark was made before the appearance of modern "communication" and that it thus might have had a different truth value then than now is important although it may also dodge the issue somewhat. While the communication environments of the past were very different from what this environment is today and while counting procedures have changed enormously—probably decisively enough to talk about the emergence of new discursive formations in the world of politics (and everywhere else)—the politicians of representation have in a basic sense always been networking the numbers. They have always been interacting with a political subject that was no more self-identical or accurately portrayed today than in, for example, the eighteenth century when John Adams invoked the "portrait in miniature" as the ideal image of representation in an era when the active political subject—the electorate—consisted exclusively of a portion of the unindentured, white, male population. There is a sense in which "the heartbeat of America"[40] has always been close to the surface—not buried in the depths of an organic body politic—even if opinion may seem to have been more definite, decided, and even thoughtful before electricity and the advent of electronic information and telecommunications technologies, when life's velocity was slower and people spent more of their spare time reading (for instance, literacy rates in America during the period of the Revolution were quite high,[41] which may have something to do with the relative caliber of political discourse at that time).

As mentioned with a different emphasis in an earlier chapter, Article I, Section 2 of the Constitution of the United States inscribes the subject of politics as number, as it supplies the calculus for determining the apportionment of representation: "Representatives and direct taxes shall be apportioned among the several States which may be included within this Union, according to their respective numbers, which shall be determined by adding to the whole number of free persons, including those bound to service for a term of years, and excluding Indians not taxed, three-fifths of all other persons." Inscribed differently elsewhere, the political subject is summed up in this passage by pluses, minuses, and fractions. If it had not been numbers determining the political subject and the associated representative practices rendered by the framers—America's fifty-five white patriarchs—slaves would never have acquired this curious, radically contingent but politically powerful value of three-fifths of a person (three-fifths is a power-value). It is worth marking not just the contingent power of that particular determination but also the persistent centrality of numbers in political representation more generally. Going back to the eighteenth century and the problems connected to the double representation of people

and property, the dominant sides of the debate over how to
determine the apportionment of federal legislative representatives broke down into those who argued that people were
what should be counted and those who argued that a state's or
electoral district's wealth should determine the value of representation (both sides arguing here not over counting versus
some other method and not just over what should count but
over what should literally be counted, over which numbers
should be the key to representation). However, there was difficulty in figuring how to count multiform wealth (a.k.a. capital), how, that is, to quantify it in a way practicable for the
purpose. It was decided that the only practical way (for one
side of the debate) or right way (for the other)[42] to calculate
the number of representatives was to count the population as
the numbers to be represented. That is, there was a conflict of
opinion regarding what was to be counted in the calculus used
to determine the number of representatives, and the counting was clearly part of a vast network of other ideas, including
that of the image of balance between not just different parts of
(mixed) government but also between different dimensions—
more specifically, different factions—of society. Nevertheless,
counting was the key to reckoning the number of representatives. It was a move toward the image of a representative
democratic republic in perfect internal balance. Counting
helped determine the identity of the political subject, not
externally, but from within.

   The subject of democratic political representation has
been closely associated with numbers and counting techniques for quite some time now. It might be a mistake to
emphasize a basic continuity in the history of representation here because, while numbers have been a determinative form of the political subject for a long time, only fairly
recently has it become possible and would it have made such
perfectly acceptable sense to describe an election as an "historic job approval rating."[43] This, and the endless procession
of opinion polls—which do not necessarily lie even if they
are not true in a traditional sense—is not the sort of discursive complex to which numbers have always been attached

(the Founding Fathers simply did not say things like that nor would such a phrase have been available to them). This techno-talk is not just new beltway lingo (it is that, too, although the lingo is not something superficial but symptomatic and characteristic of new discursive formations); the phrase marks a new kind of representation, one expressed in spreadsheets, graphs, and flow charts, in addition to other technological phenomena. In other words, what is historic is not the rating[44] but the way of articulating, perceiving, and practicing representative politics.

Leaving the differences of the past behind and considering the fundamentally quantifiable sort of representative politics inscribed by the phrase "job approval rating" and by the numbers of public opinion, the concrete question would seem to be the following: How do we, the public, fit into this scheme? How are we constituted by and incorporated into it? (Given the diversity of its profiles, what kind of corporate republic is the United States of America?) More to the point, what are we, we the public? Who are we? What kind of a subject? We are not just made-up or invented, and we are not just products of the cathode-ray tube, but in the context of politics (which cannot be isolated from other contexts and thus other identities [e.g., the producer-consumer]), we are voters, which means that we are numbers, markers. In asserting this, I am not trying to reduce either representation or public opinion— the political subject (including the silent majority)—to either numbers or to counting (these are not the only fundamentals). I am merely emphasizing that this is one of our most significant and powerful political self-identities and one of the most effective identities of the subject of representation these days, as the "we" of we the people congeals in and becomes effectively equated with numbers. Numbers have not displaced opinion (on a more general level, hyperreality has not displaced reality, which has never been stable, self-evident, or self-identical), but numbers—connected to popular images and hi-tech culture more generally—are the most powerful and positive form of public opinion nowadays. As Michael Warner suggests, polls "do not measure something that already exists as public opinion; but when they are reported as such they *are* public opinion."[45]

Different from the portrait of the people in miniature and different from an instrumental substitution, contemporary political representation is about getting the numbers of popular opinion to line up on a given side. While attempts are continually made to manipulate the numbers, they do not line up as the result of a controlled mechanical process—the apparatuses of representation are never, finally, controlled—but as the result of ongoing conflict and conflictual strategies, which always operate against an uncontrollable, uncontainably multiple and open global horizon.

This quantifiable and quantified identity, which is the effective identity of the political subject now, is not, then, an invention or a fiction but the effect of a practice. Political discourse and practice do not make up and are not apart from the political subject but articulate it and set out its effective positions of possibility and its planes of representation. The main issue to be pushed at this point is neither that representation is an illusion nor that the people do not really exist. Such arguments would take us back to invention and instrumentality (e.g., discourse as ideology or predominantly propaganda), to paranoid suspicions of organized conspiracy and visions of ideological legitimation and control (to *1984*), to a concealed, original source and to false fronts over stable, organized, self-identical, and structurally independent subarchitecture.

Meyrowritz cites Ferdinand Mount's critical remarks on this point: "'The idea that there is a real (efficient, useful) politics which is masked by an unreal (superficial) sham show is one of the most potent delusions of our time.'"[46] Meyrowitz himself continues by asserting that there is not "necessarily any change in the 'reality coefficient' of politics. There is no clear trend from truth to artifice, or from artifice to truth. There is, however, a change in the style of the 'real yet performed' political drama." On the one hand, this means that "there is a significant change in the types of images politicians can project. And this change in style is the result of the

new staging contingencies created by electronic media. . . ."
That is, the technology itself has powerful, determinative, and
creative effects on political discourse. On the other hand, this
change indicates an uncontrolled, unchosen change not only in
the identificative possibilities of the representative but, cor-
relatively, in the political subject itself, which is integrated
into all of the communications networks and counted by, in,
and on in so many ways. Viewer and voter, audience and electorate—those particular formations of the contemporary political subject are not independent of the discourse of which they
are a pivotal subject, the discourse of representation. Nor are
they describable in traditional terms, such as active vs. passive
(e.g., to describe a television viewing audience as passive is
simply inadequate and inaccurate). Neither are they phan-
tasms or—the absolute extreme—simulacra. They are very
real, effectively so. That is, the numbers counted in representation are real and so is their power.

The power of the political subject tends to be in numbers, as in an important sense it always has been. This does
not mean that reality has been displaced by hyperreality. Nor
does it mean that "we are just numbers" now. There is no
such thing as just a number, and numbers never tell the whole
story; for one thing, numbers are always arranged in a specific
way, and in a context, that is, always in connection with other
sets of numbers. Still, it does mean that while the political
subject is not reducible to number, it is not, as number, separate from other dimensions of reality. The political subject is
most effectively a numbered subject—i.e., a subject that can be
plugged in to a range of vital counting and tallying procedures—but it exceeds this identity in a thousand ways, too,
even while it does not exist outside of it and cannot escape it.
It exceeds it, that is, not as independent, but as more than the
subject, which also includes more than producer-consumer,
white-collar or blue-collar, television viewer or radio listener,
or any other subject position made possible by the networks of
discourses and practices that constitute contemporary life.
There is no independent will, opinion, or consciousness that
falls outside of our connections with systems of marking and

tabulating—with communication networks—but that does not mean that we are confined by any one particular identity. This means that while what gets represented is, literally, numbers, the political subject cannot be reduced to this identity. Castoriadis may be helpful here:

> We have to posit that whatever exists, in any domain, lends itself to an identitary-ensemblist organization and is not thoroughly or ultimately congruent to the latter. It never ceases to lend itself to this organization, does not lend itself in an empty manner but offers a partially effective grasp, so that it is impossible to think of this organization as a sheer construction, as imputable solely to the "awesome power of understanding," to borrow Hegel's expression. We can construe what is as an ensemble only because what is is capable of being so construed; we can categorize it only because it is categorizable. However, any ensemblizing, and categorizing, any organization that we establish/discover there proves sooner or later to be partial, lacunary, fragmentary, insufficient—and even, more importantly, intrinsically deficient, problematic and finally incoherent.[47]

To Castoriadis' "finally incoherent," it would be useful to add "finally incoherent and coherent," to introduce, that is, a position in tension, which would render not only the effectively productive character of an ensemblist identification of the people or political will in numbers but also would stress that it is productive perhaps not despite but because of an equally powerful dimension of incoherence, dissonance, and conflict. (The republican harmony embodied in representation is transgressed by the dissonance and conflict that it depends upon, which is the real conflict synonymous with democracy.)

A reading aligned with Castoriadis' passage hits the mark; pushed by the power of analysis, the coherence of the people in numbers is, finally, obscure and incoherent, perhaps even more so now in the age of digitalized "communications" than in the past. At the same time, if it were really "finally incoherent," then postmodern—i.e., contemporary—systems of representation would cease to function (this could be an outright bad, self-convinced, and possibly paranoid science fiction). In fact, though, the machinery of representation continues to work in its own quasi-stable, open-ended way, which means in part that it continues counting and recounting, constituting both represented and representative, and producing both the government and the people. It communicates democracy, which in the modern period is not and never has been a message independent of the discourses and practices of representation.

Is there communication in the circuits connecting people and the government, society and the state? Is that what those numbers are about? Is that what they do or serve, as they plug public opinion into the apparatuses of representation (as they make public opinion something that can be plugged in)? Baudrillard's image of postmodern (i.e., hi-tech) communication as simulated reciprocity helps us to see that 'Great Communication' is great communication even if is not derived from an ideal speech situation (political philosophy's perennial dream) but yet is also the consequence of neither ideological mirages nor old-fashioned coercion. Practices of persuasion (and attempts at manipulation) have clearly always been a fundamental part of "communication" and not just distortions introduced into it. Embedded in profoundly new technological capabilities, "communication" has become a key condition for the emergence of specific formations or representations of power; this means, for one thing, that communication has become a key condition for the identity of the subject of political representation, which in its most effective form has a positively digital—on/off, either/or, yes/no—profile these days. In other words "communication" and the subject are coextensive with each other.

Finally, it must be reiterated here that this perspective does not imply something monolithic or homogeneous. The identities of reason, communication (communicative possibilities), popular opinion, and political will continue changing and will never be independent of the discourses and practices from which they emerge. The representative democracy in which they are now located and function remains open and diverse. The diversity may in some senses become neutralized as context deteriorates (e.g., "Shall we eat Indonesian, Ethiopian, or Mexican tonight?") and as competition encourages similarity (ABC, NBC, CBS) at the same time that it fosters alternatives (i.e., "freedom of choice"). Even as they come into increasing contact with each other, differences do not disappear, do not get diluted (there is no melting pot), but they clash and compete with each other, sometimes within the formal structures provided by democracy and sometimes at its margins or outside of it.[48] The different positions that contribute to the constitution of representation all battle each other for domination—they all aim to have a corner on the discourse and practice of the republic and to push their truth and their perspective—but domination is achieved only in "partial, lacunary, fragmentary" ways (not totalizing, but these ways are nevertheless often tentatively effective). Because there are many different subject positions articulated in the numbers, and these positions will continue to compete with each other in representation. The democratic feature to which I refer here may not be the pluralism of the liberal tradition but a more conflictually conceived diversity of voices at war with one another, voices marked and legitimated as number. Still, there is consensus, and consensus always has a number; 51 percent equals consensus in general representative politics in America (two-thirds for representation to override a Presidential veto).[49]

As Vollrath writes, "The relation of power and opinion is thus numerical; at least it has a quantitative aspect. Or, as Madison says elsewhere: 'Men generally derive confidence from their numbers.' In a republican communality, expressly based on opinion, this signifies: all questions are decided by the greater number, by the majority."[50] When the economy of representation plugs these voices in as numbers—when it constitutes the political subject as number—the losses can be severe. As Sartre notes, 49 percent equals zero.[51] Zero = 0 here, but this does not mean that the formula adds up to nothing, since that 0, which is not nothing, is "represented," too. This is one of the reasons that in one of its profiles, representative democracy is an ongoing war, in which on one plane everything gets represented and is representable, everything, that is, that adapts to the conditions of representation.

Chapter VI

Assuming Positions:
Representative Democracy and Warfare

> But the truth is that if division and violence define
> war, the world has always been at war and always
> will be; if man is waiting for universal peace in order
> to establish his existence validly, he will wait indef-
> initely: there will never be any *other* future.
>
> —Simone de Beauvoir[1]

> War is the ultimate game because war is at last a
> forcing of the unity of existence. War is god.
>
> —Cormac McCarthy[2]

> War is both king of all and father of all, and it has
> revealed some as gods, others as men; some it has
> made slaves, others free.
>
> —Heraclitus[3]

State of War

The contrast between various, sometimes contemporaneous and competing formations and formulations of political
representation indicates that representation harbors enormous
conflict, a characteristic which provides some clues for alternative conceptualizations of the sort I have been developing.

Let us begin with an infamous tactical metaphor, nearly a
cliché, drawn from Carl von Clausewitz: War is an extension

of diplomacy, a means of continuing negotiation and "communication."[4] Following Clausewitz, war is thus neither outside of the state nor the Other of politics. This logic has resonances with Machiavelli, who, while different from Clausewitz, also cultivates a nonpolarized relation between war and politics. In *The Prince*, Machiavelli initially couples law and force by noting that "the main foundations of every state . . . are good laws and good arms. . . ." Then, without pause, he transgresses this first statement, asserting that "you cannot have good laws without good arms, and where there are good arms, good laws will inevitably follow." "Good arms" are thus transformed into the fundamental foundation of every state, so he adds, "I shall not discuss laws but give my attention to arms."[5] A little later in the text, Machiavelli strengthens the relation between law and force, asserting that "you must understand, therefore, that there are two ways of fighting: by law or by force."[6] Here, the position held by the state in the first quotation has been displaced by fighting, and law becomes just another means for playing out power, another weapon.[7] While straightforwardly affirming Machiavelli's conflation would make for a clumsy metaphysic, the historical instances examined in Part One provide many obvious examples of representation as an effect of various forms of power.

I invoke Clausewitz and Machiavelli here not to assert a literal truth about or to clarify the ambiguous relationship between war and "legitimate" political institutions,[8] but to emphasize an image that might contribute to an understanding of representation and representative democracy, an emphasis that allies itself with Foucault's suggestion that "one's point of reference should not be to the great model of language (langue) and signs but to that of war and battle. The history which bears and determines us has the form of a war rather than that of a language: relations of power, not relations of meaning."[9] Pushing further—and in an inversion of Clausewitz—Foucault asks, "Isn't power a sort of generalised war which assumes at particular moments the forms of peace and the State? Peace would then be a form of war, and the State a means of waging it."[10]

Applying these suggestions to the issue at hand, it would be instructive to argue that the dynamics of representative democracy—which are dynamics of power, of multiple, clashing powers—are dynamics of war. To begin with, the historic emergence of representation is literally tied to events of division and war; for example, the Declaration of Independence was no more George III's idea than Runnymede was John's. Recent historical attention to the debates between Anti-Federalists and Federalists highlights the contentious atmosphere surrounding the process of the ratification of the American Constitution. More to the point, representation and representative democracy are characterized by continual conflict, contestation, combat, ground gained, ground lost, defections, truces, surrenders, devastations, compromises, transitory wins, 'total' losses, shifting configurations of police and surveillance powers (i.e., shifting configuations of the relation between "state" and "society"), and so on. The battle of representative democracy is above all a battle for the political subject; it is a battle for the numbers, and it is an unending battle to dominate and define political reality itself, that is, to define the subject of politics.

Foucault reinforces a new critical strategy through his power images, which are images that deflate, denaturalize, or enormously complicate the determinative value of the traditional, hierarchized, axiomatic, metaphysical dyads: reason/desire, mind/body, order/chaos, peace/war, freedom/coercion, right/might, civilized/barbaric, legitimate/illegitimate, etc. Through suggestions such as Foucault's, all of these terms become connected to the articulation of power, rather than half of them—the "good" half—being granted a value privileged over and opposed to power (a power opposed to power). To be clear, this does not reverse the traditional axiomatic hierarchies, but it does defuse or denaturalize their established explanatory value, and it thus transforms the nature of the problem and suggests different stagies for making sense of representative democracy.

Following through with the ramifications of this transformation, it may be productive to view representative democracy as an ongoing war, particularly a war for the political subject. Representative democracy is not like a war but is a form of war (the metaphor is not a simile). With its real wins and real losses, its battles are clearly not just play,[11] not even when the play of representation is bloodless.[12]

The discourse and practice of representative democracy is a semi-organized[13] complex of competing forces, as well as an idea; this is one of its most material profiles and one of the values it embodies. Disengaging from the instrumental or technological perspective of rationalism, the hierarchy implied by "serving purposes"—end/means, intention/instrument—falls away or loses power and practices become forces, which have effects or incur accomplishments (achievements) that outstrip and transgress any ideas or any naturalized connection with particular ideas or meanings associated with them. This disengagement, in any event, is one way of contracting some of the provisionally outer limits or edges of political representation. If we look at representation as a complex of competing forces, we are led to a different way of considering the flexibility of the meanings associated with the discourse and practice of representation, a way that may seem to conflict with the emphasis I have placed on the coextensiveness of discourse and practice, which was not meant to suggest some fundamental or organic isomorphism.

While the two intimately linked spheres that together constitute discourse and practice function inseparably, there is another sense in which they do not touch each other, never penetrate each other at all, because such an interpenetration—the link of necessity—would have to be a penetration of meaning. Their relation is a strategic alliance—a link of contingency[14]—rather than a semiological (or a dialectical) connection. This is a mutually productive relation, surely, and there are no practices without discourses (discursive formations) or discourses without practices (nondiscursive formations). There are no words disconnected from actions and no actions disconnected from words. However, the necessity of their connections is of the order that follows a dice roll, which is the contingent opening of what becomes, only after the fact, a necessary connection or logic.[15]

A good example of what I mean here is articulated by Nietzsche in his discussion of mnemotechnics in *The Genealogy of Morals*. There, he claims that guilt originates from the notion of debt, which was connected to practices of punishment predating the presupposition of choice and free will that are so central to the discourse of guilt but that get linked to the practice of punishment in modern systems of justice. The practice (punishment) and the meaning (debt) are absolutely congruent with each other and inseparable at any given time, but this does not make for some logically necessary connection between them. As Nietzsche says:

> The cause of the origin of a thing and its eventual utility, its actual employment and place in a system of purposes, lie worlds apart; whatever exists, having somehow come into being, is again and again reinterpreted to new ends, taken over, transformed, and redirected by some power superior to it; all events in the organic world are a subduing, a becoming master, and all subduing and becoming master involves a fresh interpretation, an adaptation through which any previous "meaning" and "purpose" are necessarily obscured or even obliterated. . . . The "evolution" of a thing, a custom, an organ is thus by no means its progressus toward a goal, even less a logical progressus . . . but a succession of more or less profound, more or less mutually independent processes of subduing, plus the resistances they encounter, the attempts at transformation for the purpose of defense and reaction, and the results of successful counteractions. The form is fluid, but the "meaning" is even more so.[16]

Playing the mad scientist here, Nietzsche sounds as if he were describing a natural or metaphysical process, and in part he is (where does the "organic world" begin and end?). More useful for us here, though, is to notice all of the war metaphors in this passage and to recognize that, according to Nietzsche's perspective, "meaning" is connected to processes of conflict, to the play of power. There is never a clear division between discursive formations and practices, but the connection between them is a strategic power connection rather than one supported by a natural isomorphism or a grounding configuration of sense, essence, or logic. This observation can be applied to the discourse and practice of political representation.

According to the canon, political representation first appears in the service of the English monarch and the community of the realm, as, perhaps, one of the last major developments of the feudal order of power. Later, it is linked to very different discourses, including the discourses of virtual and actual representation. Always altered by the discourses attached to it, the practice of representation shows itself to be quite adaptable as far as its meaning goes. In a sense, the discourse and the practice, or the discursive formation and the nondiscursive formation, never touch each other. This does not imply some sort of parallelism, as if discourse and practice coincided purely spontaneously or arbitrarily or were held in contemporaneous position by mysterious forces rather than by specific, concrete power connections (power of the throne, power of the people, power of the vote, power of numbers, power of the consumer, power of the Congress, power of the dollar, power of the military-industrial complex, etc.). Reinforced now by the emphasis on power, the earlier cited remark by Castoriadis about objects and things lending themselves to "identitary-ensemblist organizations" is pertinent here, as is Deleuze's remark that "discursive relations become associated with non-discursive milieux, which are not themselves situated either inside or outside the group of statements but form the . . . limit, the specific horizon without which these objects could neither appear nor be assigned a place in the statement itself."[17] Considering practices as "non-discursive" (here we encounter the inadequacy of these terms), the connections between the discourses of representation and the practices of representation are more than just a matter of good fit and more than mutually productive; they are mutually dependent, and these dependencies are dependencies of possibility. They are formulated in terms of strategic advantage, which every formation of the political subject strives to seize, as each formation moves to make the numbers line up on its side.

One of the specific dependencies here is the dependency of democracy upon some practice of representation. The two have become inseparable from each other, an inseparability not of logic but of historical contingency, which is to say an inseparability belonging to an order of necessity established in the wake of chance event. Democracy emerged in the modern period intimately wed to the discourse and practice of representation, and now it could not have been any other way. Notice, then, that we press the notions of necessity and representation beyond their limits when we recognize an inevitability that is something like the opposite of a determinism. That is, the relation between representation and democracy has become a necessary relation, as well as a vital relation, particularly and perhaps only if representative democracy is viewed from the standpoint of war rather than as a progressive effect of developing reason.

We might speculate that if democracy were to move "beyond" representation, it would not be toward some direct or immediate expression of the political subject—not to the pure voice of the popular sovereign, the organic will of the people—but to a technologically organized hegemony that would mark the end of conflict. That is, if representative democracy ever ceases being a war—if peace is made, if democracy's conflictual character disappears, or if representation is surpassed—then will, interests, and truth will be fused or networked as One, and democracy will be complete (finished?), the artifact of a curious past, a past that may no longer be either remembered or "communicated," as the transition is made from an increasingly archaic and inadequate typographic communication environment to other kinds of more efficient communication environments, constituted and determined, above all, by radio, television, and the other communications networks, which provide the architecture for the emergence of new discursive formations.

Before this or any other future, the political subject remains numbered and multiple and not just confined to the conflicted subject-object multifariously rendered as "the people." Whatever its other futures, then, democracy and the battle for all of the terms of representation will continue to be a form of war. On its effective and visible surface—where it counts—representative democracy is a war about the political subject constituted as number, and there is no reason to believe that different orderings of numbers will not continue to assert themselves and to clash on all levels (the most general and yet perhaps also most specific level consists of the complexes of numbers associated with the expanding world population, which strains every one of the planet's resources, including its political resources).

The war goes on with continual casualities and what sometimes seem to be occasional gains for democracy. Meanwhile, it is not just a war within the formal systems for representing the political subject (the people) through government since this is by no means the only kind of representation effectively at play in contemporary democracy.[18] The political subjects and objects represented formally and informally in contemporary democratic government are many, and the many in question here is not just a plural version of the people. Whatever it is that gets embodied in the apparatus of formal political representation, "the people" is just one of the players or contenders in democracy, one always in competition with other contenders. There are many power positions—many formations of the political subject—and no given master, no ultimate control, other than intentions or contentions of advocacy aimed toward domination rather than some neutral zone of rationality, where the struggle and the fighting would stop.

INFORMING THE SUBJECT

> I've gone off on a tangent, but everything that organizes an individual is external to him. He's only the point where lines of force intersect.
>
> —Viktor Shklovsky[19]

It would be neither possible nor desirable to "abandon" representation or, more specifically, to surpass the inscriptions that continue to inform the constitution of representative democracy in America, such as the idea in this remark of Thomas Jefferson's: "We had not yet penetrated to the mother principle that governments are republican only in proportion as they embodied the will of their people, and execute it."[20] While expressing what could be taken to be an archaic set of values, Jefferson's words have not been rendered meaningless or reduced to the status of museum objects (which always touch us through their enclosures) even if their significance has been drastically transformed. The cultivation of an understanding of "will" (i.e., of one prominent form of the political subject) that is different from Jefferson's may provide the possibility for maintaining an ambivalent alliance with him and with some of the other diverse figures of democratic (and not just republican) conviction who belonged to that remarkable generation of Americans. For Jefferson and the Enlightenment's illumination of democratic possibilities generally, the ultimate source of that will was autonomous, rational individuals, who do not lose their individuality when, to use Rousseau's formulation of the social contract, they exchange their natural liberty for civil liberty, thereby constituting the general or public will and becoming political subjects, and citizens. Here is the point at which a different understanding of this situation may help sustain an alliance with Jefferson and company. This alliance is above all political, but it is also textual and historical. An alternative understanding may be pursued through a questioning of the substance (i.e., being, presence) of any natural or self-evident source in the sphere of representation. As Castoriadis says, "The individual is not the fruit of nature, not even a tropical one, but a social creation and institution."[21] This observation may be extended by explicitly adding that the individual—and, by extension, the political subject—is a continually changing social creation and institution, which is not to say any less real than alternative images; this change refers not simply to diachronic developments but also to the synchronicity of mul-

tiple identities. "Will" has not vanished because in one sense
it never was and because in another sense it has changed form,
mutated as "communication" and the range of possibilities
for "expression" has mutated.

What remains is the constituted and often contested right
of the (also constituted) political subject to express its will,
opinions, and interests. However, contemporary "expression"
now involves plugging into the democratic process differently,
interacting with the apparatuses of representation that count,
jacking in to a kind of counting that cannot be reduced to the
right to vote (as if this were a self-identical or self-evident gesture). Public opinion does not exist outside of the technological topos in which it gets aired (a topos that is never entirely
controlled, despite the maintenance forces continually at work
there).[22] It is in the production of "information" that the political subject gets produced, at least the one we associate with
public opinion, with "the people." Given the nature of this
information and the ways that political agendas get articulated in it, this could be seen as a problem for the possibilities
of representative democracy since it plays an intimate and
determinative role in the processes of representation.

One immediate response to the current conflicts of representative democracy might be a classical affirmation of education's prospects for informing and thus constituting the
political subject, the citizen. As always—from Plato through
Jefferson through liberalism today—education and the general
cultivation of the mind seems to be the obvious answer.
Answer to what—to "bad information"? Such oppositions
revolve around a continued faith in enlightenment while
underestimating the postmodern light emitted by the cathode-ray tube; now that the lights can be left on all night, the
kind of grounding clarity provided by the light of day may no
longer be primary.

Employing part of the very discourse I am trying to exam-
ine here, numbers can be used to represent one reason why
light can no longer be associated with traditional images of
clarity. "Children between the ages of 2 and 12 watch an aver-
age of 25 hours of television a week. By the time they graduate

from high school, American children each will have spent 15,000 hours in front of a television set, compared with only 11,000 hours in the classroom."[23] In the face of this numbered reality,[24] it would seem untenable, then, to view electronic entertainment as either bad or as marginal—an accessory to education. The television is now clearly a significant dimension of the process of education and thus of informing (i.e., constituting) the political subject of representative democracy. Communication and information are only proliferating, and this is at least as much a part of the political subject's education or formation as learning how to read. Whatever else might be said by way of evaluating this reality, there is no longer any choice here; the insinuation of technologized communication into the processes of human (and thus political) development will not have been "chosen," at least not as long as the electricity holds out. The question has less to do with the good or bad effects of technology on politics than it has to do with the efforts of theory to come to terms with new discursive regimes in the sphere of politics.

THE WAR ROOM:[25] AFFIRMING CONFLICT

It is possible to imagine representative democracy through images of difference and conflict rather than the stable identities and plotting points provided by traditional, dyadic, metaphysical values. Perhaps above all we must embrace the conflict embodied in the practice of democracy and learn from the art of war, which means learn to think strategically rather than teleologically.

As it pertains to the issues at hand, the most general difference between teleological and strategic perspectives or logics is that the teleological remains dominated by the command of Reason and order—by a final, original, underlying identity, an arboreal source—while the strategic is a site-specific logic, a logic not tied to any firm or safe land, a mobilized architecture, independent of foundation and an adaptable, flexible, fluid force that is not insecure but 'unsecure' as well as unpredictable. That is, the teleological perspective works from the standpoint of a Ground, which above all aims to consolidate and secure itself; on the other hand, the strategic requires a territorial perspective, a perspective which for all of its contingency is not arbitrary because, by a certain necessity, it is always somewhere, which renders it not insecure but 'unsecure,' because it could be somewhere else. Both perspectives are governed by purpose—strategy is the shadow of teleology—but "purpose" means different things for each. For teleology, "purpose" is given, objective, ultimately self-evident, even natural; picture Aristotle here. Teleology asks, "What is this thing about, what is its nature?" In contrast, strategy asks, "What is this thing for, what will it achieve, what effects will it produce?" For strategy, "purpose" is plan, something human, selective, circumstantial, and intimately wed to chance;[26] it is the assertion of will, something like a will to power. Teleology assumes purpose. Strategy asserts purposes, and its determinants are thus essentially contextual and contingent rather than given (even if also invariably connected to orienting dimensions of what Castoriadis calls the "social imaginary").[27] Pushing further and selectively extending a familiar distinction from Deleuze and Guattari,[28] what I am here calling the teleological perspective is a State perspective while the strategic perspective is the uncontainable logic of a war machine, a logic resistant to the consolidative hierarchies of stable order. In short, we might contemplate the possibility that teleology is the logic of republican order, while strategy is the operative and effective logic actually embodied in the practice of representative democracy, yet repressed by the conceptual logic of the history of representation.

    After the flow of images of the subject of political representation, the moment of truth—the moment the political subject emerges in one of its most visibly active roles—is the vote and tally, and vote we must.[29] The tally undertaken here indicates a necessary ambivalence about "the people" and reinforces the truth that representation never was simple replication. This is not just because politicians deviate from their constituencies' wishes, but—more philosophically important—because the identity of the political subject of representation is not fixed or clear. There was a time when replication was the ideal of political representation, and the problem seemed to be the practical one of just how to go about producing this replication. However, there is no univocal answer to the question, "What is it that gets represented in contemporary democracy?" Creation embedded in conflict is what representation is about. It is creation not just of a "form" but, simultaneously, of a "content," of both representative and represented, and of government and the people for whom government is an active substitute.

Derrida has written of democracy as "something that remains to be thought and *to come*... a democracy that must have the structure of a promise . . .";[30] the implication is that democracy is a promise, not the fulfillment of a promise, not something to arrive, but something intrinsically yet to come, the promise of a future without a teleology. Inheriting and participating in this promise, the vote must be for democracy; if it is not, then it is not a vote (and vote we must). The vote for democracy is inseparable from the discourse and practice of representation, comprising a complex that cannot be transcended even if or perhaps because democracy has not yet arrived and may be intrinsically incompletable, as the forces of substitution embodied in the formal and informal apparatuses of representation continue evolving and battling each other.

Still, while conflict has not worked itself out, there may come a time when representative democracy will disappear. Motivated not by Reason but by a reasonable insight, Thomas Paine, a friend of democracy, wrote, "Monarchy, aristocracy, and democracy, are but creatures of the imagination; and a thousand such may be contrived, as well as three."[31] The force of this promise or image is certainly more than a simple optimism; it is, rather, an acknowledgment or even celebration of our limited imaginations and thus an openness which here could involve a vulnerable ambivalence in the face of the future.[32]

Here in the present, it is inevitable that whatever complications it offers, the vote must be for representation even if the vote is a troubled one. This is because the processes of representation are characterized by multifarious forms of conflict. If there is an absolute value, it must for now remain democracy, not because democracy is the end or telos of representation, but precisely because the conflictual logic of actual democracy admits the ascendance of no absolute value, of no final story or final representation of the truth. That is, the promise of representation would not be the end of representation. Without representation, democracy becomes the dangerous dream of an unmediated subject, which might turn out to be synonymous with a goose-stepping army or with "'The good human being' (the sheep, the ass, the goose, and all who are incurably shallow squallers, ripe for the nut house of 'modern ideas')."[33] For now, the appropriate stance seems to be a necessarily defensive but not passive strategic engagement. It is a call for creative intervention, with democracy, for the promise of democracy.

What does this mean for philosophy? That is, what is the most appropriate battle plan? It is the same as it ever was; to engage the enemy critically and to continue its criticism of itself, that is, to confront the desire for Truth. Strategic logic has always been one of philosophy's most powerful impulses, an impulse all too often obscured or repressed by the logic of representation, which is perhaps one reason why Socrates disturbed his fellow citizens, who seem to have mistaken his brand of rhetorical warfare for manipulative duplicity. Philosophy may continue to make a difference only if it recognizes rather than rejects the martial dimension of its subject and the ramifications of this for representative democracy, rather than falling back on its stock gesture, the one that provoked Nietzsche's laughter, which is pointing somewhere else, at its own desire for Truth.

Notes

INTRODUCTION

1. Cf. Jacques Derrida, "Sending: On Representation," trans. Peter and Mary Ann Caws, *Social Research* 49 (1982): 295-326 henceforth cited as *SR*.

2. Hanna Fenichel Pitkin, *The Concept of Representation* (Berkeley: University of California Press, 1967), henceforth cited as *CR*. One of the things clarified by Pitkin's ordinary language analysis is not that "there is no real representation," but that what representation is is very diverse and that many discourses and concepts have competed and continue to compete with each other here.

3. Derrida writes that, "This interpretation of representation would presuppose a representational pre-interpretation of representation, it would still be a representation of representation." (*SR*, 320) But further, "The essence of representation is not a representation, it is not representable, there is no representation of representation." (*SR*, 314) Part of the point, one that will be clarified by looking at some historical fragments of political representation, is that there is no original representation to found representation or to be represented, only the differentially constituted complex of traces and, in the broadest sense, the discursive relations and practices that have constituted "representation." Representation itself, then, will always and necessarily be deferred.

Castoriadis emphasizes a different and more generalized version of this point when he says, "Since Plato, it has been known that every demonstration presupposes something which is not demonstrable" ("The Greek Polis and the Creation of Democracy," in *Philosophy, Politics, Autonomy*, trans. David Ames Curtis [New York: Oxford University Press, 1991], 87, henceforth cited as *GPCD*).

4. John Adams, "Thoughts on Government," in *The Political Writings of John Adams*, ed. George A. Peek, Jr. (New York: The Liberal Arts Press, 1954), 86. This piece was written in January 1776,

the same month that Tom Paine's powerful pamphlet, *Common Sense,* appeared on the streets of Philadelphia.

5. Derrida, *SR,* 311.

6. "New struggles. After Buddha was dead, his shadow was still shown for centuries in a cave—a tremendous, gruesome shadow. God is dead; but given the way of men, there may still be caves for thousands of years in which his shadow will be shown. And we—we still have to vanquish his shadow, too," Friedrich Nietzsche, *The Gay Science,* trans. Walter Kaufmann (New York: Vintage Books, 1974), sec. 108, 167.

7. Among the most important of these sources will be Michel Foucault's view that as material forms of "power," *discourse and practice constitute subjects and objects.*

8. I refer the reader to Castoriadis' conception of "absolute creations," and his articulation of the difference between what is natural and what is made, in Cornelius Castoriadis, "Technique," in *Crossroads in the Labyrinth,* trans. Kate Soper and Martin H. Ryle (Cambridge: MIT Press, 1984), henceforth cited as *CL,* e.g., 239 & 241, and to his discussion of history as creation in *GPCD,* 81ff.

9. "Inaccessible content": This concept belongs to an archaic discourse, since everything is now interconnected through networks (nets) of information and, theoretically, is all accessible to what reason has become (intelligence). We now live in an age when access, a term tied to computer/"communications" technology and the discourse of information, is becoming increasingly significant as a form of socio-epistemic exchange as its architecture. This term is also at the heart of postmodern formations of power; information (e.g., intelligence) is power. We live in a world in which nothing seems inaccessible as long as one has the power to access, whether this power is a legitimate code or an effective intrusion (the icebreaker, the postmodern picklock's tool).

10. J. G. A. Pocock, *The Machiavellian Moment: Florentine Political Thought and the Atlantic Republican Tradition* (Princeton: Princeton University Press, 1975), 183, henceforth cited as *MM.*

11. "It is not possible for us to describe our own archive, since it is from within these rules that we speak, since it is that which gives to what we can say—and to itself, the object of our discourse—

its modes of appearance, its forms of existence and coexistence, its system of accumulation, historicity, and disappearance," Michel Foucault, *The Archaeology of Knowledge*, trans. A. M. Sheridan Smith (New York: Pantheon Books, 1982), 130, henceforth cited as *AK*. However, in its introduction, Foucault also describes *Discipline and Punish* as a contribution to an archaeology of the present.

12. To be explicit, but in shorthand, what is metaphysical here is the assumption of a transcendental signified, a self-identical source ("the really real").

13. Dick Howard, *The Politics of Critique* (Minneapolis: University of Minnesota Press, 1988), 205.

14. Several philosophy graduate students from the State University of New York at Stony Brook interviewed Derrida in his Yale office in the spring of 1986. On the ferry back across Long Island Sound after the visit, they pieced together a written transcript of the conversation, which was largely about deconstruction and politics. This written draft of the conversation mysteriously disappeared in Stony Brook's Old Metaphysics building almost immediately afterward.

15. In 1777 and in direct reference to the double representation of people and property already mentioned, one radical Pennsylvanian argued that, "To say, there ought to be two houses, because there are two sorts of interests, is the very reason why there ought to be but one, and *that one to consist of every sort.*" Quoted by Gordon S. Wood, *The Creation of the American Republic, 1776-1787* (New York: W. W. Norton & Co., 1972), 231 (italics mine), henceforth cited as *CAR*.

CHAPTER I

1. Jacques Derrida, "White Mythology," in *Margins of Philosophy*, trans. Alan Bass (Chicago: University of Chicago Press, 1982), 258.

2. J. A. O. Larsen argues that the agenda-setting boule of Athens—the council of 500—functioned in part as a representative body within the *ekklesia*, the primary assembly as a whole, which itself embodied "direct democracy" instead of something more akin to representation (cf. J. A. O. Larsen, *Representative Government*

in Greek and Roman History [Berkeley: University of California Press, 1966]). He argues further that various other Hellenic and Hellenistic governments may be characterized as representative, too, particularly the federations.

M. V. Clarke maintains that while the city-state was too compact for representation to develop in a political context, there is strong evidence that the idea of representation is nevertheless very much present in Greek law (M. V. Clarke, *Medieval Representation and Consent*, reissue of 1936 edition [New York: Russell & Russell, Inc., 1964], henceforth cited as *MRC*, 279). She adds here that, "Representation was not so much a principle as a temporary administrative convenience." Like Larsen (but writing thirty years earlier), Clarke, too, sees the boule as embodying something close to a political use of representation, and she implicitly stresses practice here rather than language or intention, which is an important emphasis.

Others, however—following in the tracks of J. J. Rousseau— insist that there simply was no such thing as representation for the Greeks. For instance, Castoriadis contends that

> Representation is a principle alien to democracy. This hardly bears discussion. Once permanent "representatives" are present, political authority, activity, and initiative are expropriated from the body of citizens and transferred to the restricted body of "representatives," who also use it to consolidate their position and create the conditions whereby the next "election" becomes biased in many ways. (*GPCD*, 99)

Castoriadis' stance here is not as straightforward as it may sound, which is evident (1) in his use of "permanent" representative, a phrase that is utterly ambiguous in the sphere of practical politics, and (2) when positioned, for instance, in relation to the eighteenth-century American discourse about the differences between republic and democracy, and also about the necessity of representation for the formation of a democratic republic in such a large territory. There, we find conservatives arguing that a republic is not—god forbid, what chaos!—a democracy and that selective representation helps insure this. We find the radicals arguing that, given a large population, it is only through representation that democracy will be possible (cf. Robert W. Shoemaker, "'Democracy' and 'Republic' as Understood in Eighteenth-Century America," *American Speech* 41 [1966]). Representation is represented here as extremely malleable.

In "The Concept of Representation," in *Representation*, ed.

Hanna Fenichel Pitkin (New York: Atherton Press, 1969), henceforth *R*, Pitkin also asserts that there was no representation for the Greeks. However, in a different text, Pitkin makes the qualifying statement that, "Although the ancient Greeks had a number of institutions and practices to which we could apply the word 'representation,' they had no corresponding word or concept" (Pitkin, *CR*, 241).

I mention these diverse views not to resolve the issue, but to emphasize once more that controversy is characteristic of the discourse about political representation, which reflects the fluidity and differences found in its many formations.

3. Cf. Irene Harvey, *Derrida and the Economy of Differance* (Bloomington: Indiana University Press, 1986).

4. Cf. Jacques Derrida, "Différance," in *Margins of Philosophy*, trans. Alan Bass (Chicago: University of Chicago Press, 1982).

5. Michel Foucault, "The Discourse on Language," in *The Archaeology of Knowledge*, trans. A. M. Sheridan Smith (New York: Pantheon Books, 1982), 218, henceforth cited as *AK*.

6. "This business about discontinuity has always rather bewildered me. In the new edition of the Petit Larousse it says: 'Foucault: a philosopher who founds his theory of history on discontinuity.' That leaves me flabbergasted," Michel Foucault, "Truth and Power," in *Power/Knowledge*, ed. Colin Gordon (New York: Pantheon Books, 1980), 111, henceforth cited as *TP*.

7. Foucault, *AK*, 7.

8. Ibid., 138-39.

9. Foucault, *TP*, 114.

10. "I would like to write a history of this prison, with all the political investments of the body that it gathers together in its closed architecture. Why? Simply because I am interested in the past? No, if one means by that writing a history of the past in terms of the present. Yes, if one means writing the history of the present," Michel Foucault, *Discipline and Punish*, trans. Alan Sheridan (New York: Vintage Books, 1979), 31, henceforth cited as *DP*.

11. This fluid alternative is utilized by Ernesto Laclau and Chantal Mouffe in *Hegemony and Socialist Strategy: Toward a Radical Democratic Politics*, trans. Winston Moore and Paul Cammack (London: Verso, 1985).

12. As will be discussed at the appropriate time, these divisions come from Greek political thought, most powerfully from Aristotle. Their application in seventeenth and eighteenth-century English and then American political thought was preceded and influenced by the role they played in late fifteenth and early sixteenth century Italian republican theory (cf. J. G. A. Pocock, *The Machiavellian Moment* [Princeton: Princeton University Press, 1975]).

13. Friedrich Nietzsche, *Philosophy in the Tragic Age of the Greeks*, trans. Marianne Cowan (Chicago: Henry Regnery, 1962), Henceforth cited as *PTAG*.

14. Ibid., 45.

15. "Greek philosophy seems to begin with an absurd notion, with the proposition that water is the primal origin and the womb of all things," ibid., 38.

16. Nietzsche's account of this figure in *PTAG* may appear to emphasize this point. However, we should note (1) that this is a very early text, and the later Nietzsche probably would have disrupted this opposition head on and (2) more practically, that the opposition must be articulated in order to deconstruct it (i.e., this articulation is part of the process of deconstruction).

17. It is this trope that makes Heraclitus' fire/desire a deviant metaphysics since the hierarchical configurations of the One/the many and Being/becoming collapse with his refusal to separate their terms, to privilege one side over the other. Necessity and the law itself are inscribed (not prewritten) in and by the very processes of change and in games of chance. Cf. the Heraclitus section in *PTAG*, and also, Gilles Deleuze, *Nietzsche*, trans. Hugh Tomlinson (New York: Columbia University Press, 1983), 25ff.
While on the topic of metaphysical (helio)tropes, it would be a mistake to omit mention of Jacques Derrida's, "White Mythology: Metaphor in the Text of Philosophy," in *Margins of Philosophy*, trans. Alan Bass (Chicago: University of Chicago Press, 1982).

18. In political systems dependent upon it, representational discourse-practice can account for itself as the way that society constitutes itself in the form of a state, i.e., as the practical dimension of the foundation of the state. Eighteenth-century revolutionary America was aggressively aware that the practice of "actual" repre-

sentation offered (1) an alternative to a system of government founded on the power of the sovereign monarch (of the sovereign's identity) and (2) for the Federalists, a means necessary for the development of a more perfect union.

19. Hobbes, *Leviathan*, ed. Michael Oakeshott (New York: Collier Books, 1962), 127.

20. The danger is in mistaking artificial light for that of the sun, the natural purity of which is the light of understanding (or of being convinced). Artificial light is not wrong or defective, but it can always be altered or redirected, i.e., it does not necessarily always push the same features into the foreground. There is no pure sunlight (ozone or no ozone).

21. Dick Howard, *The Marxian Legacy*, 2d ed. (Minneapolis: University of Minnesota Press, 1988), 189.

CHAPTER II

1. A. F. Pollard, *The Evolution of Parliament* (New York: Russell & Russell, 1964, reissue of 1926 edition), 151. Henceforth cited as *EP*.

2. Helen M. Cam, "The Theory and Practice of Representation in Medieval England," *History* 38 (1953): 18. Henceforth cited as *TPR*. Why, "naturally," a *man*?

3. Ibid, 19.

4. J. R. Pole, *Political Representation in England and the Origins of the American Republic* (London: Macmillan, 1966), 205. Henceforth cited as *PRE*.

5. M. V. Clarke, *Medieval Representation and Consent* (New York: Russell and Russell, 1964), 278, henceforth cited as *MRC*.

6. This translation in Bertie Wilkinson, *The Creation of Medieval Parliaments* (New York: John Wiley & Sons, 1972), 103-4. The original Latin text is in William Stubbs, *Select Charters: from the Beginning to 1307*, 9th ed., revised by H. W. C. Davis (Oxford: Clarendon Press, 1951 [First Edition 1870]), 394, henceforth cited as *SC*.

7. Etienne Balibar, "Citizen Subject," trans. James B. Swenson,

Jr., in *Who Comes after the Subject?* ed. Eduardo Cadava, Peter Connor, and Jean-Luc Nancy (New York & London: Routledge, 1991), 47.

8. Pollard, *EP*, 157.

9. Deferring to the earlier arguments of Bishop Stubbs, McIlwain criticizes the argument that "'The Church originated representative institututions; the State adopted them'" (C. H. McIlwain, "Medieval Estates," in *Cambridge Medieval History*, (Cambridge: Cambridge University Press, 1932), 7:670-71, henceforth cited as *ME*). McIlwain notes not only that there were no Dominicans in England until 1221 but also that this argument underestimates the significance of existing Anglo-Saxon practices for the development of English representative practices in the thirteenth century. From a philosophical perspective, the point cannot be one of attempting to locate where English representation really originates. Rather, it illustrates the impossibility of locating an origin and the efficacy of an alternative approach, one articulated around the notion of grafting or fusion.

10. Later, the clergy and baronage became formally united in the House of Lords (spiritual and temporal), the Crown comes to be considered a separate estate (rather than an altogether ontologically different entity), and thus the three estates become the Crown, Lords, and Commons. Although it will be addressed in the next chapter, it is worth mentioning that this tripartite political structure became the model of mixed government that informed the Americans as they constructed their democratic republic from scratch.

11. Stubbs, *SC*, 44.

12. According to McIlwain (*ME*, 664), feudalism,

was a period of the complete territoriality of law, in the absence more or less complete of all coercive central, a regime when small territories, and each with its own customary law binding upon all within its boundaries, were the rule; and for a time the process of subdivision was making these little territorial units ever more numerous and more minute. When this process of subdivision reached its limit, and the counter-process began of the gradual accretion of fiefs which was ultimately to develop into the great national States of Western Europe, the course and direction of that development were determined by the institutions and ideas which had become established within the scattered territorial units from which the later States were ultimately formed. Prominent among these institutions and ideas was that of law as the custom of the people within a territory, the *mos utentium*, a *ius non scriptum* whose beginning was beyond memory and whose transmission was by oral tradition.

13. Cam, *TPR*, 19.

14. Clarke, *MRC*, 285.

15. Villeins were freemen, except in relation to their liege lord, who continued to hold total power over them. Here, 'free' is determined by the boundaries of feudal codes.

16. The courts themselves—the hundredmoots and shiremoots—were representative assemblies, the representative embodiments of the hundreds (the wapentakes) and the shires which were geoeconomic units of community (or of communes).

17. Cf. Helen M. Cam, *TPR*, 22. Also, Pollard points out (*EP*, 114) that by the end of the fourteenth century, communes are associated not only with the knights who represent the shires but also with the representatives of the cities and boroughs.

18. Pollard, *EP*, 109. Further, "Representation was, in fact, an unpleasant incident of feudal service. This is the popular attitude in the middle ages toward parliament, as towards the shire court; it is not a question of who is anxious to serve, but of who is obliged to attend" (ibid., 153). Reinforcing this observation, Pollard also notes that "there is hardly a parliament of the first half of the fourteenth century the opening of which had not to be postponed owing to defective attendance" (ibid., 114).

19. This metaphor comes from the opening of Ingmar Bergman's film, *The Serpent's Egg* (1978). The story takes place in Berlin in the late 1920s, on the eve of the ascendance of Hitler, as the value of German currency is collapsing.

20. Cf. Jacques Derrida's remarks on grafting in "Dissemination," in *Dissemination*, trans. Barbara Johnson (Chicago: University of Chicago Press, 1981), 355ff.

21. I will pursue this issue at greater length in Chapter V.

174
The Trace of Political Representation

22. Cf. Michel Foucault, "Truth and Power," trans. Colin Gordon et al. in *Power/Knowledge*, ed. Colin Gordon (New York: Pantheon Books, 1980), 118.

23. "who have opened schools for sophistry, and made establishments for anarchy. . . ." Applicable to politicians and political theorists and activists (particularly French ones) whose fundamental reference point is "natural rights," this derogatory phrase (and variants of it) is used by Edmund Burke in *Reflections on the Revolution in France* (Harmondsworth, Middlesex: Penguin Books, 1986), edited by Conor Cruise O'Brien, 348 (and elsewhere), henceforth cited as *RRF*. Regardless of his intentions, though, the main general point of our ensuing discussion of Burke is that the theory of virtual representation is thoroughly and classically metaphysical.

24. Cited by Louise Fargo Brown, "Ideas of Representation from Elizabeth to Charles II," *Journal of Modern History* 2 (March, 1939): 28. Henceforth cited as *IR*.

25. Among the most dramatic formal examples, of course, are the British East India Company, chartered in 1600 (its Dutch counterpart was chartered in 1602, and its French counterpart in 1664) and the Hudson's Bay Company, chartered in 1670 (this is not to mention the various individual corporations associated with each of the chartered British colonies in America and the West Indies).

26. These are not the only factors contributing to the transformation of the discourse of representation, but they are the most obvious ones (others might have to do with the status of religion and of science as well as the philosophical discourse of Reason with which the image of popular sovereignty is connected).

27. Cf. Alfred De Grazia, *Public and Republic: Political Representation in America* (Westport, Conn: Greenwood Press, 1951), 18, henceforth cited as *PR*, and many instances in Edmund S. Morgan, *Inventing the People* (New York: W. W. Norton & Co, 1988), henceforth cited as *IP*.

28. Cf. Pitkin, *CR*, chap. 8.

29. For example, Burke was an outspoken critic of the network known as "the King's Friends." More specifically pertinent here, he was a strong critic of George III's (and Lord North's) American policies, policies which of course turned out to be disastrous for Great Britain,

as America extricated itself from the Empire. However, his criticism needs to be understood in a broader context, including that provided by his later, polemical *Reflections on the Revolution in France* , where he condemned the French Revolution in no uncertain terms, defended England's constitutional monarchy, and provoked a number of published responses, including his friend Tom Paine's, *Rights of Man* (Harmondsworth, Middlesex: Penguin Books, 1985), which aggressively attacked Burke's ideas and did not neglect also to criticize his mode of exposition ("learned jargon"), and to cast doubt on his character and personal integrity (a "pensioner," i.e., of the King).

30. Cf. ibid., chap. 7. Pitkin's characterization of the debate about representation in terms of "mandate-independence" highlights the controversy over the identity of the representative.

31. Note the sense in which the word "constituent" does not really describe the electorate in the context of virtual representation since the electorate (a tiny percentage of the population to begin with) only makes the gesture—the vote—that puts the virtual representative into place, and thereafter is no longer a necessary or active component or element of the dynamics of representation (i.e., having voted, the electorate no longer constitutes the representative). This constituted reality is perhaps what leads to Rousseau's famous remark that, "The English people think that they are free, but in this belief they are profoundly wrong. They are free only when they are electing members of Parliament. Once the election has been completed, they revert to a condition of slavery: they are nothing. Making such use of it in the few short moments of their freedom, they deserve to lose it" (Jean-Jacques Rousseau, "The Social Contract," in *Social Contract*, ed. Sir Ernest Barker [London: Oxford University Press, 1960], 260.)

32. There is no reason to assume that the use of the masculine here is "neutral," particularly given the patently paternal characteristics of the representative as trustee.

33. Edmund Burke, "Speech to the Electors of Bristol," in *The Works of Edmund Burke*, Vol. 2 (Boston: Little, Brown, and Company, 1880), 96.
It is worth noting that my use of this passage reinscribes its institutional, canonized value. Often excerpted or framed identically, and just to mention a cluster of relatively recent volumes (selected here by virtue of their current presence on my desk), this

passage is quoted by Anthony Arblaster, *Democracy* (Minneapolis: University of Minnesota Press, 1987), henceforth *D*, 83; by Bernard Bailyn, *The Ideological Origins of the American Revolution* (Cambridge: Harvard University Press, Belknap Press, 1967), henceforth *IOAR*, 163; by De Grazia, *PR*, 38; by Edmund S. Morgan, *Inventing the People* (New York: W. W. Norton & Co., 1988), henceforth *IP*, 216; by Pitkin, *CR*, 171; included in Pitkin, *R*, 175-76; by Pole, *PRE*, 441; by Gordon S. Wood, *The Creation of the American Republic: 1776-1787* (New York, W. W. Norton, 1969), henceforth *CAR* 175; by Gordon S. Wood, *Representation in the American Revolution* (Charlotteville: University Press of Virginia, 1969), henceforth *RAR* 4; and doubtless many others.

34. "Concrete-abstraction" is my own, clumsy construction, but regarding the "social imaginary," cf. Cornelius Castoriadis, *The Imaginary Institution of Society*, translated by Kathleen Blamey (Cambridge: MIT Press, 1987), and Claude Lefort, *The Political Forms of Modern Society*, edited by John B. Thompson (Cambridge: MIT Press, 1986). Also, in a seminar taught by him in the philosophy department at S.U.N.Y./Stony Brook in fall 1986, Lefort invoked a notion of the "material-symbolic" to emphasize the effective reality rather than ideality of the social imagination.

35. By "meaningless," I mean going nowhere other than into a continuing play of repetition (Heraclitus, Nietzsche, Freud), which is always repetition with a difference.

36. Note the singularity of interest here. While a given borough might not be confined to just one interest in the discourse of Parliament, the abstractive formulation of the interest of the nation, an eidetic maneuver, tends to pare interests down to the fewest possible. This is the movement of simplification—breaking things down into definite, general identities and manageable categories—another metaphysical gesture.

37. It is worth mentioning that while "interests" are central to the discourse and republican conceptions of the Federalists, the relationship between the general public interest and other interests is far more problematic for them than for Burke, since the various interests represented in government ("a landed interest, a manufacturing interest, a mercantile interest, a money interest, with many lesser interests. . . .") are the source of factions and division rather than in some fundamental state of harmony (cf. Madison's famous *Federalist 10*).

38. To put it in shorthand, one important difference between mobilized ground and floating signifiers is the difference between history and semiology; regardless of his critical intentions, Baudrillard remains wholly subject to the authority of the Sign (in fact, his may be the only pure semiology, since it recognizes only signifiers). Cf. Jean Baudrillard, *Simulations*, trans. Paul Foss, Paul Patton, and Philip Beitchman (New York: Semiotext[e], 1983).

39. "Sales became increasingly numerous until, when newspapers began to appear in England, seats in the House of Commons were advertised for sale," De Grazia, *PR*, 34.

40. Ibid., p. 35. That such a requirement was not formalized until this late date seems to accentuate this new anxiety, an anxiety that was well-founded since anyone in a position to run for Parliament was probably also in a position to purchase whatever it took to fulfill the land requirement, thereby circumventing the reactionary, self-protective intent of the law. This is a major transformation in the ground of values, and the traditional aristocracy was in a panic as it watched no-names become somebodies.

41. Cf. John Locke, *An Essay Concerning the True Original, Extent and End of Civil Government*, chap. 5 in *Social Contract*, ed. Sir Ernest Barker (London: Oxford University Press, 1960).

42. While it would be tempting to argue the latter—that Locke's discourse is an effect—it might be more philosophically productive to try avoiding causal explanations and to view all of these events—discursive conditions and nondiscursive events—as coextensive with each other.

43. Speaking of the period during the English Civil War—before Locke and well over a century before Burke's writings—Brown points out (*IR*, 35) that the conservative group believed that the representative system had a property basis. Their view prevailed in the Heads of proposals, which redistributed the electoral units according to the amount of subsidy paid by each county and disenfranchised "poor decayed or inconsiderable towns." The radical group believed that the basis was population and aimed at manhood suffrage. After acrimonious discussions, in which the radicals denied that they were anarchists and refused to be bought off by a concession of votes for soldiers, they succeeded in getting an approach to this, in the Second Agreement of the people.

This 17th-century conflict is just one instance of precedents for later conflicts in the understanding of political representation.

44. Fear of the seizure of property fueled the republican logic embodied by the Federalists in America, as will be discussed in the next chapter.

45. Pitkin, *CR*, 185.

46. Ibid., 189.

47. Quoted by Pitkin, *R*, 173. Note the "natural." Here is another piece of artillery in the battle to break with the feudal order, a divorce from social practices as well as from ideas (metaphysics). In this instance, "natural" may be counterposed against "conventional," against, that is, the power associated with the conventional mythology of an aristocracy based upon bloodlines. A similar, related example of this type of self-conscious break would be Hobbes, who reinscribes tradition by supporting the sovereign but who breaks with it (or believes himself to be doing so) by asserting that hereditary (again bloodlines) is not the basis for the monarch's legitimacy. Rather than heredity, Hobbes (and the earlier Machiavelli) would affirm something like competence, excellence, or quality (minimally, the ability to avoid being overthrown), perhaps prefiguring Burke's notion of a natural aristocracy, the basic meaning of which is that some few people are simply better than others.

48. Pitkin, *CR*, 188.

49. e.g., Burke, *RRF*, 141.

50. The idea that property and wealth ensure independence of judgment was a common one on both sides of the Atlantic in the eighteenth century, as these sorts of criteria became an issue. The logic of this reason determined, for one thing, that poor people are susceptible to bribes, while wealthy men are freed from the temptations of anything but reason. Of course, this is a political joke of the largest magnitude, particularly in the context of a discourse whose central term is interests. It is also still an effective and timely joke. Those who must laugh the most at this joke are those very judges whose 'independence' is insured by the objective interests associated with their wealth.

51. Cited by De Grazia, *PR*, 46.

52. Pole, *PRE*, 441.

53. The "Intolerable Acts," as the colonists called them, were five extremely coercive laws imposed by Parliament in the spring of 1774, four of which were in direct response to the Boston Tea Party. The major effect of these laws was not what was spelled out in them, but in their aggravation of revolutionary conditions. Three of the laws crippled Massachusetts economically (the Boston Port Act), judicially (the Administration of Justice Act), and legislatively (the Massachusetts Government Act); not too surprisingly, the first battles of the Revolution were fought the following spring in Massachusetts.

54. Cf. Gordon S. Wood, *The Radicalism of the American Revolution* (New York: Alfred Knopf, 1992).

55. Actually, the English infatuation with tea was extremely recent and the direct product of the European expansionism at work in the development of virtual representation. According to Fernand Braudel (*SEL*, 250-51), "The first cargoes of tea are thought to have arrived" in Europe "at Amsterdam in 1610 on the initiative of the Oost Indische Companie," while tea was apparently not launched as a fashionable or popular practice in London until 1657 ("But the East India Company only began to import it from Asia in 1669").

CHAPTER III

1. It is probably not necessary to remind the reader that *Common Sense* was the title of Tom Paine's widely read, revolutionary pamphlet, originally published in January, 1776. It was widely acknowledged at the time that this book helped fuel and fan the fire of a revolution already underway (cf. Robert Middlekauf, *The Glorious Cause: The American Revolution, 1763-1789* (New York: Oxford University Press, 1982), 317ff.). The battles of Lexington and Concord had occurred the previous April, and Bunker Hill on June 17, but a certain hesitation was hanging in the air by the following winter. As well as opening up the critical question of the fundamental legitimacy of the institution of English monarchy in general, this important pamphlet also offered suggestions about how to set up the new Continental government.

2. It may seem somewhat ironic that Burke himself did not believe that the American colonies were either virtually or actually represented in Commons.

Furthermore, Burke's opposition to "the King's Friends" (see note 29 in the previous chapter) shared with the Americans a deep suspicion of an active, deliberate, behind-the-scenes conspiracy within the British government, a conspiracy which, from the 1760s on, the colonists increasingly saw at work in every move perceived as against them (cf. Bailyn, "The Logic of Rebellion," and "A Note on Conspiracy," 94-159). The perceived plotting was seen, that is, as moves of (corrupt, organized, and itself invisible) power against liberty (cf. Bailyn, "Power and Liberty," *IOAR*, 55-93). At the same time, English administrators and Tories in America saw conspiracy on the other side, in seditious colonists who professed loyalty to King George but who were surreptitiously working together to sever the bond to England.

3. Thomas Whately, quoted by Bailyn, *IOAR*, 166.

4. Ibid.

5. Wood, *RAR*, 3.

6. At the same time, the federative images of unitary order and common interest would also be opposed by the Anti-Federalists, who contributed significantly to the general political debate after the war with England even if they tend to be remembered (or forgotten) for having 'lost' the battle over the Constitution.

7. Bailyn, *IOAR*, 168.

8. Wood makes the point that

. . . Perhaps precisely because the Crown had also sought in 1767 to prevent any expansion of the electorate and because the Revolutionaries needed as much support as they could muster, many states in 1776 did perceptibly enlarge the basis of consent, without however elevating the right to vote into a major issue of the Revolution. Indeed, the Revolution came in time to mark a decisive turning point in the development of American thinking about voting. Although not as a result of clearly intended theory the right to vote and the electoral process in general were set on a path to becoming identified in American thought with the very essence of American democracy. But at the outset in 1776 it was not at all obvious that voting itself was crucially important, and all of the states retained some sort of tax-paying or property qualification for the suffrage. Few in 1776 considered such qualifications a denial of the embodiment of democracy. . . . (*CAR*, 167-68)

That voting was an essential element in the representative process would eventually become a given (of sorts). As shall be discussed in a later chapter, though, the adjoining issue of the scope of suffrage became the subject of massive political debates and practices, which may or may not have ended with the civil rights movement in the South in the late 50s and early 60s, culminating in the 24th Amendment to the Constitution in 1964 (Sec. 1: "The rights of citizens . . . shall not be denied or abridged by the United States or any State by reason of failure to pay any poll tax or other tax") and with the Voting Rights Act of 1965.

9. As shall be discussed later, consent is formulated as the medium of exchange between the representative and what it represents, and voting as the instrument of consent.

10. Is this a necessary tendency? It is certainly necessary to philosophy that it "discover"—i.e., articulate—the unity in things, that it offer univocity in place of dispersion, that it find a logic at work. This may be one of Foucault's limitations; with his emphasis on regularities, he offers us coherent, relatively discrete packages of discourse, and he makes historical formations seem neater than they may be. On the other hand, one advantage offered by a Foucauldian approach is that it may highlight the common terms underlying the different positions in, for example, a debate (cf. the following footnote).

11. This is one of the important and interesting conclusions drawn by Michael G. Kammen in *Deputyes and Libertyes: The Origins of Representative Government in Colonial America* (New York: Alfred A. Knopf, 1969), henceforth *DL*.

12. "Get organized": This phrase is not intended to suggest that representation exists in some finished form in America since it is being continually transformed, as other aspects of culture change. In the foreground, some of the key changes have been in the expansion of suffrage, which is embodied most dramatically in the extension of the vote to women and native Americans and in the effects of the civil rights movement on the ability of blacks to vote and to hold office (in fact, it is worth mentioning that the original Constitution for the new State of New Jersey allowed women to

vote although this right was rescinded in 1807). Perhaps the most significant background transformation, maybe even more difficult to
read, is the impact of electronic communications media on the political process, an issue that will be be addressed in Part Two of this
project.

13. Wood, *CAR*, 183.

14. Cf. De Grazia, *PR*, 54. Here, it is important to mention
Kammen's qualifying assertion that, given the differences between
different colonies and between them and England, "It should therefore be clear that the traditional view—epitomized by Professor De
Grazia: 'on the whole . . . the colonial representative systems were
modeled after the English law'—is simplistic and perhaps mislead-
ing" (Kammen, *DL*, 54). In fact, turning the tables somewhat,
Kammen states of the seventeenth century that, "One might indeed
argue that English politics at mid-century were as much influenced
by New Englanders or men with strong connections there, such as
young Henry Vane and Richard Hutchinson, who had cut their parliamentary teeth in Massachusetts during the 1630s" (Kammen, *DL*,
55).

Kammen's point is an interesting one. However, it must be
supplemented by other, closely related considerations regarding
dependency, which are: (1) the colonists' reliance on the uncritically
formulated axioms of English political discourse (e.g., "mixed government"), (2) their dependence on English common law, as evidenced by references in the literature of pamphlets at the time (cf.
Bailyn, *IOAR*, 30ff.), as well as (3) their deference—strategic or not—
to English Parliamentary procedure, invoked in terms of precedence
(cf. Pole, *PRE*, 277).

Also—a point about residency requirements—Pole notes (*PRE*,
295) that residence requirements, rather than being the product of
"ideological" concerns, were sometimes (e.g., in cases in
Massachusets, Pennsylvania, and Virginia) the result of individual
political players trying to disqualify particular individuals from the
legislature rather than the result of a pure insistence on a simple
link in the logic of representation; here again, chance contributes
to the shape of history.

15. Cf. Pole, *PRE*, 401. Residential requirements for English
Parliament were finally repealed in 1774, a move that at least elim-
inated a certain institutional hypocrisy that may have conveniently
fit the theory of virtual representation. As Morgan sarcastically puts

it, "A statute of 1413 required that a representative be a resident of the borough that chose him, but the lawyers in the House of Commons quickly interpreted this to mean that he need not be a resident of the borough that chose him" (*IP*, 47).

16. Tom Paine, whose vision is oriented towards the future, understands the pitfalls of seeking origins—a transcendental signified—and legitimation in the past, the problem of trying to establish a source, which can always be pushed back further and which may not be so palatable once it is revealed. In *Common Sense*, he observes;

> This is supposing the present race of kings in the world to have had an honorable origin; whereas it is more than probable that, could we take off the dark covering of antiquity and trace them to their first rise, that we should find the first of them nothing better than the principal ruffian of some restless gang, whose savage manners or pre-eminence in subtilty obtained him the title of chief among plunderers and who, by increasing in power and extending his depredations, overawed the quiet and defenseless to purchase their safety by frequent contributions. (Paine, *Common Sense and Other Political Writings* [New York: Bobbs-Merrill Co. Inc., 1953], henceforth *CS*, 14)

Paine continues; "William the Conqueror . . . A French bastard landing with an armed banditti and establishing himself king of England against the consent of the natives is in plain terms a very paltry, rascally original" (*CS*, 15). Later, in *RM*, he cleverly turns Burke's invocation of tradition (in *RRF*) against him more than once. For example: "Hard as Mr. Burke laboured the Regency Bill and Hereditary Succession two years ago, and much as he dived for precedents, he still has not boldness enough to bring up William of Normandy, and say, There is the head of the list! there is the fountain of honour! the son of a prostitute, and the plunderer of the English nation" (henceforth cited as *RM*, 118). Paine repeatedly makes the point that those who look to the past for legitimation never go back far enough to reveal the destabilizing force of truth. Is this something like a protodeconstructive operation, a deconstruction of origins?

17. I will fly loosely for the moment, inserting "place" in the place of the subject of representation, the variable subject position, which, as we have seen, had already been filled by land and then by

national interests. Roughly speaking, this place is what becomes the electoral district.

18. De Grazia, *PR*, 56. Kammen cites basically the same list of features commonly differentiating early colonial representative assemblies from Parliament, *DL*, 67.

"Place-holding" meant holding Crown appointments, which would have conflicted with the balance believed to be achievable by "mixed government," by government made up of the Crown, the House of Lords (temporal and spiritual), and the House of Commons.

19. Here, the impelling, chance impact of geography determines an east-west pattern that recurs in different American colonies. By and large, commercial interests—those, generally, of seaboard merchants—tended to dominate the eastern counties, while frontier districts (not necessarily formalized yet into the geopolitical division of the county) tended to be more directly focused on and tied to the land itself. We might point out that "land" here has a significance very different from what it had meant in England. In England, it had involved an entire complex of feudal significations, while for the pioneers, land was what directly supported them in the present, and it was the ground of their future rather than of their past.

Of course "directly supported" is not as self-evident, self-identical, or direct as it may seem. It translates into such things as a political interest in and a desire to control potentially hostile natives, who, in turn, felt their territory, their land (and way of life), threatened, but who were also utterly excluded from the systems of direct and indirect representation that were marking up that land and destroying the tribes. They were not, however, excluded from the economic dimensions of representation (e.g., the fur trade) or from being used in war by Europeans against other Europeans (the most outstanding example is the French and Indian Wars).

The tradition offers the image of eastern Indians as stupid or gullible (in addition to being heartless savages); the archetype here is the story about the twenty-four dollars worth of trinkets exchanged for Manhattan. However, recent historians (e.g., Roy Harvey Pearce, Francis Jennings, and James Axtell) take a very different perspective, often presenting the "Indians" (another leveling category that obscures the differences between tribes) as quite cognizant of the threat posed by the whites, and, among other things, desperate, using every strategy possible to delay the inevitable and wringing what they could out of a no-win situation (e.g., Staten Island was sold as a whole by one local tribe on three separate occasions, twice to the Dutch and once to the English; one wonders if the Indians considered the whites to be stupid, as well as heartless, destructive savages).

20. Pole, *PRE*, 173ff. Pole points out that thirty qualified voters implied a population of roughly 150. Also, only officially recognized towns and districts qualified for this right, which left other settlements outside the network of direct representation.

21. Ibid., 177.

22. A common theme in twentieth century histories of this period is that colonial representation actually revived medieval English forms of representation (more direct from the outset), insofar as representatives stood in and could speak for only the local geopolitical territory from which they came (cf. Bailyn, *IOAR*, 162-64; Wood, *CAR*, 184). While this is an interesting and worthwhile analogy, it should be grasped only loosely, and this for at least two reasons. One—an obvious point—is that while it is important to point out the way that history repeats itself, it is a mistake to let the recognition of repetition obscure critical differences; no historian would argue with this point. Second, though, this analogy may be based upon a slightly distortive, traditional reading of medieval representation. When the king went to war—not an infrequent occurrence in the Middle Ages—his necessary attempts to persuade his lords to support him (via assembled representatives), could not always be restricted to "local" issues. Also, and to repeat a vital, correlative point made in an earlier chapter, the barons were aware of themselves and of their power as a group—more than just in terms of individual name and territory—from, generally speaking, Magna Carta on, and so power-discourse had a horizontal tangent amongst the barons—an effective displacement of the local sphere by the concerns of the community of the realm—as well as an apparently vertical tangent connecting the Crown to the individual barons. Thus, while certain characteristics of American colonial representation may appear to be regressive and to revive old medieval forms, this coincidence should not be pushed too hard, or taken too literally. There can be no return to the past.

23. Pole, 69-70.

24. Ibid., 282.

25. Ibid., 286.

26. Kammen, *DL*, 62ff.

27. Bailyn explores this binary opposition in Chapter III of *IOAR*, "Power and Liberty: A Theory of Politics." It is worth noting that the metaphysical opposition between these two identities continues to have a powerfully determinative effect in political theory, as embodied in formulations such as "a politics of rational (free) discourse" versus "a (non)politics of coercion," or "free talk" versus "violence" ("right" versus "might," etc.). This is a very dangerous dyad, since it is based upon a classical, self-serving misreading of power, one that renders the philosopher either (1) ineffectual in the fight against power or (2) the natural choice for king (or e.g., vanguard of the proletariat). The deconstruction of the opposition between power and liberty is one of the most significant deconstructions for political theory.

28. To suggest that an idea is "in the air" is not to claim that it appears from out of the blue. One of the grander genealogical narratives pertinent here would be Nietzsche's in *Genealogy of Morals*, where he links the ascendance of reason and the demise of Christianity to the Christian value of honesty; here, honesty eventually leads to confessing that God is a fiction.

The significance of the pseudo-technical phrase "in the air" will acquire a different significance, one with more weight, in Chapter VII of this volume, when the focus shifts to representation in the contemporary age of "information," in a "communications" culture, in which politics is largely a media affair and ideas are literally in the air and on the air, transmitted on the airwaves, picked up by radio and TV.

29. Cf. Dick Hebdige, *Subculture: the Meaning of Style* (London: Methuen, 1979), 12ff.

30. Now, two hundred years later, it is obvious that "nature" is a fragile thing and a thing that requires a tremendous effort to produce. The production of "natural" rights continues to demand enormous labor, including the labor of/for democracy, a true battle.

31. As with all metaphysical oppositions, the division between the two sides turns out not to be so clear and exclusive as each side would like to believe. In this case, the actual representation that had so much discursive support in America ended up involving the continued institution of virtual representation as well, as may become clear in later chapters.

32. Here we may encounter some resonances with the traditional assessment of Athenian democracy, which tends to emphasize that the limitations of this democracy were limitations of the practical scope of freedom. The limitations here are associated with the restricted scope of participation since women, slaves, and foreigners were formally excluded from the active political process. The historical irony is that American democracy has harbored some strikingly similar exclusions—women, slaves, and foreigners—and thus limitations for much of its history.

33. It is worth remarking here that the popular civics notion that eighteenth century Americans had no perspective on slavery and just lived with (and by means of) and accepted it, for example— that they (white people) were somehow naive (compared to us) and that they just did not understand—is simply historically inaccurate. Many were led to question and vigorously criticize the institution of slavery, some through a secularized discourse of natural rights—one logic of which necessarily stressed the universality of equality—others through humanitarian versions of basic Christian morals. Going way back, it was clear to many that the slavery issue would eventually explode.

It is worth drawing attention to the following semi-random but pertinent textual-historical notes here: 1) While the first cargo of twenty African slaves was delivered to Virginia in 1619, an early protest was registered against the slavery of blacks in a February 18, 1688 resolution passed by Germantown Mennonites in Pennsylvania (cf. Henry Steele Commager, ed., *Documents of American History* [New York: F. S. Crofts & Co., 1935], 37-38); 2) The first pamphlet published by Paine in America was entitled "African Slavery in America," a direct attack on the slavery of blacks in the colonies (published March, 1775); 3) Benjamin Rush, one of the signers of the Declaration of Independence and a member of the Continental Congress, among other distinctions in his life, founded the first American antislavery society; 4) While it cannot be forgotten that Jefferson himself was a slaveowner, his Declaration of Independence, with its list of grievances against the King, included a paragraph protesting the King's suppression of American legislation to prohibit or restrain the slave trade (the Continental Congress deleted this paragraph since not all slaveowners shared Jefferson's perspective that this was a grievance); 5) James Madison, another Virginian slaveowner, acknowledges the problem of slavery, albeit utterly

188   *The Trace of Political Representation*

uncritically, when he says, "and it is admitted that if the laws were
to restore the rights which have been taken away, the negroes could
no longer be refused an equal share of representation with the other
inhabitants" (*Federalist 54*), a statement that is by no means part of
an antislavery argument but which nevertheless ambivalently recognizes "natural rights," while at the same time granting legitimacy
to the laws that negate these rights.

34. "Natural/artificial." It is worth tagging this opposition even
if it would be beyond the scope of this project to deconstructively
engage this classical, metaphysical dyad as it operates in the economy of the discourse of natural rights or of social contract theory.

35. Jean Baudrillard uses the phrase "scene and mirror" in
Simulations to describe the scene of representation, a very effective
image, against which he counterposes what he asserts has displaced
this scene, namely, "the screen and network."

36. The difficult relationship between these two will be
touched on shortly.

37. John Locke, "An Essay Concerning the True Original,
Extent and End of Civil Government," in Ernest Barker, ed., *Social
Contract: Essays by Locke, Hume, and Rousseau* (London: Oxford
University Press, 1960), 29-30, henceforth cited as *ST*.

38. Locke advances a definition of property that is not just
coincidentally similar to Marx's much later one (in short, property is
labor mixed with matter and congealed in products). The determinative appearance of what could be seen as a variant of Locke's definition of private property in Marx's labor theory of value is a strong,
specific example of what is implied by Foucault's provocatively
phrased challenge to the notion that Marx's theory is revolutionary:

> At the deepest level of Western knowledge, Marxism intro-
> duced no real discontinuity; it found its place without diffi-
> culty, as a full, quiet, comfortable and, goodness knows, satis-
> fying form for a time (its own), within an epistemological
> arrangement that welcomed it gladly (since it was this arrange-
> ment that was in fact making room for it) and that it, in return,
> had no intention of disturbing and, above all, no power to mod-
> ify, even one jot, since it rested entirely upon it. Marxism exists
> in the nineteenth-century thought like a fish in water: that is, it
> is unable to breathe anywhere else. (Michel Foucault, *The*

Order of Things, trans. anon. [New York: Vintage Books, 1973], 261-62.]

39. Locke, *ST*, 55 and 70ff.

40. Cf. Plato, *Crito*.

42. Locke, *ST*, 55.

43. Ibid., 73.

43. Ibid., 96.

44. Ibid. 133.

45. Nighttime eyes skyward, taking in the stars, stumbling into a ditch with Thales, who, we know it has been said, once predicted a bumper olive crop on the basis of astronomical observations and then quietly rented out all of the local, Milesian olive presses early in the season, thereby setting up a monopoly that enabled him to make a killing that year. With Thales, I ask if there is not a sense in which (1) ground has always been the stuff beneath our feet and (2) property or, rather, profit(ing) has always been the good(s). It may be Nietzsche who helps most here, as he answers indefinitely, yes and no: yes insofar as profiting is linked to power (a power to which even Thales had to submit in order "to make his point" about philosophy to the community); no insofar as property (and its movement) is not the essential explanation.

46. "Put on exhibit." This phrase could refer both to museum displays and to the courtroom, where exhibits are used to help make a case.

47. Aristotle, master of division, delineated three good versions of these—monarchy, aristocracy, and polity—and three bad versions—tyranny, oligarchy, and extreme democracy or anarchy—in order to distinguish those types that hit the mark from those that miss it (cf. *Politics*, Bk. 3, chap. 7). For Plato, however, the internal logics of the three political types may destroy the possibility of a just polis, a terrifying possibility which emerges when Plato violently deconstructs them in Book XIII of the *Republic*.

It can be argued that Book XIII of the *Republic* is a deconstruction rather than an external critique since (in Plato's narrative) it is the very logic of each of the three governmental forms discussed there that is their undoing, that is, it is not outside forces or (critical)

discourses that destroy them in Plato's narrative. Nor is this deconstruction a dialectic since there is no productive exchange, no
advance, and no truth recovered, except that the ideal Republic—the
city in words—degenerates from one political form to another—from
the Republic to timocracy, to oligarchy, to democracy—ending up in
the very despotism which must stand opposed to the justice Plato's
characters seem to be seeking.

48. Wood, *CAR*, 199. Wood's discussion of the issue of mixed
government and the representation of property is extremely helpful.

49. By the seventeenth century, the Crown had come to be
considered as a separate estate, while the Church (the Lords
Spiritual) had ceased to be thought of as a separate estate, having
been incorporated into the nobility and commons. This is one significant difference between medieval and modern politics.
In order to understand the conceptually convoluted problem
of how the King could represent himself (construed as a separate
estate), it is necessary to refer again to the Theory of the King's Two
Bodies, which originated in early medieval theories about the dual-
natured Christ. The reason that Charles I was beheaded in the name
and under the authority of Charles I via the medium of Parliament,
was that he, Charles of the flesh, was doing a bad job representing
the estate of the Crown, representing the other Charles, whose
authority was derived from God Himself and whose body was the
body politic, a body ill-served by Charles of the flesh (cf.
Kantorowicz, *KTB*).

50. Morgan argues that at least the immediate model for the
bicameral legislature was not Parliament but the colonial (i.e.,
already American) legislatures (*IP*, 248-49).

51. Cf. Pole, *PRE*, 292.

52. Wood, *CAR*, 217.

53. Cf. Pole, *PRE*, 82. According to this plan, which was never
adopted (and which was not William Penn's favorite), the acreage
had to be purchased from the colonial proprietor (i.e., from the Penn
family) and if the holder's estate dropped to below 2,000 acres, his
membership in this upper house would be dissolved.

54. Wood, *CAR*.

55. Howard Zinn, *A People's History of the United States* (New York: Harper and Row, 1980), 82. Henceforth cited as *PH*.

56. Wood, 218.

57. Pole points out (*PRE*, 300) that in the debate about representation—and the issue of and anxiety about the representation of property in particular was about the security of property—"slavery indeed introduced one of those distinctions of interest which gave to the debate on the representation of interests and persons a hard and material urgency. This was never a debate about unsubstantial theories but always about the substance of power."

Once more, circumstances force critical analysis beyond straightforward oppositions between ideas (e.g., liberty) and forces (e.g., power), transforming their relationship into one of complicity, the force (and discourse) of power-knowledge.

58. While on the topic of Federal authority over political/legal practices within the individual states, it is important not to forget conservative Federalist's (e.g., Hamilton's) opposition to a Bill of Rights. Eventually, the Constitution would tell the states how to conduct their voting practices, a developing process that took its first direct form in the 15th Amendment to the Bill of Rights, which was adopted in 1870 (Sec. 1. The right of citizens of the United States to vote shall not be denied or abridged by the United States or by any State on account of race, color, or previous condition of Servitude; Sec. 2. The Congress shall have power to enforce this article by appropriate legislation). In this sense, it is a mistake to imagine that the Federalists beat the Anti-Federalists since the latter, though they lost one battle, were partially responsible for the oppositional political movement and discourse that led three years later to the adoption of the Bill of Rights.

59. The pertinent passage of the Constitution reads: "Representatives and direct taxes shall be apportioned among the several States which may be included within this Union, according to their respective numbers, which shall be determined by adding to the whole number of free persons, including those bound to service for a term of years, and excluding Indians not taxed, three fifths of all other persons."

An Anti-Federalist response to this specific passage:

"In a free state," says the celebrated Montesquieu, "every man, who is supposed to be a free agent, ought to be concerned in his own government, therefore the legislature should reside in the whole body of the people, or their representatives." But it has never been alledged that those who are not free agents, can, upon any rational principle, have any thing to do in government, either by themselves or others. If they have no share in government, why is the number of members in the assembly, to be increased on their account? Is it because in some of the states, a considerable part of the property of the inhabitants consists in a number of their fellow men, who are held in bondage, in defiance of every idea of benevolence, justice, and religion, and contrary to all the principles of liberty, which have been publickly avowed in the late glorious revolution? If this be a just ground for representation, the horses in some of the states, and the oxen in others, ought to be represented—for a great share of property in some of them, consists in these animals; and they have as much controul over their own actions, as these poor unhappy creatures, who are intended to be described in the above recited clause, by the words, "all other persons" (Brutus, *Essay III*, included in Pole, *AC*, 44).

However, and to avoid simply repeating an erroneous piece of Americana, it is worth repeating one of the key, convincing points of Kenyon's important essay, which is that "The Anti-Federalists were not latter-day democrats" (Cecelia Kenyon, "Men of Little Faith: The Anti-Federalists on the Nature of Representative Government," *William & Mary Quarterly* 12 (January 1955), henceforth *MLF*, 42), regardless of their opposition to a constitution "which they thought to be aristocratic in origin and intent" (ibid., 5).

60. Fortunately for American representative democracy, intent does not lie latent in texts. By which I mean not only to draw attention to the obvious point that there is no intent tucked away in the Constitution (minds do not adhere to pieces of paper) but also to the fact that this is one of the things that makes the American Constitution workable. It is not a finished or completable text. Like all texts, it remains open both to interpretation and supplementation and to amendment. The legislative and judicial branches of government continue writing it.

It is worth remembering that Thomas Jefferson believed that the Constitution should be rewritten every generation, an aggressive, unmetaphysical vision of the future.

61. Pole, *PRE*, 356ff.

62. Wood, *CAR*, 163.

63. Philosophers may be interested to know that the emblem of the participants of the working-class Shays' Rebellion was a sprig of hemlock.

64. "This was just the sort of episode they had heard of before." Pole, *AC*, 10.

65. Quoted by De Grazia, *PR*, 100.

66. The final chapter of this project will include reference to the Trilateral Commission's *Report on the Governability of Democracies* (Michel Crozier, Samuel P. Huntington, Joji Watanuki, *The Crisis of Democracy: Report on the Governability of Democracies to the Trilateral Commission* [New York: New York University Press, 1975] henceforth cited as *CD*). The dominant value in play in this report (its bias) is inscribed in the title itself, which provides an image of harnessed democracy, or democracy in control.

67. "Dominant opinion": Part Two of this investigation will try to determine the meaning of this in connection with procedures of counting.

68. Pole, *AC*, 222.

69. Robert W. Shoemaker, "'Democracy' and 'Republic' as Understood in Late Eighteenth-Century America," henceforth "DR," *American Speech* 41 (1966), 89, 95. See note.

70. Paine, *CS*, 7. Paine's valorization of simplicity can be read a variety of ways. For one, it can and should be read as the archetypal metaphysical dream (which, alternatively, could be read as a Freudian dream). For another, it can be read as an anticipation of the productive horrors of the kind of modern state apparatus embodied in massive bureaucracy.

71. Ibid., 8.

72. Quoted by Wood, *CAR*, 225.

73. Ibid., 231.

74. This image of diversity belongs in part to the liberal tradition of pluralism, which is the tradition of tolerance. It escapes the

confines of this tradition if democracy is viewed from the stand-point of institutionalized political warfare, rather than from the standpoint of consensus (the latter is a nodal point for liberalism and for all rationalist philosophies of liberation). "Equality," for instance, may refer less to an actual (or potentially realizable) status than it does to the (relational) possibility of effectively engaging in this warfare and of asserting difference.

I will pursue these kinds of possibilities in the final chapter of this project. Here, I will cite only these important remarks about Foucault: "And Foucault shows that the law is now no more a state of peace than the result of a successful war: it is war itself, and the strategy of this war in action, just as power is not the property of the dominant class but the strategy of that class in action," Deleuze, *F*, 30.

75. Wood, *CAR*, 385.

76. Cited by Kenyon, *MLF*, 25. While his conception of "different branches" would be different from Madison's, the point here is that the Federalists and the Anti-Federalists shared common conceptual ground (not perhaps anything as fancy or basic as an *episteme*, but they were speaking the same political language), in their confidence that it is the issue of "the security of the people" that is "generally understood." Kenyon emphasizes other common ground shared by the Federalists and Anti-Federalists, as well.

77. From a vantage point across the ocean, this all seemed very strange:

> The French *philosophes*, as they gradually became aware of the nature of the new state governments, tempered their initial excitement at watching republics being created with their amazement at seeing the institution of upper houses in the new states. They could only conclude that the new American constitutions were too much the children of the parent, too much influenced by the English form of govenment. . . . For the philosophes the nation could have only a single interest. Indeed, this was the assumption of republicanism. . . . Since, as Condorcet pointed out, "the representatives of a single nation naturally form a single body," there was no place for a senate in an egalitarian republic (Wood, *CAR*, 236).

78. An argument could be made that it is not until 1964, with the adoption of Article XXIV, that the connection between property

and suffrage is "finally" laid to rest (i.e., most recently addressed) in the Constitution: "Sec. 1. The right of citizens of the United States to vote . . . shall not be denied or abridged by the United States or any State by reason of failure to pay any poll tax or other tax."

79. While Charles Beard (*An Economic Interpretation of the Constitution of the United States* [New York: Macmillan Co., 1939]) may seem to push too much for a kind of economic determinism (a charge he vigorously denied), he documents some rather startling, specific, and almost systematic connections between, in particular, individual Federalists and financial interests ("money, public securities, manufactures, and trade and shipping"), concluding that "The Constitution was essentially an economic document based upon the concept that the fundamental private rights of property are anterior to government and morally beyond the reach of popular majorities," and that "The Constitution was not created by 'the whole people' as the jurists have said; neither was it created by 'the states' as Southern nullifiers long contended; but it was the work of a consolidated group whose interests knew no state boundaries and were truly national in their scope" (324-25).

Howard Zinn (*PH*) marshals a wide range of similar, not-so-surprising evidence about what cashes out into the power of capital in connection not just with the Constitution but with the Revolutionary and post-Revolutionary period as a whole.

One way of stating my position would be to suggest that despite these marked interests that actively helped determine the shape of American representation (which should be taken seriously but not in a paranoid spirit), America nevertheless generated political and specifically democratic transformations. Some might think it non-committal to compromise democracy with "scare-quotes," but it is not, since the effect is not to negate it but simply to highlight the problematic profile of its identity.

80. Marking a closely related point and in contrast with the previous footnote, Pole pushes things to one of the mundane, everyday places they should be pushed when he says that "there was nothing inevitable about the Constitution that emerged from the deliberations at Philadelphia. As one reads the debates, it is not difficult to imagine that a majority might have favored a different arrangement" (*AC*, 13). Images of contingency like his should help keep historians, political scientists, and philosophers (who are trained to seek and formulate necessity rather than contingency,

logic rather than chance), more sober than they might be without them.

81. While a Marxist analysis of the configurations of post-Revolutionary American political opposition might throw some light on things—property and opposition to it certainly played an important role—it might tend to clarify the terms of opposition more than conditions of that time warrant, that is, to make things too clear. For instance, Kenyon points out that the Anti-Federalists were not great believers in the potential wisdom of "the people," that is, of the majority (e.g., it would simply be inaccurate to reduce the Federalist/Anti-Federalist opposition to a property/people opposition).

82. Again, the observation that a "text" is not (just) a "book" is more than academic hairsplitting.

83. Once more, intention (consciousness) is not what is at issue here; the claim is not that anyone actually believed such a story about the status of the Constitution (in fact, cynicism was widespread on all sides at the time), but that this is the philosophy implied and inscribed by their arguments and actions. Here, intention refers us once again to the hermeneutic of original intent, a philosophy produced by and completely in line with the logic of conservative American political discourse, which seeks stable, transcendental conditions—the origin of the origin—behind the manifest text. In response to this philosophy, Gore Vidal asked during the Bork hearings: Who knows what those fifty-five, mostly well-to-do white men had in mind 200 years ago? Vidal's question is certainly one of the more concrete, to-the-point refutations of this particular kind of ontology.

84. On the one hand, it may be true that the new aristocracy gave up enough popular government to keep the masses happy and that the Bill of Rights has this palliative aspect. Once inscribed, the intentions of those aristocrats no longer defined or completely controlled either the masses or the Bill of Rights, and this is part of the movement of democracy in America.

85. A constitution constitutes a strange metaphysics, insofar as it is both law and not law, both law and the ground of law. Insofar as it is the ground of law, it is difficult for it to be law on the mundane level, a tension captured by the conflict between Article XVIII (1919),

Prohibition (law on the mundane level) and Article XXI (1933), its repeal, which is at the same time an admission of the sense in which laws do not belong inside the Constitution even though laws cannot be outside of it, either. Here, of course, my implicit invocation of law and Law invites a necessary deconstruction.

86. The "openness" referred to here should not be equated with "open-mindedness" (which always has its limits), so much as with openness to change, which refers to an intrinsic potential for malleability or transformation of limits, as well as to struggle, which includes the struggle over interpretation.

For a thoughtful discussion of these issues about writing, one related specifically to the American Constitution, cf. Sanford Levinson, "Writing and Its Discontents," *Tikkun* 3, no. 2 (March/April 1988).

87. At a dinner party, Castoriadis once expressed surprise at the suggestion that Plato was a conservative, noting that conservatives are people who do not want to change things, while Plato's drastic changes—orchestrated by the One (i.e., by Plato, the one with the hotline to Truth)—constitute the extreme reordering (toward a 'better' world) that is the hallmark of fascism.

88. One of the most consistent and shameful illustrations of the fact that written guarantees guarantee nothing (or certainly very little), is the history of treaties between white governments and Native American tribes (cf. Vine Deloria, Jr., *On the Trail of Broken Treaties* [New York: Delta Books, 1974]). Here, it must be acknowledged that Canada has done far more to compensate for these deficiencies in recent years.

89. Cf. Montesquieu, *The Spirit of the Laws*, bk. 8, chap. 16 in *Selected Political Writings* (Indianapolis: Hackett Books, 1990). If there was one, unifying concern amongst the Anti-Federalists in all of their scepticism, this was it, which was why they wanted to keep power on the side of local government and why they opposed a strong, centralized federal government.

90. Paine, *RM*, 180. In Paine's use of "miniature," it is difficult not to detect very contrasting, even if apparently arbitrary, surface resonances with John Adams' famous image (this as actually a common analogy) of the representative assembly as a miniature portrait of the people as a whole. Paine's association of "miniature" with

Athens and not with America, which he associates with "magnitude," might be read as a signal recognizing that the type of simple representative relationship—a relationship of correspondence—connoted by "miniature portrait" is not what representation can be about here in this vast land with its diverse populations, which might be directly contrasted with the different, less complex, apparently more simply unifiable range of possibilities available to a city-state.

91. It is worth emphasizing here (1) the general point that an anxiety about the continuing unity of the community has been central to western political philosophy from the outset and (2) that we see an similar concern with "factions" in, outstandingly, Aristotle and Machiavelli.

In the *Politics* (bk. 4, chap. 11 in *The Basic Works of Aristotle* edited by Richard McKeon [New York: Random House, 1941]), Aristotle argues that the best condition for a good political community is the presence of a large middle class to mediate and defuse the natural tensions between the wealthy and the poor: "Where the middle class is large, there are least likely to be factions and dissensions" (*Politics*, line 1296a8-9).

In *The Prince* (chap. 9, "The Constitutional Principality"), Machiavelli notes that the wealthy and the poor are invariably at odds with each other and that the prince must account for this in the construction of his power base in the community: "The people are everywhere anxious not to be dominated or oppressed by the nobles, and the nobles are out to dominate and oppress the people" (*The Prince*, trans. George Bull (Harmondsworth: Penguin Books, 1982), p. 67).

92. At the same time, though, factions is precisely what democracy is an embodiment of, which is one reason why the image of institutionalized warfare (not just a game!) seems so appropriate for democracy.

93. "The American states were neither simple democracies nor traditional mixed governments. They had become in all branches governments by representation," Wood, *CAR*, 387.

94. The difference between the use of the lower-case with "democracy" and the upper-case with "Republic" is a metaphysical difference, with the metaphysics in the Republic, and the difference in the democracy.

95. Marxists might argue that this range hangs between two very definite poles, that of property (capital) and that of the people (labor), two poles that translate on the practical level into the opposition between capitalism and socialism. However, it may be better not to sink these poles too deeply into the ground. That is, while recognizing these poles, we would like to keep the field open for other possibilities, too, such as the productive effects of communications technologies. We will address these issues in Part Two.

96. It is conceivable that if an investigation of "sign" was initiated from the image of this type of signing, the results would be very different from those of an investigation oriented to the traditional, metaphysical, immaterial, binary sign to which semiology tends to submit itself. In conjunction with this image of "sign" as associated with the act or event of signing (e.g., a document), the image of markmaking, lifted from the discourse and practice of art, might also be fruitful.

97. For a compact but informative description of this inclusion, cf. Zinn, *PH*, the chapter entitled, "The Intimately Oppressed," 102-123.

98. "More than half the colonists who came to the North American shores in the colonial period came as servants," (ibid., 46) which was usually in the form of an indenture entered into in exchange for ship's passage to America.

99. Cf. C. H. McIlwain, "Medieval Estates," in *Cambridge Medieval History, Vol. 7* (Cambridge: Cambridge University Press, 1932), 668, and, more recently, Edmund S. Morgan, *Inventing the People* (New York: W.W. Norton, 1988), henceforth cited as *IP*.

100. Morgan, *IP*, 14.

Chapter IV

1. Shorthand; both of these formations of representation count on a transcendental condition, a transcendental signified, something outside of themselves (I will talk more about counting in the final chapter).

Postured as it is against the metaphysics of virtual representation—in opposition to which direct or literal representation is differentially constituted—it is easy and tempting to begin believing that direct representation is real, i.e., is real representation in contrast with a representation centered around interests, with the deliberative, representative discourse-practice that calls itself virtual. Once again, it is a story of the sophistic (the virtual) pitted against the philosophical (the actual), of desire against reason, of power and corruption against the truth, of might against right (for a shorthand version of the progress of this problem, and of the determination of the value of these values, cf. (a) Plato, (b) Nietzsche, and (c) Foucault on truth and power).

However, while the wild and perilously metaphysical character of virtual representation was as apparent to the advocates of direct representation back in the 18th century as it is to us today, it is worth repeating here that Burke condemned the possibility of an actual representation based upon natural rights philosophy (based upon the subject [as opposed to objective interests]) as, specifically, "metaphysical" (cf. Burke, *RRF*, 348).

2. Cf. Pitkin, *CR*, chapters 4 and 5 (as well as 6) for some interesting and helpful discussions of the various meanings of "standing for," a phrase that, among other things, embodies a wide range of connections with action.

3. "Truth as necessary error": The connection may not become clear until the end of this project, where I will argue that representation cannot be abandoned and that to believe that it should be—the call either to go beyond representation or to return to some simpler politics—is both dangerous, deluded, and a new and ancient metaphysic (again, cf. Derrida, *SR*, 311).

4. Cf. Jacques Derrida, "White Mythology," in *Margins in Philosophy*, trans. Alan Bass (Chicago: University of Chicago Press, 1982).

5. Paine, *RM*, 184.

6. J. Roland Pennock, "Political Representation: An Overview," in *Representation*, ed. J. Roland Pennock and John W. Chapman (New York: Atherton Press, 1968), 8.

7. Jürgen Habermas, *Legitimation Crisis*, trans. Thomas McCarthy (Boston: Beacon Press, 1975), 97, henceforth cited as *LC*.

8. "Hence the importance of Nietzsche," Michel Foucault, "Truth and Power," in *Power/Knowledge*, ed. Colin Gordon (New York: Pantheon Books, 1980).

9. Michel Foucault, *The History of Sexuality, Volume I: An Introduction*, trans. Robert Hurley (New York: Vintage Books, 1980).

10. "Contexts" is necessarily plural, partly because every "context" embodies different planes, including social, economic, cultural, political, technological, aesthetic, and the discursive planes and planes of representation associated with each of them. I refer again here to Braudel's advocacy of "concrete, pluridimensional history" (Fernand Braudel, "On a Concept of Social History," *OH*, 131), and also again to his remark;

> But even the word society is rather vague: we really ought to talk of socio-economies. Marx asked the right question: who owns the means of production, the land, the ships, the machinery, the raw materials, the finished products and, no less, the leading positions in society? It is, however, clear that the two coordinates: society and economy, are still not sufficient: the State, in all its forms, simultaneously cause and consequence, makes its presence felt, disturbs and affects relationships whether it seeks to or not, and often plays a very forceful role in those architectural systems that can be classified into a typology of world socio-economic systems: those based on slavery, those with serfs and overlords, those where there are businessmen and pre-capitalists. This is to return to the language used by Marx, and to walk some of the way with him, even if one rejects his precise words or the rigorous processes by which he saw every society moving from one stage to the next. (Braudel, *SEL*, 561)

11. Analogically, picture here the relationship between filmmaking hardware and the film that it makes possible; the camera constitutes the movie, but covers itself over, that is, does not appear in any direct way in the audio-visual scene. As Benjamin puts it, "The equipment-free aspect of reality here has become the height of artifice; the sight of immediate reality has become an orchid in the land of technology" (Walter Benjamin, "The Work of Art in the Age of Mechanical Reproduction," in *Illuminations*, trans. Harry Zohn [New York: Schocken, 1969] 233). It may be that avant-garde filmmakers such as Godard have changed this by using shooting techniques that draw attention to the equipment (e.g., handheld cameras, aggressively anti-"realist" framing, subjects looking and talking directly into the camera, etc., an aesthetic which has gained great

popularity in the advertising industry). However, it is also likely that such self-conscious techniques only generate different possibilities for the technology to cover itself up, particularly as an anti-realist aesthetic begins to acquire its own reality, that is, begins to be taken as the truth (e.g., this is the way life *really* looks). In recent years, and in pursuit of an image of authenticity, the advertising industry has followed the avant-garde into the world of handheld cameras.

NOTE: It could be argued that the condition of the possibility of a political cover-up is the self-covering that is one of the dimensions of productive discourse and practice.

12. Lefort, "Outline of the Genesis of Ideology in Modern Societies," *PFMS*, 184. Henceforth "OGI."

13. Lefort, "The Logic of Totalitarianism," *PFMS*, 282.

14. Ibid.

15. Cf. Maurice Merleau-Ponty, esp. *The Visible and the Invisible*, translated by Alphonso Lingis (Evanston: Northwestern University Press, 1969).

16. In contrast with a form of society Castoriadis describes as *instituting*—conscious of itself as the author of its identity—society sometimes appears as the "already-instituted." One form of the already-instituted would be the metaphysical assertion of an ontologically prior and independent reality, and one form of this, in turn, would be the assertion of an autonomous political subject. Cf. Castoriadis, *IIS*, 215.

17. Dick Howard, *The Marxian Legacy*, 2d Ed. (Minneapolis: University of Minnesota Press, 1988), 216.

18. Again, "Hence the importance of Nietzsche" (Foucault, "Truth and Power," *PK*, 131, 133). This statement could be read as an encapsulated version of one of the two vast sides currently debating each other in the field of social and political philosophy, the other side being critical theory, which, in particular, would dispute Foucault's association of (rather than opposition between) truth and power, arguing that Foucault represents the forces of postmodern irrationalism. Also, "Nietzsche" could be said to be one name for the point of disjunction between these two general camps (cf. Habermas' "The Entry into Postmodernity: Nietzsche as a Turning Point," in

The Philosophical Discourse of Modernity, translated by Frederick Lawrence [Cambridge: MIT Press, 1987]).

19. Again, cf. Braudel, *SEL*, 561.

20. Pitkin, *CR*, 180.

21. Henry Ford, *Representative Government* (New York: Henry Holt & Co., 1924), 175. Henceforth cited as *RG*.

22. Cornelius Castoriadis, "Technique," in *Crossroads in the Labyrinth*, trans. Kate Soper and Martin H. Ryle (Cambridge: MIT Press, 1984), 229. Henceforth cited as *T*.

23. Ibid., 237.

24. Ibid., 229.

25. Ibid., 239.

26. Ibid., 240.

27. Ibid., 241.

28. Ibid.

29. "Desire," "will to power," or something like these necessary and necessarily clumsy formulations.

30. Castoriadis, *IIS*, 135.

31. Cf. Martin Heidegger, "The Question Concerning Technology," in *Basic Writings*, ed. David Farrell Krell, trans. William Lovitt (Harper and Row: New York, 1977).

32. Karl Marx, "Wage Labour and Capital," *The Marx-Engels Reader*, ed. Robert C. Tucker (New York: W. W. Norton & Co., 1978), 207.

33. Going back to the fourteenth century, Swiss pikemen—footsoldiers, commoners—had already made significant and very concrete contributions on the battlefield to the demise of the feudal warrior, the mounted and heavily armored noble, the knight. While still far from the modern organization of the army, the firearm sealed the stunned and humiliated knight's fate. The effects of the firearm were slow in coming, and clearly by no means isolated from other factors, but they contributed to this transformation, which was coextensive with the demise of feudalism.

34. Heidegger, "The Question Concerning Technology."

35. Cf. Jacques Derrida, "Differance."

CHAPTER V

1. Rousseau, "The Social Contract," in *Social Contract*, ed. Ernest Barker (New York: Oxford University Press, 1979), 190, henceforth cited as *SC*.

2. A. F. Pollard, *The Evolution of Parliament* (New York: Russell & Russell, 1964), 152.

3. President Reagan's "Farewell Address," delivered January 11, 1989, transcript printed in *The New York Times*, January 12, 1989, B8.

4. Quoted by Neil Postman, *Amusing Ourselves to Death* (New York: Penguin Books, 1985), 125. Henceforth cited as *AOD*.

5. For example: the Iran-Contra scandal (which dissolved into memories of the Oliver North Special), the various Meese scandals, the various Pentagon procurement scandals, the Bork debacle (followed by the clumsy Ginsburg nomination), and the fact that by spring 1988 at least 110 members of the Reagan administration had been indicted or were under investigation for various forms of corruption. The scandals perpetuated during his presidency continued surfacing well after it was over (e.g., the multifaceted H.U.D. scandal), as did their general tendency to dissolve unresolved, which was perhaps paradigmatically exemplified by the overturning of the Nofziger conviction for influence-peddling and by the Iran-Contra affair's remarkable lack of impact, sealed by President Bush's pardoning of Caspar Weinberger and other high-ranking officials.

6. This observation does not imply that these configurations and values continue to mean the same thing.

7. While I will limit my comment simply to pointing it out, it is not accidental that all of these oppositions map onto each other, that the sides all line up. For example, all are capable of being fit into something like a "mandate-independence" framework. However, while they map onto each other, they do not map onto the specific opposition that I am about to mention, the one they all assume and share in common. This one provides a condition for the possibility of

taking a position rather than itself being a position in the same sense, that is, rather than being a position within an established discourse. It could be said that this is a form of the metaphysical gesture in general, that is, the hierarchically cast relation between the real and its representation.

8. Heinz Eulau, "Changing Views of Representation," in *Contemporary Political Science: Toward Empirical Theory*, ed. Ithiel de Sola Pool (New York: McGraw-Hill, 1967), 79.

9. Note the gender-free formulation, which, as is the case with any instrument, underscores the neutrality and nonpersonal identity associated with the representative.

10. Locke, *SC*, 123.

11. Ibid., 124.

12. Of course this is not what Lenin intends to describe in *State and Revolution* (New York: International Publishers, 1932), but an argument can be made that it is what the logic of his words is destined to inscribe.

13. The term "leveling" is one with dense connotations in the history of western political discourse. Conservatively inclined thinkers have used it to express disdain for more democratic forces and for the mediocrity these forces are seen to represent. The Marxist tradition has used it to describe the effects of capitalism, as it reduces value to exchange value, quality to quantity and human beings to machines.

14. "For Nietzsche, it was not a matter of knowing what good and evil were in themselves, but of who was being designated, or rather who was speaking when one said Agathos to designate oneself and Deilos to designate others. For it is there, in the holder of the discourse and, more profoundly still, in the possessor of the word, that language is gathered together in its entirety," Michel Foucault, *The Order of Things*, trans. anon. (New York: Vintage Books, 1973), 305, henceforth cited as *OT*.

15. Pitkin, *CR*, 163.

16. Cf. for example, Paul Virilio and Sylvere Lotringer, *Pure War*, trans. Mark Polizotti (New York: Semiotext[e], 1983).

17. Crozier et al., *CD*, 96. In the distant shadow of Huntington's

words here is Rousseau's observation, cited in below in the main text.

18. Niccolò Machiavelli, *The Prince*, trans. George Bull (Harmondsworth: Penguin Books, 1982), 90-91.

19. Here it becomes clear that "observation" and "prescription" are no more opposed to (or clearly distinct from) each other than are "objective" and "subjective," a couplet related to the observation/prescription couplet. Cf. Nietzsche's famous critique of objectivity as a symptom of ascetic ideals and his suggestion of the necessity for a "future 'objectivity'":

> There is only a perspective seeing, only a perspective "knowing"; and the more affects we allow to speak about one thing, the more eyes, different eyes, we can use to observe one thing, the more complete will our "concept" of this thing, our "objectivity," be. But to eliminate the will altogether, to suspend each and every affect, supposing we were capable of this—what would that mean but to castrate the intellect? (*The Genealogy of Morals*, 3d Essay, Sec. 12, trans. Walter Kaufmann (New York: Vintage, 1969) 119. Henceforth cited as *GM*).

20. Even during elections, support is a very flexible and often malleable phenomenon.

21. Neither does Michael Domhoff's analysis of power in America suggest the conclusion that it is "the people" who govern (cf. *Who Governs America Now?* [Englewood Cliffs, N.J.: Prentice-Hall, 1983]).

22. With "Ritual of election," the archaeology of political representation takes an ethnographic turn.

23. This conflict could be thought through a Foucauldian inversion of von Clausewitz' famous image of war as "not merely an act of policy but a true political instrument, a continuation of political intercourse, carried on with other means" (Carl von Clausewitz, *On War*, ed. and trans. Michael Howard and Peter Paret [Princeton: Princeton University Press, 1984] 87); it might be strategically asserted that politics is an extension of war by other means (cf. Foucault, "Truth and Power," in *Power/Knowledge*). This might have the effect of forcing a more serious consideration of conflict although consensus on this theoretical or metaphorical move

remains unlikely (as consensus always remains unlikely, we never agree with each other). I will address this possibility later.

24. "Agreement among whom?," is one way of approaching the question of the political subject, of asking what it is that gets represented. Reducing the issue to the binary alternatives of the mandate-independence controversy or of popular sovereignty versus an elite sovereign (e.g., an elite social class) obscures important historical and cultural specificity, specificity that puts into question the notion of a self-evident political subject. Cf. the brief discussion of the Levellers a few paragraphs down in the main text.

25. Henry Ford, *RG*, 159.

26. Those who use "activist" to describe a type of judge, do it to contrast that type with themselves. On the one side, it is asserted, are the liberal activists, who actively and interventively interpret the law in conjunction with their own personal, subjective perspective (i.e., political or ideological perspective). On the other side— the conservative, objective, and grounded side—are the ontologists, whose reading of the law is based upon the worship of a phantasm, the original text or original intent, a perspective which is itself a thoroughly political metaphysics. The originalists are equally as "active" in their readings of and rulings on the law since they are just as much interpreters as any other kind of judge (meddlers all!) and since their interpretations are no less perspectival than any others. The ongoing effects of the massive reformation of the Supreme Court in the 1980s and 1990s have made this clear and will continue to do so for many years.

The basic point is that there is no Law behind the law that would make possible a grounded, nonintervening, non-contextual reading/ruling, every one of which occurs within a discourse more specific than, for instance, some objective, absolute, universal "American Law."

27. Rousseau, *SC* (ed. Barker), 262.

28. Ibid., 260.

29. Foucault, *DP*, 194.

30. The mass-media are anti-mediatory and intransitive. They fabricate noncommunication—this is what characterizes them, if one agrees to define communication as an exchange, as a recipro-

cal space of a speech and a response and thus of a responsibility (not a psychological or moral responsibility but a personal, mutual correlation in exchange). We must understand communication as something other than the simple transmission-reception of a message, whether or not the latter is considered reversible through feedback. Now, the totality of the existing architecture of the media founds itself on this latter definition: they are what always prevents response, making all processes of exchange impossible except in various forms of response simulation themselves integrated in the transmission process, thus leaving the unilateral nature of the communication intact. This is the real abstraction of the media. And the system of social control and power is rooted in it. (Jean Baudrillard, "Requiem for the Media," in *For a Critique of the Political Economy of the Sign,* trans. Charles Levin [St. Louis: Telos Press, 1981], 169-170.)

As usual, Baudrillard's description is limited—closed off—by its absolutes (e.g., "always," "unilateral"), but he is getting at a very important development in "communication."

31. Gilles Deleuze and Félix Guattari, *A Thousand Plateaus,* trans. Brian Massumi (Minneapolis: University of Minnesota Press, 1987), 389.

32. A vote's power-value to use a Nietzschean strategy.

33. C. B. MacPherson, *The Political Theory of Possessive Individualism* (Oxford: Oxford University Press, 1962), 128, henceforth cited as *PTPI*. MacPherson cites strong evidence (*PTPI*, chap. 3) that despite dominant historical memory, the Levelers were radical liberals rather than radical democrats since they were clearly not in favor of "manhood suffrage," which itself would have excluded women, criminals, and deliquents, resulting at the time in an electorate comprised of about 1,700,000 Englishmen. Instead, the Levellers generally favored a "non-servant franchise," which excluded wage-earners (servants) and alms-takers (beggars), and constituted an electorate of 417,000 men. In fact, they supported an even more restrictive franchise at various points in their debates with Cromwell and the New Model Army; under one formulation, the electorate would have consisted of about 375,000 men.

Here we are talking numbers. But these numbers are more than just symbols or just signifiers; they are vehicles but vehicles with substance.

34. While over two-thirds of all Native Americans were citizens by the end of World War I, an enormous number (125,000) were not. The Indian Citizenship Act of 1924 was "designed as a reward for the loyal service of thousands of Native Americans in World War I. . . ." (James S. Olson and Raymond Wilson, *Native Americans in the Twentieth Century* (Urbana: University of Illinois Press, 1984), 24, henceforth *NA*). This inclusion was not as straightforward as it seems. For one thing, many Native Americans were understandably wary of this mechanism of assimilation. For another, this Act did not secure the right to vote, and "states such as New Mexico and Arizona kept erecting voting barriers and did not allow most of their Native Americans to vote until after World War II" (*NA*, 84ff).

35. The scare-quotes serve specifically to put into the question the notion that data exists independently of its collection, which is always a selective and thus productive process, as it breaks public opinion down into a predominantly binary reality with an occasional shade of difference marked by categories such as those black holes of statistics, "no opinion," "don't know," and "undecided."

36. Jean Baudrillard, "The Orders of Simulacra," trans. Philip Beitchman, in *Simulations* (New York: Semiotext[e], 1983), 122.

37. The most dramatic shift in the recent history of American representative politics was Democratic candidate "Mike" Dukakis' 17% loss in support between the peak of the 1988 Democratic National Convention and the peak of the Republican National Convention just several weeks later.

38. Joshua Meyrowitz, *No Sense of Place* (New York: Oxford University Press, 1985), cf. chap. 14. Henceforth cited as *NSP*.

39. Quoted in Charles W. Roll, Jr. and Albert H. Cantril, *Polls: Their Use and Misuse in Politics* (New York: Basic Books, 1972), 41.

40. This phrase has been the centerpiece of an ongoing advertising campaign for Chevrolet.

41. Cf. Postman, *AOD*.

42. Again, I am not trying to suggest here that this split was just ideological or dialectical (i.e., the Marxist reading that would reduce it to people versus property). That reading certainly tells an important part of the story, but there are others, including the problem rep-

resented by how to count slaves; clearly, it was not in the obvious interests of the North to have slaves counted as persons, which is why the figure three-fifths is a compromise with more than one profile. Another complicating element in this story is that, given the ambiguity in determining wealth, those in favor of it as the basis of apportionment decided that counting people was the most accurate method for representing wealth anyway. Estimates made in Massachusetts at the time suggested that this was true, i.e., that the proportional correlation between population and wealth was a consistent one (cf. De Grazia, *PR*, 95). In any event, this early, constituting identification of people and property in the counting procedures injects one more profound ambiguity into the history of American representation.

43. Michael Deaver in an interview on "The McNeil/Lehrer News Hour," January 18, 1989.

44. The reference suggests specifically that Bush's election was a sign of electoral approval of Reagan. In fact, this was not an historic but an antihistoric rating, if anything, given that it required immediate amnesia (active forgetfulness of yesterday's sleaze factor) on a scale unprecedented in recent American history.

To use Postman's image (*Amusing Ourselves to Death*), the appropriate metaphorical reference may be not Orwell's *1984* but Huxley's *Brave New World*, the story of a future power constituted not by coercion but through pleasure, or simulated pleasure, i.e., entertainment: "In the Huxleyan prophecy, Big Brother does not watch us, by his choice. We watch him, by ours. There is no need for wardens or gates or Ministries of Truth" (*AOD*, 155).

45. Michael Warner, "The Mass Public and the Mass Subject," in Bruce Robbins, *The Phantom Public Sphere* (Minneapolis: University of Minnesota Press, 1993), 236.

46. Meyrowitz, *NSP*, 276 (quoting Ferdinand Mount, *The Theatre of Politics*) and, following, 279.

47. Castoriadis, *ISS*, 273.

48. The articulation of an inside and an outside to democracy takes its formal structures and apparatuses too seriously. Is it really accurate, for instance, to see the global power of Islam as outside of American democracy, given its effects on America, which are effects not of American openness to Islam but of necessary coexistence?

49. It would be too much of a detour here to address alternative systems of representation, such as the proportional representation (in contrast with two-party) found in many democracies in the world (e.g., France, Germany, and Israel). While these alternatives have some features strongly in their favor and may seem to be more directly representative, they tend to depend upon coalitions in order to function, and, in addition to other problems they seem to engender, these coalitions go a long ways toward taming the apparent diversity marked by the proportional mixture. Another way to put it is that the apparent mirror gets distorted in its need for alliances and coalitions, in, that is, the necessity of establishing a consensus.

50. Ernst Vollrath, "That All Governments Rest on Opinion," *Social Research*, 43 (spring 1976), 48.

51. Jean-Paul Sartre, "Elections: A Trap for Fools," in *Life/Situations*, trans. Paul Auster and Lydia Davis (New York: Pantheon Books, 1977), 205, henceforth cited as *ETF*. Sartre is actually quoting a journalist here.

Chapter VI

1. Beauvoir, Simone de, *The Ethics of Ambiguity*, trans. Bernard Frechtman (New York: Citadel Press, 1976), 119.

2. Cormac McCarthy, *Blood Meridian* (New York: Vintage International, 1992), 249.

3. Heraclitus, Diehls fragment 53, trans. Kathleen Freeman, in *Ancilla to the Pre-Socratic Philosophers* (Cambridge: Harvard University Press, 1971), 30.

4. "War is simply a continuation of political intercourse, with the addition of other means," Carl von Clausewitz, *On War*, ed. and trans. Michael Howard and Peter Paret (Princeton: Princeton University Press, 1984), 605. While prominent threads of Clausewitz' thought seem highly instrumentalist, these threads compete with others.

5. Niccolò Machiavelli, *The Prince*, trans. George Bull (Harmondsworth: Penguin Books, 1982), 77.

6. Ibid., 99.

7. Since it is far less costly than the exertion of actual military force, law is generally preferable to battle, but Machiavelli does not deem it worth addressing in a guidebook for princes beyond the confident note that good laws will follow good arms.

8. Nor are my assertions intended to conflict with Deleuze and Guattari's fascinating discussion of "the war machine," in *A Thousand Plateaus*, translated by Brian Massumi (Minneapolis: University of Minnesota Press, 1987), although it is beyond the scope of the current project to explain why and to provide an account of why their discussion is an important one.

9. History has no 'meaning,' though this is not to say that it is absurd or incoherent. On the contrary, it is intelligible and should be susceptible of analysis down to the smallest detail— but this in accordance with intelligibility of struggles, of strategies and tactics. Neither the dialectic, as logic of contradictions, nor semiotics, as the structure of communication, can account for the intrinsic intelligibility of conflicts. 'Dialectics' is a way of evading the always open and hazardous reality of conflict by reducing it to the Hegelian skeleton, and 'semiology' is a way of avoiding its violent, bloody and lethal character by reducing it to the calm Platonic form of language and dialogue. (Michel Foucault, "Truth and Power," *PK*, 114-15.)

10. Ibid., 123.

11. If it is play, so is war. This note further compromises the line of bifurcations ordered as: game of violence/real violence, conventional/natural, etc.

An excellent example of a cultural practice from American history may help here. For many of the buffalo-hunting, nomadic, horse-riding Plains tribes (e.g., Cheyenne, Sioux, Blackfeet, and Arapaho), war was a game. One of the more significant forms of this game—a way of scoring points—was stealing an enemy's horses. This involved a range of highly coded practices, having to do with various interrelated factors, including the quality of the horse, how well guarded it was, the identity of the owner, etc. Another significant form of war-as-game for the Plains tribes was the practice of counting coup. Killing an enemy constituted a coup, but a more valuable coup was for an unarmed warrior to touch an armed enemy in battle with his hand or with a coup stick (not a club—not a real weapon—but a game weapon used in situations of real risk, in real blood combat), an event which had to be witnessed by a comrade.

12. The literal blood shed in covert actions, for example, cannot be viewed as outside of democracy; in its connection with security, this is part of what representative, republican democracy is.

13. To describe the institution of political representation as, more straightforwardly, organized would restrict the focus to its formal elements and would obscure the significance of the multifarious informal dimensions of its practice.

14. "To link is necessary; how to link is contingent," Jean-François Lyotard, *The Differend*, trans. Georges Van Den Abbeele (Minneapolis: University of Minnesota Press, 1988), 29 (and elsewhere).

15. On the theme of necessity and, specifically, the throw of the dice, cf. Deleuze, *Nietzsche and Philosophy*, and Derrida, "The Double Session" in *Dissemination*.

16. Friedrich Nietzsche, *The Genealogy of Morals*, trans. Walter Kaufmann (New York: Vintage Books, 1969), 77-78.

17. Gilles Deleuze, *Foucault*, trans. Sean Hand (Minneapolis: University of Minnesota Press, 1988), 10.

18. Oliver North, for example, certainly believed himself to be an active representive of American democracy in his extensive covert operations, which were not merely tactical but the deployment of a semi-covert policy. To argue that "that is not representation" is not to argue some literal truth, but is, rather, to take up an idealistic and literal-minded position in the war of American democracy (which is clearly neither just a bunch of words nor a parade of floating signifiers). Of course, the truth is that Oliver North did represent American democracy, and thereby contributed to the (un)constitution of its nature in the process of his operations.

A fruitful site for a sober deconstruction would be the appearance of "democracy" in the transcript of the Oliver North hearings.

19. Viktor Shklovsky, *A Sentimental Journey: Memoirs, 1917-1922*, trans. Richard Sheldon (Ithaca: Cornell University Press, 1970), 188.

20. Jefferson, quoted by Pole, *PRE*, 301.

21. Castoriadis, *IIS*, 311.

22. The failed democratic revolution in China in spring and early summer 1989 was apparently depicted in drastically inaccurate form in the Chinese news media. However, thanks particularly to radio technology and international broadcasting networks (e.g., the BBC and the VOA), the population of China knew about the events in Tiananmen square, including the bloodshed.

23. Jane Brody, "Personal Health," *The New York Times* (Wednesday, January 21, 1987), C8.

24. This is probably more extreme in the United States than anywhere else at this point in time. However, the trend toward deregulation and commercialization of communications media in many parts of the globe are also making it more true elsewhere. More generally, the presence of the networks of communication is a global phenomenon.

25. "The War Room" is the title of a documentary film of the Clinton presidential campaign, directed by Chris Hegedus and D.A. Pennebaker, 1993.

26. Cf. Clausewitz, "Moral Factors," in *On War*, bk. 3, chap. 3, 184-85.

27. I would not want to push this as literal, but perhaps strategic logic can be associated with the instituting moment of the radical imaginary. Cf. Cornelius Castoriadis, *The Imaginary Institution of Society*, trans. Kathleen Blamey (Cambridge: MIT Press, 1987), and "Power, Politics, Autonomy," in *Philosophy, Politics, Autonomy*, ed. David Ames Curtis (New York: Oxford University Press, 1991).

28. Gilles Deleuze and Felix Guattari, "1227: Treatise on Nomadology—The War Machine," in *A Thousand Plateaus*, trans. Brian Massumi (Minneapolis: University of Minnesota Press, 1987), chap. 12.

29. Echoing Sartre, we have no choice but to choose. However, this is not an ontological imperative but a practical imperative. If it is a duty in a Kantian sense, it is a duty derived not from the structure of reason but from the contingent necessities of situation.

30. Jacques Derrida, *The Other Heading: Reflections on*

Today's Europe, trans. Pascale-Anne Brault and Michael B. Naas (Bloomington and Indianapolis: Indiana University Press, 1992), 78 (and elsewhere).

31. Paine, *RM*, 142.

32. How could it not be given the recurring dream image of something beyond state capitalism, in which the competition between multinational corporations overtly displaces the enlightened, liberal, weak pluralism currently embodied by the United Nations? (Here, picture the nightmare image of corporate peacekeeping forces.)

33. Friedrich Nietzsche, *Gay Science*, trans. Walter Kaufmann (New York: Vintage Books, 1974), aphorism #350, 293.

Bibliography

Adams, John. *The Political Writings of John Adams*. Edited by George A. Peek, Jr. New York: Liberal Arts Press, 1954.

Allison, David B., ed. *The New Nietzsche*. New York: Delta, Dell Publishing Co., 1977.

Althusser, Louis. *Lenin and Philosophy and Other Essays*. Translated by Ben Brewster. New York: Monthly Review Press, 1972.

Arac, Jonathan, ed. *After Foucault*. New Brunswick, N.J.: Rutgers University Press, 1988.

Arblaster, Anthony. *Democracy*. Minneapolis: University of Minnesota Press, 1987.

Aristotle. *Politics*, in *The Basic Works of Aristotle*, edited by Richard McKeon. New York: Random House, 1941.

Arrow, Kenneth. *Social Choice and Individual Values*. New York: John Wiley, 1963.

Bagdikian, Ben H. *The Media Monopoly*, 3d ed. Boston: Beacon Press, 1990.

Bailyn, Bernard. *The Ideological Origins of the American Revolution*. Cambridge: Harvard University Press, Belknap Press, 1967.

––––––. *Pamphlets of the American Revolution, 1750-1776*. Cambridge: Harvard University Press, Belknap Press, 1965.

Banks, Iain M. *Use of Weapons*. New York: Bantam, 1991.

Barker, Sir Ernest, ed. *Social Contract: Essays by Locke, Hume, and Rousseau*. London: Oxford University Press, 1960.

Baudrillard, Jean. *For a Critique of the Political Economy of the Sign*. Translated by Charles Levin. St. Louis: Telos Press, 1981.

———. *Simulations.* Translated by Paul Foss, Paul Patton, and Philip Beitchman. New York: Semiotext[e], 1983.

Beard, Charles A. "The Teutonic Origin of Representative Government." *American Political Science Review* 26 (1932): 28-44.

———. *An Economic Interpretation of the Constitution of the United States.* New York: Macmillan Co., 1939.

Beard, Charles A. and John Lewis. "Representative Government in Evolution," *American Political Science Review* 26 (1932): 223-40.

Benjamin, Walter. *Illuminations.* Translated by Harry Zohn. New York: Schocken, 1969.

Beauvoir, Simone de. *The Ethics of Ambiguity.* Translated by Bernard Frechtman. New York: Citadel Press, 1976.

Bloom, Harold. *The Anxiety of Influence.* New York: Oxford University Press, 1973.

Bobbio, Norberto, "Are There Alternatives to Representative Democracy?" *Telos* 11 (1978): 17-30.

Botsford, George Willis and Charles Alexander Robinson, Jr. *Hellenic History.* New York: The Macmillan Co., 1950.

Braudel, Fernand. *On History.* Translated by Sarah Matthews. Chicago: The University of Chicago Press, 1980.

———. *The Structures of Everyday Life: The Limits of the Possible.* Vol. 1, *Civilization and Capitalism: 15th-18th Century.* Translated by Sian Reynolds. New York: Harper & Row, 1981.

———. *The Wheels of Commerce.* Vol. 2, *Civilization and Capitalism: 15th-18th Century.* Translated by Sian Reynolds. New York: Harper & Row, 1982.

Brown, Louise Fargo. "Ideas of Representation from Elizabeth to Charles II." *Journal of Modern History* 2 (1939): 23-40.

Burke, Edmund. *Reflections on the Revolution in France.* Edited by Conor Cruise O'Brien. Harmondsworth, Middlesex: Penguin, 1986.

Burke, Edmund. *The Works of Edmund Burke. Vol. 2.* Boston: Little, Brown, and Company, 1880.

Cadava, Eduardo, Peter Connor and Jean-Luc Nancy, eds. *Who Comes after the Subject?* New York & London: Routledge, 1991.

Cam, Helen M. *Liberties and Communities in Medieval England.* London: Merlin Press, 1963.

——. "Medieval Representation in Theory and Practice." *Speculum* 29 (1954): 347-55.

——. "The Theory and Practice of Representation in Medieval England." *History* 38 (1953): 11-26.

Castoriadis, Cornelius. *Crossroads in the Labyrinth.* Translated by Kate Soper and Martin H. Ryle. Cambridge: MIT Press, 1984.

——. *The Imaginary Institution of Society.* Translated by Kathleen Blamey. Cambridge: MIT Press, 1987.

——. *Philosophy, Politics, Autonomy: Essays in Political Philosophy.* Edited by David Ames Curtis. New York: Oxford University Press, 1991.

Certeau, Michel de. *Heterologies.* Translated by Brian Massumi. Minneapolis: University of Minnesota Press, 1986.

Clarke, M. V. *Medieval Representation and Consent.* New York: Russell and Russell, 1964. Reprint of 1936 edition.

Clausewitz, Carl von. *On War.* Edited and Translated by Michael Howard and Peter Paret. Princeton: Princeton University Press, 1984.

Commager, Henry Steele, ed. *Documents of American History.* New York: F. S. Crofts & Co., 1935.

Crozier, Michel J., Samuel P. Huntington, and Joji Watanuki. *The Crisis of Democracy: Report on the Governability of Democracies to the Trilateral Commission.* New York: New York University Press, 1975.

Dahl, Robert. *Dilemmas of Pluralist Democracy.* New Haven: Yale, 1982.

De Grazia, Alfred. *Public and Republic: Political Representation in America.* Westport, Conn.: Greenwood Press, 1985.

Deloria, Vine, Jr. *Behind the Trail of Broken Treaties.* New York: Delta Books, Dell Publishing Co., 1974.

Deleuze, Gilles. *Foucault.* Translated by Sean Hand. Minneapolis: University of Minnesota Press, 1988.

―――. *Nietzsche and Philosophy.* Translated by Hugh Tomlinson. New York: Columbia University Press, 1983.

―――. "Plato and the Simulacrum." Translated by Rosalind Krauss. *October* 27 (Winter 1983): 45-56.

Deleuze, Gilles and Félix Guattari. *A Thousand Plateaus.* Translated by Brian Massumi. Minneapolis: University of Minnesota Press, 1987.

Derrida, Jacques. "Declarations of Independence." Translated by Tom Keenan and Tom Pepper. *New Political Science* 15 (Summer 1986): 7-15.

―――. *Dissemination.* Translated by Barbara Johnson. Chicago: University of Chicago Press, 1981.

―――. *Margins of Philosophy.* Translated by Alan Bass. Chicago: University of Chicago Press, 1982.

―――. "No Apocalypse, Not Now." Translated by Catherine Porter and Philip Lewis. *Diacritics* (Summer 1984): 20-31.

―――. *The Other Heading: Reflections on Today's Europe.* Translated by Pascale-Anne Brault and Michael B. Naas. Bloomington & Indianapolis, Ind.: Indiana University Press, 1992.

―――. *Positions.* Translated by Alan Bass. Chicago: University of Chicago Press, 1981.

―――. "Sendings: On Representation." Translated by Peter and Mary Ann Caws. *Social Research* 49 (Summer 1982): 294-326.

Domhoff, Michael. *Who Rules America Now.* Englewood Cliffs, N.J.: Prentice-Hall, 1983.

Dowse, Robert E. "Representation, General Elections and Democracy." *Parliamentary Affairs* 25 (Summer 1962).

Encyclopedia Britannica. 1970 edition.

Eribon, Didier. *Michel Foucault.* Translated by Betsy Wing. Cambridge: Harvard University Press, 1991.

Eulau, Heinz. "Changing Views of Representation." In *Contemporary Political Science: Toward Empirical Theory.* Edited by Ithiel de Sola Pool. New York: McGraw-Hill, 1967, 53-85.

Ford, Henry. *Representative Government.* New York: Henry Holt & Co., 1924.

Foucault, Michel. *The Archaeology of Knowledge.* Translated by A. M. Sheridan Smith. New York: Pantheon Books, 1972.

———. *The Birth of the Clinic.* Translated by A. M. Sheridan Smith. New York: Vintage Books, 1975.

———. *Discipline and Punish.* Translated by Alan Sheridan. New York: Vintage Books, 1979.

———. *Foucault Live.* Translated by John Johnston. New York: Semiotext[e], 1989.

———. "Governmentality." *Ideology and Consciousness* 6 (autumn 1979): 5-21.

———. *The History of Sexuality. Vol. 1.* Translated by Robert Hurley. New York: Vintage Books, 1980.

———. *Language, Counter-Memory, Practice.* Edited by Donald F. Bouchard. Translated by Donald F. Bouchard and Sherry Simon. Ithaca: Cornell University Press, 1977.

———. *The Order of Things.* New York: Vintage Books, 1973.

———. *Power/Knowledge.* Edited by Colin Gordon. Translated by Colin Gordon, Leo Marshall, John Mepham, and Kate Soper. New York: Pantheon Books, 1980.

———. "The Subject and Power." In Hubert L. Dreyfus and Paul Rabinow, *Michel Foucault: Beyond Structuralism and Hermeneutics*, 2d Edition. Chicago: University of Chicago Press, 1983.

Freeman, Kathleen, trans. *Ancilla to the Pre-Socratic Philosophers.* Cambridge: Harvard University Press, 1971.

Freud, Sigmund. *The Future of an Illusion.* Translated by W. D. Robson-Scott. Revised by James Strachey. Garden City, New York: Anchor Books, 1964.

Gibson, William. *Burning Chrome.* New York: Ace, 1987.

———. *Count Zero.* New York: Ace, 1987.

———. *Mona Lisa Overdrive.* New York: Bantam, 1988.

———. *Neuromancer.* New York: Ace, 1984.

Habermas, Jürgen. *Legitimation Crisis.* Translated by Thomas McCarthy. Boston: Beacon Press, 1975.

———. *The Philosophical Discourse of Modernity.* Translated by Frederick Lawrence. Cambridge: MIT Press, 1987.

———. *The Structural Transformation of the Public Sphere: An Inquiry into a Category of Bourgeois Society.* Translated by Thomas Burger. Cambridge: MIT Press, 1989.

Harvey, Irene. *Derrida and the Economy of Différance.* Bloomington, Ind.: Indiana University Press, 1986.

Hebdige, Dick. *Subculture: the Meaning of Style.* London: Methuen, 1979.

Hefner, Richard D. *A Documentary History of the United States.* New York: New American Library, 1985.

Heidegger, Martin. *Basic Writings.* Edited by David Farrell Krell. Translated by William Lovitt. Harper and Row: New York, 1977.

Hermens, Ferdinand Aloys. *The Representative Republic.* Notre Dame, Ind.: Notre Dame University Press, 1958.

Hill, B. W., ed. *Edmund Burke on Government, Politics and Society.* Sussex: The Harvester Press, 1975.

Hirsh, Arthur. *The French New Left.* Boston: South End Press, 1981.

Hobbes, Thomas. *Leviathan.* Edited by Michael Oakeshott. New York: Collier Books, 1962.

Horkheimer, Max, and Theodor W. Adorno. *Dialectic of Enlightenment.* Translated by John Cumming. New York: Continuum Publishing Co., 1986.

Howard, A. E. Dick. *Magna Carta: Text and Commentary.* Charlottesville, Virginia: University of Virginia Press, 1964.

Howard, Dick. *Defining the Political*. Minneapolis: University of Minnesota Press, 1989.

————. *The Marxian Legacy*, 2nd Ed. Minneapolis: University of Minnesota Press, 1988.

————. *The Politics of Critique*. (Minneapolis: University of Minnesota Press, 1988.

Hoy, David Couzens. *Foucault: A Critical Reader*. Oxford: Basil Blackwell, 1986.

Jennings, Francis. *The Ambiguous Iroquois Empire*. New York: W. W. Norton & Co., 1984.

Kammen, Michael G. *Deputyes & Libertyes: The Origins of Representative Government in Colonial America*. New York: Alfred A. Knopf, 1969.

Kantorowicz, Ernst H. *The King's Two Bodies: A Study in Medieval Political Theology*. Princeton: Princeton University Press, 1981.

Kellner, Douglas. *Television and the Crisis of Democracy*. Boulder, Colo.: Westview Press, 1990.

Kenyon, Cecilia M. "Men of Little Faith: The Anti-Federalists on the Nature of Representative Government." *William and Mary Quarterly* 12 (January 1955): 3-43.

Laclau, Ernesto and Chantal Mouffe. *Hegemony and Socialist Strategy: Towards a Radical Democratic Politics*. Translated by Winston Moore and Paul Cammack. London: Verso, 1985.

Larsen, J. A. O. *Representative Government in Greek and Roman History*. Berkeley: University of California Press, 1966.

Lefort, Claude. *Democracy and Political Theory*. Translated by David Macey. Minneapolis: University of Minnesota Press, 1988.

————. *The Political Forms of Modern Society*. Edited by John B. Thompson. Cambridge: MIT Press, 1986.

Lenin, Vladimir. *State and Revolution*. New York: International Publishers Co., 1932.

Levinson, Sanford. "Writing and Its Discontents." *Tikkun* Vol. 3, no. 2 (March/April, 1988).

Luke, Tim. "Televisual Democracy and the Politics of Charisma." *Telos* 70 (Winter 1986-87): 59-79.

Lyotard, Jean-François. *The Postmodern Condition: A Report on Knowledge*. Translated by Geoff Bennington and Brian Massumi. Minneapolis: University of Minnesota Press, 1984.

——. *The Differend: Phrases in Dispute*. Translated by Georges Van Den Abbeele. Minneapolis: University of Minnesota Press, 1988.

Lyotard, Jean-François and Jean-Loup Thébaud. *Just Gaming*. Translated by Wlad Godzich. Minneapolis: University of Minnesota Press, 1985.

Machiavelli, Niccolò. *The Prince*. Translated by George Bull. Harmondsworth: Penguin Books, 1982.

McCarthy, Cormac. *Blood Meridian*. New York: Vintage International, 1992.

McIlwain, C. H. *The American Revolution: A Constitutional Interpretation*. Ithaca: Cornell University Press, 1958. Reissue of the original 1923 edition.

——. "Medieval Estates," in *Cambridge Medieval History*, Vol. 7. Cambridge: Cambridge University Press, 1932.

MacPherson, C. B. *The Political Theory of Possessive Individualism*. Oxford: Oxford University Press, 1962.

Marsh, Henry. *Documents of Liberty: from Earliest Times to Universal Suffrage*. Devon: David & Charles Publishers, 1971.

Marx, Karl. *The Marx-Engels Reader*. Edited by Robert C. Tucker. New York: W.W. Norton & Co., 1978.

Merleau-Ponty, Maurice. *The Visible and the Invisible*. Translated by Alphonso Lingis. Evanston: Northwestern University Press, 1969.

Meyrowitz, Joshua. *No Sense of Place*. New York: Oxford University Press, 1985.

Middlekauf, Robert. *The Glorious Cause: The American Revolution, 1763-1789*. New York: Oxford University Press, 1982.

Montesquieu, Alain. *Selected Political Writings*. Indianapolis: Hackett Books, 1990.

Morgan, Edmund S. *Inventing the People*. New York: W.W. Norton & Co., 1988.

Nietzsche, Friedrich. *The Gay Science*. Translated by Walter Kaufmann. New York: Vintage Books, 1974.

—————. *The Genealogy of Morals*. Translated by Walter Kaufmann. New York: Vintage Books, 1969.

—————. *Philosophy in the Tragic Age of the Greeks*. Translated by Marianne Cowan. Chicago: Henry Regnery, 1962.

Nelson, Jenny L. "Television and Its Audiences as Dimensions of Being: Critical Theory and Phenomenology." *Human Studies* 9, no. 1 (1986).

Olson, James S. and Raymond Wilson. *Native Americans in the Twentieth Century*. Urbana: University of Illinois Press, 1984.

Paine, Thomas. *Common Sense and Other Political Writings*. New York: Bobbs-Merrill Co., 1953.

—————. *Rights of Man*. Harmondsworth, Middlesex: Penguin Books, 1985.

Palmer, R. R., and Joel Cotton, *A History of the Modern World*. 4th Edition. New York: Alfred A. Knopf, 1971.

Pateman, Carole. *The Problem of Political Obligation*. New York: John Wiley & Sons, 1979.

—————. *The Sexual Contract*. Stanford: Stanford University Press, 1988.

Pennock, J. Roland and John W. Chapman, eds. *Representation*. New York: Atherton Press, 1968.

Pitkin, Hanna Fenichel. *The Concept of Representation*. Berkeley: University of California Press, 1967.

—————. "Hobbes' Concept of Representation." *American Political Science Review* 58 (1964): 328-40, 902-18.

—————. ed. *Representation*. New York: Atherton Press, 1969.

Plato. *The Republic*. In *Plato: The Collected Dialogues*. Edited by Edith Hamilton and Huntington Cairns. Princeton: Princeton University Press, 1980.

Pocock, J. G. A. *The Machiavellian Moment: Florentine Political Thought and the Atlantic Republican Tradition.* Princeton: Princeton University Press, 1975.

Pollard, A. F. *The Evolution of Parliament.* New York: Russell & Russell Co., 1964. Reissue of 1926 edition.

Pole, J. R. ed. *The American Constitution, For and Against: The Federalist and Anti-Federalist Papers.* New York: Hill and Wang, 1987.

——— . *Political Representation in England and the Origins of the American Republic.* London: MacMillan, 1966.

Postman, Neil. *Amusing Ourselves to Death.* New York: Penguin Books, 1985.

Rajchman, John. *Michel Foucault: The Freedom of Philosophy.* New York: Columbia University Press, 1985.

Robbins, Bruce. *The Phantom Public Sphere.* Minneapolis: University of Minnesota Press, 1993.

Roll, Charles W. Jr. and Albert H. Cantril. *Polls: Their Use and Misuse in Politics.* New York: Basic Books, 1972.

Rorty, Richard. *Contingency, Irony, and Solidarity.* Cambridge: Cambridge University Press, 1989.

Rossiter, Clinton, ed. *The Federalist Papers.* New York: New American Library, 1961.

Said, Edward. "Opponents, Audiences, Constituencies, and Community." In *The Anti-Aesthetic: Essays on Postmodern Culture.* Edited by Hal Foster. Port Townsend, Washington: Bay Press, 1983.

Sartre, Jean-Paul. "Elections: A Trap for Fools." In *Life/Situations.* Translated by Paul Auster and Lydia Davis. New York: Pantheon Books, 1977.

Schwartz, Nancy L. *The Blue Guitar: Political Representation and Community.* Chicago: The University of Chicago Press, 1988.

Shklovsky, Viktor. *A Sentimental Journey: Memoirs, 1917-1922.* Translated by Richard Sheldon. Ithaca: Cornell University Press, 1970.

Shoemaker, Robert W. "'Democracy' and 'Republic' as Understood in Late Eighteenth-Century America." *American Speech* 41 (1966): 83-95.

Silverman, Hugh J. ed. *Postmodernism in Philosophy and Art.* London: Routledge, 1990.

Stockton, David. *The Classical Athenian Democracy.* Oxford: Oxford University Press, 1990.

Strauss, Leo and Joseph Cropsey. *History of Political Philosophy.* 3d Edition. Chicago: University of Chicago Press, 1987.

Strayer, Joseph R. *Medieval Statecraft and the Perspectives of History.* Princeton: Princeton University Press, 1971.

——— . *On the Medieval Origins of the Modern State.* Princeton: Princeton University Press, 1970.

Stubbs, William. *Select Charters: from the beginning to 1307,* 9th ed. Edited by H. W. C. Davis. London: Oxford University Press, 1951. Reprint of 1913 edition.

Sun Tzu. *The Art of War.* Translated by Samuel B. Griffith. New York: Oxford University Press, 1971.

Tuchman, Barbara. *A Distant Mirror.* New York: Ballantine Books, 1979.

Ullman, Walter. *Principles of Government and Politics in the Middle Ages.* London: Methuen & Co., 1961.

Van Creveld, Martin. *Command in War.* Cambridge: Harvard University Press, 1985.

Virilio, Paul and Sylvere Lotringer. *Pure War.* Translated by Mark Polizotti. New York: Semiotext[e], 1983.

——— . *Speed and Politics.* Translated by Mark Polizzotti. New York: Semiotext[e], 1986.

Vollrath, Ernst, "That All Governments Rest on Opinion." *Social Research* 43 (1976): 46-61.

Warner, Michael. *Letters of the Republic: Publication and the Public Sphere in Eighteenth-Century America.* Cambridge: Harvard University Press, 1992.

White, Hayden. *The Content of the Form*. Baltimore: Johns Hopkins University Press, 1987.

———— . *The Tropics of Discourse*. Baltimore: Johns Hopkins University Press, 1978.

Wilkinson, Bertie. *The Creation of Medieval Parliaments*. New York: John Wiley & Sons, 1972.

Wittgenstein, Ludwig. *Philosophical Investigations*. Translated by G. E. M. Anscombe. New York: Macmillan Publishing Co., 1968.

Wood, Gordon S. *The Creation of the American Republic: 1776-1787*. New York: W. W. Norton & Co., 1969.

———— . *The Radicalism of the American Revolution*. New York: Alfred Knopf, 1992.

———— . *Representation in the American Revolution*. Charlottesville: University of Virginia Press, 1969.

Zinn, Howard. *A People's History of the United States*. New York: Harper and Row, 1980.

Index

Adams, John, 97, 165n
Althusser, Louis, 113
America, 7, 11, 182n; eighteenth century, 7, 49ff.
American Revolution, 35, 48,
  68, 179n, 180n
Anti-Federalists, 81, 88, 153,
  191-92n
apportionment, 53-54, 131
archaeology, 8, 20-21
Aristotle, 19, 48, 65, 162, 189n,
  198n
Articles of Confederation, 63, 75
artificial person, 19
Athens, 19

Bailyn, 63
Balibar, Etienne, 32
Battle of Bunker Hill, 53, 179n
Baudrillard, Jean, 43, 138, 140,
  177n
Beauvoir, Simone de, 151
Benjamin, Walter, 201n
bicameral legislature, 68, 72,
  78-79, 190n
Bill of Rights, 36, 81ff., 136,
  191n, 194n, 196n
body politic, 25, 65, 122
Boston Tea Party, 48
Burke, Edmund, 9, 19, 38ff., 49,
  55, 104, 175-76n, 179n

Cam, Helen, 29-30
capitalism, 9, 13, 28, 37, 42ff.,

100, 142, 174n, 215n
Castoriadis, Cornelius, iv, 40,
  102, 109ff., 146, 156, 159,
  162, 165n, 166n, 168n, 176n,
  197n, 202n
Clarke, M.V., 30
Clausewitz, Carl von, 151-52
Commons, 34, 35, 36, 49, 76
communication, 2, 11, 12, 19,
  24, 114ff., 119, 125, 131ff.,
  139, 146, 157, 207n, 214n
community, 29, 39; of representation, 31, 33ff.; of the realm,
  9
conflict, 105, 144, 146-149,
  151ff.
congress, 40, 47; Continental,
  47
consensus, 11, 64, 148
consent, 58ff., 64, 124, 131, 135;
  tacit, 61ff.
constituency, 26, 39
Constitution,the American 63,
  69ff., 75, 81, 88, 118, 136,
  141, 153, 191n, 195n, 196n
counting procedures, 12, 117,
  135ff.

Declaration of Independence,
  59, 67, 91
Delaware, 67
delegate-trustee controversy, 39
Deleuze, Gilles, 135, 156, 162,
  212n